Premier's Progress

This book is dedicated to Premier's passengers

Premier's Progress
1936 – 1986

The History of Premier Travel Limited

Compiled and edited by M.M.E.L.

Premier Travel Group in association with
The Pevensey Press

Frontispiece: *First Metroliner, B192 JVA. Birmingham Motor Show 1985*

Published by Premier Travel Group in association with
The Pevensey Press, Cambridge

© Premier Travel Group, Kilmaine Close, Cambridge

Compiled and edited by M.M.E. Lainson
Subedited by Julia Harding
Designed by Tina Dutton
Production by The Pevensey Press in association with Book Production Consultants, Cambridge

Map on page 150 by Jon Harris
Cartoons by Brian Warwick

Typesetting by The Burlington Press (Cambridge) Ltd., Foxton, Cambridge
Printed in England by The Burlington Press (Cambridge) Ltd., Foxton, Cambridge

Contents

		page
List of Abbreviations		8
Foreword and Acknowledgements		9
1	Undergraduate Roadways	11
2	The First Five Years	14
3	War	20
4	The Founding Members	30
5	Running the Show	35
6	The Senior Team	53
7	'It's All About People' I	62
8	Grim Reality	72
9	Success in Sight	76
10	Diversion for the Chairman	80
11	Premier Airlines Ltd	89
12	'It's All About People' II	93
13	The Birth and Early Growth of Premier Travel Agency	104
14	Reports of Progress	110
15	Infusion of Youth	124
16	The Continued Growth of Premier Travel Agency	127
17	Forty Years On and a New Board	133
18	Let the Board Speak	135
Appendixes		
1	Summary of the Premier Travel Group, 1936–86	144
2	Directors and Company Secretaries	145
3	Club 25 Members	146
4	Premier Travel Agency	147
5	Stage Carriage Services, January 1985	148
6	Long-Distance and Express Services, January 1985	149
7	Operational Fleet, January 1936–December 1955	152
8	Fleet Additions, January 1956–January 1985	155
9	Time Sheet	157
10	The Rise and Fall of the First Premier Inclusive Holidays	158

Abbreviations

B.V.B.	Bill V. Burnett
E.A.L.	Edward Arthur Lainson
F.G.	Frank Grice
F.N.M.	Frank Neville Matthews
G.B.	Geoffrey Bray
J.A.M.	John Albert Matthews
M.J.G.	Maurice Jack Gifford
M.M.E.L.	Wife of E.A.L.
N.C.P.T.	Norman Charles Pennell Thompson
P.S.A.	Peter Spencer Andrews
R.A.H.	Reginald A. Howard
R.C.H.D.	Robert Charles Harris Dodkin
R.L.S.	Renford Laurence Sargent
S.P.	Sydney Pennell
W.F.M.	William Frederick Matthews
BR	British Rail
CIBS	Coach and Independent Bus Sector
ECOC	Eastern Counties Omnibus Company
ENOC	National Omnibus Company
PAL	Airlines Limited
PHL	Premier Holidays Limited
PT	Premier Travel
PTA	Passenger Transport Association
PTA	Premier Travel Agency
PTL	Premier Transport Limited
PTS	Premier Travel Services
PVOA	Passenger Vehicle Operators' Association
UCOC	United Counties Omnibus Company
UR	Undergraduate Roadways

Foreword and Acknowledgements

Premier Travel is not only a limited liability company, occupying itself with the operation of buses and coaches, with running country-wide express services and short local rural services, with inclusive holidays and continental coach tours, with a network of travel agencies, with extensive North American and Far Eastern connections, with air services from Cambridge Airport, with, indeed, every aspect of modern transport – except space travel, so far.

It is also a company in the broad, human sense of a group of friends and colleagues working together, often for the greater part of their lives, for the benefit of each other. E. A. Lainson, the founder, has always insisted that we work 'with Premier, not for it', and it is this spirit of collaboration in and identification with the joint effort that has become one of the most impressive of the Company's achievements.

The compilation of this history is a good example of our sort of co-operation. The Board, prompted by F. N. Matthews, gave me the job of recording the actual progress of the Company over fifty years and also the quality of the people who have made it possible. Immediately everyone came to my help. R. C. H. Dodkin began it all by feeding me with facts and figures, with dates and details. Then he added his own contribution to our story. M. J. Gifford wrote, lucidly and vividly, the whole of the vital engineering history from 1941 to the present day. Geoffrey Bray followed with a most valuable and detailed account of the traffic developments and general expansion of the Company. We are all deeply appreciative of these three contributions amounting to about two-thirds of the book. The remaining third of the story has been shared between more than twenty members of the staff, and I acknowledge their contributions, especially S. Pennell's, as the vital ingredient of our effort to record all aspects of these first fifty years. Dozens of other people, both within and without the Company, have lent photos and I am particularly grateful to Paul Carter and C. V. Routh of 7 Wheatfield Way, Cranbrook, Kent, whose photos of buses and coaches are outstanding. I wish we could have used many more.

To put together the subsequent montage of experience, I have had the help of Mrs Kathy Bond as typist, reader of my writing, general assistant and ever-willing, efficient and cheerful companion. I owe her deep gratitude. Julia Harding has subedited out practically all my errors, I hope, and I am grateful for her thoroughness.

Our main omission, it will be noticed, has been to avoid any reference to rogues, cheats or blackguards. We have been set back by several such types but they are of no consequence. But it means that this history is not the whole truth but that part of the truth that has been positive, exciting and successful.

I apologise to the Board for my inadequacies as an historian and ask forgiveness of everyone whose contribution I have omitted or under-valued. I only hope you have enjoyed belonging to this Company and remember – 'it's creamier by Premier'.

M.M.E.L.

1

Undergraduate Roadways

Once upon a time, fifty-five long years ago, five assorted undergraduates were lounging around in Cambridge, wondering what on earth to do with themselves on Sundays in term. One, E.A.L., suggested they run a bus company and start up a service to somewhere or other, preferably a seaside place. For some obscure reason this idea caught on and the five, having each contributed £5, found five more investors and so, with a capital of £50, they organised themselves into a company and in 1932 registered the chosen name, 'Undergraduate Roadways', under the Business Names Act 1916.

They then quite seriously and efficiently set about appointing college representatives. 'How would you like to represent Undergraduate Roadways for us, old chap? All you've got to do is contact your college secretaries and tell them we can do their transport for them. Then pass the enquiry to us and we'll do the rest.'

They called themselves 'Traffic Manager', 'General Manager', 'Publicity Manager', etc. The ten were all 'Directors'; their notepaper spelt out their names and titles. At no time did the Company own or have control over any vehicle. It was one of only twenty bus or coach companies in the country to operate on the 'Permit to Hire' basis. Their method was to engage local operators to carry out the private hires that they had obtained at a marginally lower rate than their own quotations. Amazingly, they succeeded and handled a fair proportion of the sporting fixtures of the various colleges. They carried the University ice hockey team to Purley, and European Motorways took them across Europe. On his return the driver complained to E.A.L. that the riotous team had purloined 'souvenirs' from the various hotels, disputed bills and, after a tour of over a thousand miles, had not thought to give him a tip.

A girls' private school in Essex employed UR to carry the girls between school and home at the beginning and end of the holidays; they were also required to lay on a lorry to carry the luggage. On one occasion everything went wrong and the phone buzzed: 'Hallo, Undergraduate Roadways. Traffic Manager speaking.'

'Traffic Manager! You're not fit to manage a perambulator', said the irate Headmistress at the other end. Since H.L.D.B. was only twenty years old it was probably a correct judgement.

Altogether, the first experiments were exciting enough to lead the ten 'Directors' on to further expansion and they began to reconsider their original idea of a seaside service on summer Sundays. They found Clacton and Yarmouth were already served, so they worked out a timetable for a route to Skegness, filed their application for a licence at the Traffic Commissioners and started preparing their case.

Until the Transport Act 1980, it was always necessary to find witnesses who would be willing to come to the Traffic Court to support an application for a new service, by establishing a need. Since our ten were, as undergraduates, fairly remote from the normal run of passengers, they had to seek help elsewhere. One bright spark thought of writing to the Dean of Peterborough Cathedral, pointing out that their new venture would enable people to attend matins at the Cathedral and asking for his support. They received the following reply:

I am deeply gratified to learn of the religious spirit that appears to permeate Cambridge University and the surrounding district. Most heartily do I support your contention that Peterborough Cathedral is the finest of its kind in East Anglia if not indeed in Great Britain.

As a result of this letter, E.A.L. and Mr. D. R. W. Stevenson, the Company's solicitor and greatest supporter (he was only about ten years older than his clients, and entered wholly into the spirit of their enterprise), asked for an interview with the Dean, hoping to persuade him to attend the hearing on their behalf. This is E.A.L.'s verbatim account of the interview:

'We rang the bell and the door was opened by the parlourmaid. Behind her was a rather acid-looking lady.

"We are from Undergraduate Roadways and would like to see the Dean, please."

"Egbert," the lady called, "two bus persons from Cambridge to see you."

'We had a short discussion with him and after a bit the gong rang. It was about 7 o'clock in the evening. He looked a bit disturbed but we continued talking; then the gong rang again and we heard a woman's voice in the background: "Haven't those bus persons gone yet? The Dean's fish is getting cold!"

"Excuse me, gentlemen," said the Dean in some agitation, "my wife, gentlemen, my wife", and we were hustled out. He did not appear at the Traffic Court but we had his splendid letter.'

The hearing of the application was tabled for a certain day in the spring term and H.L.D.B. and E.A.L. duly presented themselves at Ipswich Town Hall, where the Commissioners were sitting. Their photo was taken on the steps of the building in trilby hats and black coats and they look sober and serious citizens.

The case was taken for them by D. R. W. Stevenson, who, in his opening, pointed out how difficult it was to get to Skegness and said that the application represented a worthwhile venture, which would be useful not only to the University but also to members of the general public. Both Eastern Counties Omnibus Company and the London and North-Eastern Railway Company had put in objections to the application, so their evidence followed.

Mr Stevenson established that there was no other way than UR to get to Ely for matins, read out the Dean's epistle and impressed the Traffic Commissioner. Consequently the decision was held over to await the outcome of the 'Backings' in other areas.

Meanwhile, back in Cambridge, the *Cambridge Daily News* had published the following report:

UNDERGRADUATES RUN BUS SERVICE
The new organisation will open
administrative offices at the
Hermitage, Silver Street, where all the
clerical work will be carried out.

The Hermitage was one of St Catharine's College lodging houses and E.A.L. was one of its residents, so when his Tutor, Dr D.H.J. Chater, read the paper he was not pleased. He phoned the Hermitage: 'Hello, that you, Daldrey?' (Mr Daldrey was the landlord.)

'Yes, Sir.'

'You running a bus service, Daldrey?'

'No, Sir.'

'Well who the devil is?'

'Are you referring to Undergraduate Roadways, Sir?'

'I don't know what the name is. Just tell me who's in it.'

'Well, Sir, Mr Lainson is the Traffic Manager.'

'Did you say Lainson? Send him to me immediately.'

E.A.L. continues the story: 'Of course, H. and I were still away in Ipswich and so it was some time later that I presented myself before him: "You sent for me, Sir."

"Are you dabbling in transport, Sir, commercialising the college? Cambridge not good enough for you?"

"Yes, Sir, I'm very happy here, thank you, Sir."

"Any more of my men concerned in this – this *episode*?"

"Oh yes, Sir. We have two other Directors in this college."

"Directors! Tell them to withdraw immediately and do the same yourself."

'Following this interview, the Registered Office and Company were moved to 45 Jesus Lane and our names deleted from the stationery. We did not, however, have to terminate the activities of the Company and our application for a Backing for our Skegness service, due to be heard in Nottingham, went ahead. We had six objections in the East Midland area – the independents were Fleetways Ltd, Express Safety Coach Co. Ltd, the Provincial Company of Leicester and Mr Pyewell of Peterborough.

'Accordingly, Mr Stevenson, Mr Maitland-Clark the Publicity Manager (and one of the original five) and myself proceeded to Nottingham Traffic Court in Mr Stevenson's small Austin. We arrived a little after the proceedings had commenced and the court was very full. The Traffic Commissioner, whom of course we hadn't previously seen, was speaking as we entered: "I have no hesitation in dismissing this application." For a minute we thought it was ours, but not so. He continued: "I will take the Undergraduate Roadways case next", at which there was a guffaw in the crowded court. Our solicitor rose.

"Who are you?" asked the Chairman fiercely.

"Stevenson, Sir, of Squires and Company, Cambridge."

"Tell me, Mr Stevenson, is this a clumsy attempt on the part of Cambridge University to pull the legs of the Traffic Commissioners? I will tell you now, I

The founder and the tallest inspector in England, Ronald Ponsonby Griffin, 1933

don't like undergraduates."

"No, Sir, I have been an undergraduate myself and I know what can arise in the undergraduate mind. But my clients, Sir, are not men of straw. We have here the Traffic Manager and the Publicity Manager, who will be called to give evidence."

"Very well, Mr Stevenson, proceed", said the Chairman, and Mr Maitland-Clark took the witness stand.

'He produced three letters, from Varsity Express Motors, Comfort and Reliance Coaches and one other operator, confirming that they were willing to hire vehicles to Undergraduate Roadways, when they didn't require them themselves.

"These letters aren't worth the paper they are written on," said the Chairman, "they say that they will supply coaches only if they don't need them!" Laughter in court.

'However, neither LNER nor ECOC had any real grounds for opposing the application and the decision was reserved, To our delight, both the Primary and Backing Licences were subsequently granted and Undergraduate Roadways became part of a highly professional group of Express Service Coach Operators.

'We set about planning the inaugural celebrations and decided to approach Miss Jessie Matthews, who was at the height of her popularity at the time. We invited her to open the service and when the local paper appeared with the news, it added, "She will be accompanied by the tallest inspector in England, the height of this undergraduate being no less than 6ft 11in." Maitland-Clark and I went to Skegness and saw Mr Cooper, the Publicity Manager, and asked him how we should entertain the young lady.

"Gentlemen, that will be a matter for my Council – I think our Mayor would agree to a civic lunch." We were, of course, enormously impressed.

'Unfortunately these elaborate excitements fell through and on the initial journey Mr Charles F. Klapper of the Omnibus Society and myself were the sole passengers. The Varsity Express Motor was driven by Driver Robertson, who did all the subsequent journeys between Cambridge and Skegness. The coach used was rather special: it started on petrol and, having warmed up, was switched over to the Harvey Patent Paraffin Attachment. I remember the cost of paraffin at the time was 4½d [2p] a gallon, so considerable savings in fuel were possible. We had a pleasant day by the seaside and returned to Cambridge about 10 p.m. without further incident.

'Our main "Agency" was at 48 Jesus Lane, where Mrs Sampson, who was H.D.L.B.'s landlady, was a great asset to UR in every way. She was a remarkable person: Chairman of the Women's Section of the British Legion; a well-known figure amongst the University staff and personally very friendly to us. To call her a "brick" would be a fair description. She entered fully into the spirit of UR, answered the phone, took bookings and, I think, thoroughly enjoyed the whole experience. We were all very attached to her. Her daughter later joined PT as my secretary and was with us at the outbreak of war.'

When E.A.L. went down in 1934, UR was carried on by Gordon Crisp and Arthur Stockings until their time was up, after which it almost ceased to function in the University. In 1935, E.A.L. acquired the outstanding shareholdings and incorporated it into Premier Travel as a subsidiary company. Its bank account was only recently closed. Two or three of the original members became shareholders in Premier but financially UR made no great fortunes for the original ten. However, they got their money back, plus a lot of fun, an outlet for their youthful 'cheek', and gained quite a useful ration of business experience.

2

The First Five Years

FOUNDATION

In June 1934, the Depression was at its height and E.A.L., like a lot of other young graduates, found himself unemployed and, in a way, almost unemployable. He had a short, sterile spell trying to sell water-softeners to friends of his mother, but their allegiance to her didn't run to buying an expensive gadget. Luckily, he had been bitten early in his teens by the transport bug, whose remarkably deep and penetrating bite imposes upon its victims a one-track mind for the rest of their lives. The feverish devotees who throng railway enthusiasts' outings or Omnibus Society visits have all contracted the disease, one of whose side-effects is to stimulate an enormous appetite for innocent transport pleasures or, better still, transports of innocent pleasure. Consequently a simple happiness permeates their lives, to a degree not usually experienced by the adult population.

Needless to say, after the UR experience, there was no real chance of E.A.L. ever getting over the infection, so he turned his mind to entering the transport world. He and H.D.L.B., shortly to become his brother-in-law, asked for an interview at London Transport. They were received courteously and told that there might be a job for them: 'Of course, you'll have to drive.' H., always bright and quick, said: 'Drive a bus? Do you realise I'm a Cambridge graduate?'

'My dear sir,' said their interviewer, 'we have enough Cambridge men driving buses in London to form a club.' So that was that.

They made one or two further attempts to enter the industry but without success, so E.A.L. proceeded to work on a plan to start his own bus company.

He knew every bus service and operator within miles of Cambridge, so Cambridge became the heart of his ideas. He planned, on paper, a take-over of one or two of the existing companies and then an expansion of express services, which were, are, and always will be, his greatest interest. He did a very great deal of homework during this lean period and built up a reasonable prospectus to launch the new business.

He spent a good deal of time visiting various operators in the area, usually by bicycle, to talk about the possibility of their joining his enterprise. Only the discussions with Harston and District Motor Services, owned and operated by Mr Norman Pennell Thompson, and Royal Blue Coaches, owned and operated by Mr Harry J. Brown, proved fruitful.

The next step was to find the capital for the venture and a stroke of cruel fortune gave him his first opportunity. He had been appointed executor for a favourite cousin, who in 1934 had the misfortune to lose his wife. His grief undermined his confidence and within days of his wife's death he took a gun and blew himself away. This awful happening not only turned E.A.L. into a responsible executor at the age of twenty-three, it also gave him, by bequest, a small capital sum of his own.

Another move was an advertisement in *The Times* for 'Capital to launch a New Transport Company'. This only produced an enquiry from a large bus concern in the North and an offer of unlimited loans from a firm of City gentlemen, at the staggering rate of 33⅓% interest! So the search continued. E.A.L. tells the story:

'I contacted Sir Christopher Magnay, whom I knew to have been one of the Directors of Premier Omnibus Company Ltd and Premier Line in London. That business had been compulsorily acquired by constituent companies of the Tilling and BET groups, the services being divided between them. Sir Christopher was interested in my plan and, indeed, was the inspiration behind our Company's name, Premier Travel'.

So, without further delay, they were ready to go. They had E.A.L.'s own money; Sir Christopher's investment, together with that of a friend of his, Captain Kirk; and N.C.P.T.'s acceptance of part of his purchase price in shares in the new company. So, in the upshot, working together with their solicitors, Partridge and Wilson of Bury St Edmunds, with Mr Tom Wilson, the senior partner, acting as godfather, the first Company meeting took place on 17 January 1936.

The proceedings were formal to a degree, legalistic and satisfying, and, when it was all over, Sir

Christopher Magnay was in the chair, N.C.P.T. was Managing Director, E.A.L. was Company Secretary and Captain C.G.P. Kirk was a Director.

Lloyds Bank Ltd was entrusted with the first account and the Directors were authorised to make arrangements with the bank to obtain an overdraft – as they thought fit. We have been in mutual support ever since. This seems a good point to list the Managers of Lloyds of Cambridge who have guided and helped Premier in the most practical form possible – hard cash – since the Company was formed. They were not the kind who lend an umbrella when the sun is shining and ask for it back as soon as it rains. Indeed, without their understanding, strictures and patience the Company would probably not have made it, and Premier is extremely grateful.

F. W. Yelf Esq., 1934–39
A. J. Parry Esq., 1939–50
C. D. Henderson Esq., 1950–56
H. C. Roberts Esq., 1956–58
S. J. Collingwood Esq., 1958–62
E. J. Furley Esq., 1962–69
R. G. Turner Esq., 1969–78
B. F. Brown Esq., 1978–present day

WE BEGIN

And so the daily life of Premier Travel Ltd began; the Company offices were registered at 15 Market Hill, Cambridge; the telephone number was 3327; the first notepaper was printed and the very special Premier blue was adopted as the fleet livery.

Both N.C.P.T. and E.A.L. enjoyed themselves in their different spheres. The former was in charge of the engineering side, and the Minutes are full of references to his problems in that department. He was, in a way, only continuing the work he had begun early in 1922, after leaving the Navy as a lad of eighteen in 1918. He had acquired an old Army truck and fitted it with wooden benches to carry passengers; he called his venture 'Harston and District Motor Services' and set about pioneering new routes between Fowlmere and Cambridge, later extended to Royston, and between Royston and Cambridge via Barrington.

He has told of how, in the first weeks of operation, he carried only one or two people in the high wagon, because the average country woman was scared of the new-fangled machine. He would slow down as he passed them trudging back from market, often heavily laden, but they would not climb aboard. Then, one day, it was pouring with rain,

with plenty of wind about, so he stopped just ahead of a little group. They took the lesser of two evils and struggled onto the bus. That was all that was needed. They were his passengers from then on and year by year he improved and marginally extended his regular services, private hire, etc. When E.A.L. approached him in 1935, he saw an opportunity to expand his interests and he liked the terms of the agreement giving him a directorship in the projected company. So 1936 began well for him. The Company had taken over his five vehicles – three Gilfords and two Reos. From Royal Blue Coaches had come one Maudsley and an AEC, seven in all.

It was rather a hotch-potch fleet and demanded a tremendous amount of repetitive labour to keep it running. Many adaptations had to be made. For instance, the 26-seater Reo had to be reduced to 20 seats so that it could be operated without a conductor. To do this 6 seats were removed, leaving a large gap in the middle of the bus, across which passengers had to lurch from one end to the other. Only when it was packed tight with standing passengers was it safe or comfortable.

During this period, the garage was resurfaced; an electric air compressor was purchased; part of the fleet was overhauled; a special water supply was negotiated with the local authority at a cost 'not to exceed £7 5s 9d' (£7.29). N.C.P.T. reported in July 1936 that the Company was handicapped by lack of staff and the fleet was not receiving adequate attention – a shadow of things to come – but in the first two years N.C.P.T. was nevertheless enjoying the new, if slow, improvements in the fleet and garage.

In December 1936, a major step forward was taken. The Minute reads:

> It was finally resolved that a contract be awarded to Messrs Coaches and Components for the supply of a 25-seater coach of Bedford manufacture, with body-work by Messrs Duple Bodies and Motors Ltd; Messrs Coaches and Components would take a 26-seater Maudsley coach in part exchange.

This quotation demonstrates the formal, detailed, almost proud style of Minute writing adopted by E.A.L. from the beginning of the Company, giving it thereby its own momentum of importance and substance. It should, in addition, be of interest to Omnibus Society and PSV Circle members checking ancient vehicles! Most importantly it celebrates the ordering of the Company's very first brand new vehicle, BVE 668.

A year later a 35-seater Dennis, CCE 568, with body by Duple, was added to the fleet. It was a

magnificent vehicle in the heavy, stuffy style of the time. The plush seats were thick and buoyant, the Art-Nouveau decorations curled and coiled over the ceiling and, wherever this leviathan of the road appeared, there was great satisfaction all round.

Meanwhile E.A.L. was in his element. He had acquired a nucleus of services with which to start his widespread and ambitious empire, and was anxious to get off the mark. In May 1936, there were negotiations with Weeden's Motor Services of Chrishall but they came to nothing at that point for lack of money. Throughout this period he was vigorously opposing inter-availability of tickets between ECOC and ENOC, which was detrimental to his local services, though much later on in our history he was to sponsor many types of pooling

and collaboration between operators. Before those peaceful days arrived, however, he was in and out of the Traffic Courts, making applications for a series of trunk and local routes, or objecting to all and sundry who threatened the Company's services.

In June 1936 he organised an exciting and ambitious private hire – the annual staff outing of Pye Radio Ltd. It involved transporting 1,000 people from Cambridge and the surrounding district to Tower Pier, London, where they were to embark on the Royal Sovereign paddle steamer, then proceed by water to Southend, where coaches were to pick up the party for the return journey. After detailed discussions with Pye, he put in a quote of 5s 9d (29p) per head, against Eastern Counties'

CCE 568, second new PT vehicle, March 1937

quote of 5s (25p). Nevertheless, he won the contract because three of ECOC's coaches had broken down on their journey in 1935.

A tremendous amount of organisation then began: it involved 32 coaches, gathered from all over the county, with a few provided by London operators, who stayed overnight at their pick-up points. Everything was done that could be done – detailed loading sheets, numbered coaches, precise instructions to every driver, strict timetabling.

The plan was to rendezvous at Pye's, Haig Road, and to proceed more or less in convoy to Tower Bridge. E.A.L. was to lead the way as passenger in the first coach. He was up at the crack of dawn, went out to start the car and found he had a flat tyre. 'For want of a nail, the battle was lost.' This

delayed him, delayed the start from Cambridge, the convoy system went haywire and every driver was on his own. At one time, as E.A.L.'s coach neared the City, he saw, to his consternation, three or four of his coaches, obviously lost, heading away in the opposite direction. Worse was to come.

When the first contingent arrived at Tower Pier, they saw the Royal Sovereign slowly edging out into midstream. Horrified, Driver Pennell rushed to the booking office.

'Stop the boat – you've left some passengers behind.'

'How many?' asked the clerk laconically.

'Over a thousand', was the answer.

Even to a blasé crowd-weary Cockney this was quite an oversight and the shore to ship communications buzzed and the steamer was stopped further downstream at North Woolwich. The East Anglian coaches were at once diverted to join the ship, so their troubles were soon over. The London operators, however, had further commitments and had no more time available for our party, so the only course open was to take their passengers to Fenchurch Street and send them by train to Southend. There they eventually rejoined the group when the Royal Sovereign docked at the pier.

For the return journey late that evening another conglomeration of coaches, including one of high-seated capacity belonging to the City Coach Company, supplemented the Cambridge contingent, and E.A.L. anxiously watched as all the coaches were loaded successfully. However, as they moved off there was further panic as two of the coaches managed to block the tramlines, thus bringing the Southend Tramways System to a halt. Eventually everyone got home safely, including E.A.L., after almost twenty hours on the road.

Although it was a near fiasco, few people at Pye's took up the offer, recorded in the Minutes of 6 October 1936, of complimentary tickets to Southend on another occasion, to make amends. This great outing remains the largest private hire commitment ever operated by Premier.

By April 1937, the Company was negotiating the acquisition of Empire's Best Express Service between Birmingham and Clacton, operated by Messrs Webber Bros, who had thought up two lovely slogans. One was:

East is East and West is West
And the Route between is Empire's Best

The second was shorter:

Out of the Smoke Zone – Into the OZONE

The price paid for this service was £505, including a

deposit of £250, plus 'a "Bill of Exchange" for £255, payable two months after the transfer of the last licence'.

The purchase of Service 5 was probably the best investment Premier ever made. E.A.L. set about increasing the frequency of journeys and days of operation until it became daily throughout the year, except for Christmas Day. Intermediate bookings were gradually incorporated as the time-table filled out, but an embargo on travel between Bedford or Northampton and Cambridge remained until the eighties. In 1982 it actually operated 303,223 laden miles on 2,527 journeys, carried 78,872 passengers and took a gross revenue of £220,295.

It also had the important side-effect of bringing the Company into the heart of the Midlands and, thanks to the courtesy of Midland Red Omnibus Company, who allowed us to pick up and set down in their central coach station at Digbeth, it gave us from the start the advantage, often denied independent operators, of excellent professional facilities for our service.

The so-called Freedom Act of 1980 has now resulted in the introduction of a new joint opera-tion with National Express on broadly the same lines as Service 5.

The acquisition of this service also marked the beginning of the development of others in the Midlands, and the connnectional timing with Yelloway at Leicester on their London–Blackpool service led eventually to close co-operation be-tween the two companies and the formation of a daily link between the North West and South East of England.

E.A.L. recalls another incident in 1937 which led to a further extension of Premier's business:

'The Eastern Counties staff went on strike and we looked for opportunities to expand traffic. One idea was to run an hourly service between Royston and Cambridge on the main road and another was to operate between Cottenham and Cambridge, on a fairly frequent service. The members of the Eastern Counties strike committee met me at 15 Market Hill and expressed their concern that we proposed to run some of their services. I said to them, "We are taking no sides in this dispute but it may well be to your advantage after the strike, if the passenger traffic is retained." After a discussion it was agreed that they would have no objection to our running the Royston to Cambridge service but they would not agree to us operating between Cottenham and Cambridge. The strike lasted several weeks and traffic in the early stages was fairly small but it improved rapidly as the strike

continued. We, I think, obtained a certain amount of credit during this time.

'Generally speaking between 1936 and 1939 we kept the pattern of the local services very much as they were in Harston and District's day, apart from diverting Service 2, Barrington–Cambridge, into Hauxton, which led to a considerable fight with ECOC.'

All in all, from an operating and expansionist point of view, the first two years of Premier's existence had fulfilled most of its expectations. Unfortunately, the money people thought other-wise, as was obvious when the second Annual General Meeting took place in February 1938.

WE NEARLY END

Mr E. E. Harmer, the Auditor, was grave. He dealt with the draft figures for 1937 in detail and showed that there was a loss on trading of £460. The list of creditors was a long one. Although stock was much higher and the debtors were also at a high figure, he viewed the position with alarm. The policy of the Company would have to be one of retrenchment – no new capital, increased revenue. He then withdrew so that the Directors could have a private discussion.

The Chairman said it was questionable whether the Company ought to carry on. They agreed to adjourn and come back for a further meeting on 28 February.

With even greater gravity they met again; the Chairman said both he and Captain Kirk were very disturbed by the financial position and doubted whether they were justified in continuing to oper-ate the Company. What were the prospects for 1938? Not good, said the Auditor; E.A.L. dis-agreed. The firm had made considerable savings in the first two months of the current year and both he and N.C.P.T. felt they might show a small profit during 1938.

No good, the Chairman responded; in his opin-ion the Company should go into voluntary liquida-tion.

E.A.L. repeated that they had already reduced the amount outstanding to creditors and the only problem was that the amount owed was greater than the debtors and stock put together. N.C.P.T. added that he felt the position was by no means hopeless and the Company ought to carry on. But the grave Auditor reiterated 'Voluntary liquida-tion'.

The Chairman proposed that if the Company did continue to operate there must be an interim statement in June. Then this Chairman, after just two years in the life of the company he had generously helped to bring into existence, declared that he wished to remain neither Chairman nor Director and resigned. He added these words: 'I am anxious, however, to assist the Company in every way possible, and I will continue to remain a shareholder.'

E.A.L. found himself able to ask whether, if N.C.P.T. and he were able to effect a substantial improvement, Sir Christopher would return as Chairman. The answer was yes.

E.A.L. then thanked him and said he was anxious to record their gratitude to Sir Christopher and Captain Kirk for not insisting on voluntary liquidation.

At the next AGM, on 24 April 1939 (five days before his wedding), E.A.L. was Chairman of Premier Travel, N.C.P.T. was Managing Director and Sir Christopher and Captain Kirk were present only as shareholders. This time there was no mention of liquidation.

The resignation of Sir Christopher from the Board must have come as a staggering blow to E.A.L. and N.C.P.T., and to the latter's great credit he stood by E.A.L. as the rest departed. A rather odd footnote is that we have a letter from Sir Christopher dated only six months prior to this fateful meeting, introducing one of his friends as a new shareholder! More extraordinary still, at the last Directors' monthly meeting on 7 December 1937, under his chairmanship, Sir Christopher spoke firmly on two subjects – the award of a bonus to all staff who had worked so hard and willingly during the ECOC strike earlier in the year, and the importance of planning for the future! Nine weeks later he was resigning his directorship and urging liquidation.

It happens all the time that financial backers are the first to be scared. They doubt their own original judgements; worry over their possible involvement with failure; mutter in their corporate beards and decide to withdraw their names and, they hope, their money. They offer to help in every way they can, bar standing firm and adding a little more capital from their usually deep purses. They belong to that special category that never mind taking a chance, provided there is no risk attached.

If Premier had been publicly quoted, it would have floundered and been overwhelmed at least three times in its life. Instead we are able to record the history of its first five decades, which should demonstrate that 'grasping nettles, with backs to the wall, whence all but we have fled' is not only a stimulating life-style but can often, and in Premier's case certainly did, lead to much richer pastures, which after a long time have become very lush indeed.

Immediately after all these Boardroom shocks, Premier got up again like a good boxer reeling from a heavy blow but by no means down or out, and as the summer months of 1939 slid inevitably into war, all the normal services of the Company were running and Service 5 was in its third season of operation. The holiday traffic from the Midlands to Clacton increased greatly, as people, presumably anticipating trouble, were determined to get away before the worst happened. Yet it is very doubtful whether many of our passengers imagined for a moment that after this long hot summer the beaches would be closed, mined and rendered u/s for the duration. The service culminated in a journey on 2 September 1939, the day Neville Chamberlain sent an ultimatum to the Germans concerning the invasion of Poland. Driver Fred Barker was travelling from Digbeth to Clacton with a load of holiday-makers. When he arrived, word was passed to him about the new development. His group, on hearing the news, voted unanimously to go home as soon as possible, if not before, so our Fred, without even opening the boot, turned round and headed back to Brum!

At more or less the same period, a large movement of evacuees took place and every vehicle was ordered to the railway station to carry them on to their various destinations. E.A.L. went himself to organise Premier's part in the exercise, which went very smoothly indeed. Apart from various troop movements and increased work contracts, Cambridge and Premier then settled into the Cold War routine. E.A.L.'s attempt to volunteer for the RASC was turned down – transport management was a reserved occupation. Gas masks, ration books, a myriad of forms and regulations were introduced, but so orderly and unruffled was the surface of affairs that Midland Red and Premier met in November to outline a plan for a skeleton coastal service for summer 1940 to provide munition workers with relaxation. Dunkirk shattered this uneasy calm. E.A.L. went quickly to volunteer, for the Navy this time, and Premier was left to N.C.P.T., with the Lainson wife on the sidelines. Here is my version of Premier's war.

3
War

1940–41

The Minutes of a meeting of the Board on 1 July 1940 were short and to the point.

> Owing to the absence of Mr E.A. Lainson on war service, the Board authorises Mr N.C.P. Thompson to be solely responsible for the operation of the Company until further notice.

To his dismay, N.C.P.T. found himself back in the hot-seat, with his younger colleague away from it all, and he felt deeply resentful. He had sold out in the hope of enjoying a quieter, easier life than small bus operators usually enjoy. Instead he now had to cope with all the endless difficulties of wartime shortages – lack of spare parts, reduced staff, new regulations – all against the background of Premier's very dicey financial position. Additionally,

because E.A.L. had appointed me to help, by keeping in daily contact with the running of the Company and in constant touch with him by letters and occasional phone calls, I became an extra irritation to N.C.P.T. by passing on the absent Chairman's questions and suggestions on every conceivable aspect of the business. We have kept the greater part of the correspondence between us during the first two years of war, so I can confirm that I called for help at every opportunity, as the avalanche of daily problems threatened to overwhelm us.

We discussed – by letter or phone – wages, waybills, bus allocations, the comings and goings of staff, the monthly revenue from services and contracts, the purchase of spare engines, spare parts, bargain equipment. I reported to him the call up of Fred Barker, and of Syd Pennell, who

Gilfords galore, 1936–37

Gilfords galore, 1936–37

remembers the day vividly. The loss of these two young, vigorous and reliable people caused a serious gap in our strength and dismayed us both. I told him of Ministry of Labour edicts, and the strictures and instructions of the Ministry of Transport Vehicle Examiners. I remember Mr Wood, a senior officer, very clearly, because he actually discussed garage problems with me, then an amateur, and worked out for me a regular docking system to suit our erratic needs. He and his colleagues kept us in touch with sources of spare parts, engines, tyres etc., and Premier owes a great debt of gratitude to this highly skilled group of engineers, both during the war and throughout our history. Incidentally it is they who established the safety standards for the industry that have made buses and coaches the most reliable form of passenger transport.

At this point the recollections of Mr J. Gifford, who joined the Company in 1941 and is now Chief Engineer and Director of Premier Travel Services, give a clear and concise description of those early days, so turbulent and rough, and yet, even to this young man, somehow challenging and worth working for.

An Engineer's War

M. J. Gifford

When I joined the Company at Harston in February 1941 as a driver, the fleet consisted of eight vehicles in various states of repair. They were HX 3464 and VE 8761, both standing derelict in the big barn; CCE 568 stood in the paint shop with its engine dismantled, having been requisitioned by the RAF and then returned because of engine trouble; the runners were BVE 668, VE 4993, WG 1284, WG 334 and TM 8464, known as 'Tom Mix' because it lurched forward a foot every time you started off. There were also the remains of a Reo in the yard.

After having spent the previous eleven years in the commercial transport industry, fortunately with companies who required a fairly high standard of fleet maintenance, I was more than a little surprised to find the vehicles in the condition they were, knowing that passenger carrying vehicles were subject to MOT regulations and inspection. No straightforward maintenance work was carried out, and the procedure was that as and when a vehicle failed to run, an employee driver–mechanic would fiddle about with it for some time to get it going again, and that was it. It is as true today as it was then, that this practice leads to the same defects becoming more and more frequent and the result is an unreliable fleet.

I applied for, and took a driving test for a PSV driving licence and was passed by our 'Mutual Friend', A. G. Prest. I then drove WG 1284 on the Cambridge to Fowlmere service. After a while, however, we were employed to transport aircraft fitters to Alconbury, Wyton and Gransden airfields, and I was given one of these jobs. This consisted of picking up the fitters from all over Cambridge and, in my case, taking them to Wyton, staying there all day and returning them at night. A pretty boring job.

During this time the vehicles left to cover service work were giving more and more trouble. One morning, after a session of hand-cranking to get them going, the then Managing Director, Mr N. Thompson, said to me, 'I hear that you can mend these things.'

'No!' I replied. I had left my previous job to get away from engineering work, but he insisted and, being rather easy going, coupled with the monotony of the aerodrome job, I said I would help. From then on, while the Wyton job lasted, I used to take the workers to the aerodrome and N.C.P.T. would fetch me back to Harston in his car to work in the garage.

It soon became apparent to me that it was the ninth wonder of the world that any of the vehicles ran at all. To see what and how repair work was done was unbelievable. Questioning one mechanic as to why he was probably making more work rather than rectifying the defects, he replied, 'Not to worry, this is the "Jog-Along Bus Company".' I also found out why all the vehicles had to be started with a starting-handle: it appeared that as the starter motors gave trouble they were taken off and dumped in the 'tunnel', a part of the garage.

This was the worst time I think I can remember from a mechanical point of view, and I was aware that financially 'Aladdin's lamp' would have been useful. N.C.P.T. hinted on several occasions that it was probably our last week. I think he expected the MOT to come at any time and out the vehicles off the road. So I thought my stay with Premier was to be very short-lived. However, we kept at it, and it took a little while to get the vehicles that would run into some sort of shape.

First on the list was CCE 568. The engine had been dismantled by a part-time fitter and parts were scattered all round the workshops, but all were found and the engine was rebuilt with the very minimum of expense and the bus was soon back in service. I then set about sorting out and repairing the starter motors and was able to get most of them back into working order and refitted to their respective vehicles. This of course eased the tremendous effort put in by our early morning 'human starter', Charlie Thompson. That morning start was an education in itself, with the 'first light' vocabulary emerging with profuse exuberance from the front of each vehicle, and, mingled with this, the frequent shout 'look out!' as Gilford handles flew across the yard. Only the nimble survived.

One day, early in 1942 I think it was, I was working in the garage on my own when two officials appeared and said they wanted to look around. After a while they spoke to me: 'Those two buses standing in the big barn will have to be made to run.' I didn't think that was very likely, for they had been dismantled, had no engines in them and had been written off. But they insisted that they would be back on the road. I said I would get the 'top brass' over, and buzzed N.C.P.T. on the extension line we had between the garage and the Marquis of Granby at Haslingfield. When I told him what these gentlemen had said they wanted done, he replied, 'They b . . . well can't do that, who do they think they are? It would cost the earth. Tell them we're not putting them back on the road.'

'I have told them that a few times already, and they say they are going to run, so I suggest you come over and talk to them.'

He soon arrived in his car, and it appeared they were government men dealing with the requisitioning of vehicles. After talking to N.C.P.T. for a while they came over to me and asked if I could put all the parts back on HX 4364 (the most recently dismantled vehicle) and make it a runner. I said I would have a go. No repair work was to be carried out; we were just to make the vehicle complete. When this was done I had to ring a Biggleswade number to get further instructions. This I did, and told them that the engine sounded like a tin of nails, but they seemed to be pleased. They then gave me instructions to collect all the remaining parts I could find relevant to the 20-seater Gilford, and load them onto the bus. Then we had to tow the vehicle to Robert's Engineering at Whitwell near Welwyn, so that they could rebuild the engine and manufacture any parts that were missing. This was done and we eventually got the vehicle back, but even with all this effort the two vehicles were very poor runners.

Whilst this was going on, CCE 568 again developed engine trouble, and to put this right it required a crankshaft regrind and new bearings. The same government men appeared in the yard again and asked what was wrong with it, so I told

'Only the nimble survive'

them. They said they would let me know what to do, and two days later they rang up and asked if I thought I could drive the bus to Newmarket without doing more damage to the engine. I said I would nurse it there and they told me to take it to Crisswell's garage in Newmarket, who would be ready to recondition the engine. This was duly completed and before we collected the vehicle they painted it all over with dark navy blue paint. It looked like 'Gulliver's hearse'. Once this vehicle was back, we had achieved that which we thought to be impossible: we had all eight vehicles running, albeit some of them a little shakily.

During this early period, a young evacuee from London had come to work for us. His name was Frank Grice. He worked with me in the garage for some time, in fact, until another man, known as 'Sailor Howard', joined the Company in December 1942 to run the office in Cambridge, and he encouraged Frank to go and work with him there. As far as I was concerned, I had known better men than Mr Howard, but I must say that he was the first man to join the Company who had enough mechanical knowledge to know that a certain number of new parts had to be put on the vehicles to keep them going, and who was interested enough to try and make it possible to purchase them. Up to that time the Managing Director would always say, 'We can't afford it, patch it up.'

Apart from the task of getting the vehicles back on the road, daily running repairs had to be carried out in the evenings, and often well into the night, so that the vehicles could be used the next day, and this caused some 'aggro' from neighbours, who 'gently' called to us over the fence.

We were thus working on a day to day basis, just keeping the vehicles going. I think the MOT examiners thought the Company was like a ship without a captain at the helm. So they gave us long lists of defects to rectify by the next week's inspection, in an attempt to raise the level of safety and reliability, and in turn keep the vehicles on the road.

At this time, vehicles carried a 'Permit to Carry Passengers', which was issued by the Traffic Commissioners, and without which a vehicle could not run. However, knowing the circumstances, these people were very fair to us, especially T.F. Turton, the Chief Certifying Officer, who gave us a lot of help and advice. He would call in at the garage quite frequently just to have a chat, see how things were going and tell us to keep up the good work. He seemed to be very interested in the Company and keen to see it succeed, and this gave us a lot of encouragement and a good anchor. My opinion is

that his influence at the top went a long way to giving us the opportunity to improve gradually and to survive.

Incidentally I must myself have had some faith in the survival of the Company, although there was no fairy godmother in sight, because one day Mr Howard, then Company Secretary, came to the garage and asked if I was interested in buuying some shares. I bought fifty.

It was now 1943, and I joined the armed forces.

MORE WAR, 1942–43

The years 1940 and 1941 were easily the worst that Premier staggered through. But time was on our side and help was around the corner. While E.A.L. was home on leave in late 1942, he had a meeting with ECOC about local services. One of their Traffic Assistants, Mr R. A. Howard, was present. Apparently impressed by the young sailor, he rang up the next morning and asked if there was a job for him with Premier. The two Directors had a short consultation and agreed there certainly was room for an administrator cum Traffic Manager and, within a week or two, he was installed at Market Hill and a new phase of our development had begun.

I remember the relief with which I heard of R.A.H.'s appointment. No longer would I have to rush backwards and forwards from Panton Street, our home, to the office (often on my mother's tricycle) or spend an enormous amount of time answering the phone and conducting long argumentative calls with N.C.P.T. No longer would I have to leave the baby asleep in her pram on the Market Place whilst I watched over her from the first floor balcony, above what is now Watches of Switzerland. I thought then that all would be easy and that I would revert to being mother of two, housewife and landlady, for we had billetees, evacuees and plain lodgers at different periods of the war. Even my good mother would benefit, since she would no longer be needed as baby-sitter and general factotum.

In one way I was right, because R.A.H. immediately took over the correspondence and we have many of his long and detailed letters by which he kept E.A.L. in managerial contact throughout the rest of the war. And of course his coming marked the end of the lowest ebb of Premier's fortunes, when domestic upheavals vied with breakdowns for priority treatment and daily rotas were worked out side by side with ration books, amidst children's hullaballoo. From this time onwards there was only one way for Premier, 'go up or go under'. R.A.H. turned out to be the right man at that moment to take us up.

Needless to say, it wasn't a smooth journey and almost immediately I was again involved in the affairs of the Company. The reason was that, within weeks of his arrival, R.A.H. and N.C.P.T. were at loggerheads. The heat of the argument rose daily as R.A.H.'s administrative and traffic plans were thwarted by the bad maintenance of the fleet. N.C.P.T., in turn, felt he was the fall-back man for everything that went wrong and I was no help to him, since I myself shared this feeling of being overwhelmed.

Luckily there was always the phone and, day after day, when he was not on patrol duty, the absent Chairman would put in a transferred charge call to Cambridge 54333. (One call amounted to thirty shillings, so I queried it with the operator, pointing out that by wartime regulation we were only allowed six minutes for trunk calls. She phoned back with the exact details of a midnight to 00.45 call, so we had to pay.) Every day E.A.L. fed new ideas, solutions, encouragement to the three of us but, notwithstanding all his efforts from afar to keep us working in constructive harmony, there came a moment when there had to be a more drastic solution. The following letter expresses the outcome succinctly.

15 March, 1943

Dear Sir Christopher,

The date of my seasonal leave having now been settled, I have arranged for the Annual General Meeting of the Company, and a Director's Meeting to be held on Tuesday, March 30th. The agendas for both Meetings are being forwarded to you and Captain Kirk and I very much hope that you will be able to be present. Should the date proposed be inconvenient to you we can hold the meetings on any of the three following days.

Although the Company is now doing much better than at any time in the past, our revenue and profit figures are much less than they should be. We have turned down a number of highly remunerative contracts owing to failure to keep the whole fleet in sound mechanical condition and have consequently not been operating at anything approaching capacity on the contract side. This is largely due to inefficiency and I feel that drastic steps are necessary to improve the position.

Howard, whom I think you have met, came to us

as Traffic Manager about four months ago and has already made considerable improvements. It is, however, practically impossible for him to achieve the maximum efficiency unless he is given full authority and I feel therefore that the best course is to appoint him a Director. He is prepared to invest £100, which I gather is the most he can conveniently manage at present. I have asked him to discuss the matter in detail with Thompson and to offer to take over 100 of his shares. I am writing to Thompson myself putting the position to him as clearly as I can. Quite frankly I have come to the conclusion that he has largely lost interest in the business. Another step which I am anxious to take is to transfer £100 of my holding to my wife and secure her own position by appointing her a Director. She now has a fairly comprehensive knowledge of the business but cannot exercise any real influence without having the appropriate authority.

These changes will, in my opinion, be beneficial to the Company and will give immediate results. Meanwhile I am not forgetting my promise to acquire two thirds of your own holding as soon as the war is over. I hope that we may at the same time be able to persuade you to resume the Chairmanship after the war; persuade is the wrong word in point of fact as I am convinced that the present and future prospects of the Company are quite satisfactory, given reasonably efficient management. The Traffic Commissioners have informed us that we may acquire one (& presumably two or three if we so desire) of the new Austerity 32-seater Bedford buses. These vehicles are priced at £800 complete and when operated on short-mileage, daily contracts at £7 10 0d per day and upwards are an excellent proposition. We can also have a double-decker on loan from London Transport at £25 per month. This bus would avoid a great deal of duplication on the local services – Howard tells me that the actual mileage saved would be 263 per week – and release two saloon buses. In order to obtain this vehicle we must improve our maintenance system, however, as the Traffic Commissioners require to be fully satisfied that we can keep the vehicle up to the standard required by London Transport and will not consent to this transfer until this is done. It is quite obvious to me that under present conditions the possibilities of the business are enormous and it is equally clear that we are not at the moment pulling our weight in the war effort.

I enclose two cuttings from Modern Transport dealing with the history and activities of the Company. Howard tells me that he gave you a copy of the issue containing the final instalment. Perhaps you will let me have your views and suggestions regarding the points I have outlined.

Yours sincerely,

Arthur Lainson.

Sir Christopher replied sharply by return:

Dear Lainson,   16th March, 1943

I was surprised to get your letter in which you say you are buying Thompson's shares before having kept your promise to buy Captain Kirk's and my own first – You are in a hole, I am sure, or I feel you would not have suggested such a thing and you must own that you got yourself into it.

I was unfortunately cut off in the middle of a telephone call that your wife put through and was therefore unable to finish the conversation. I am the last person who would refuse to offer help – and I feel that your wife has made quite an effort to keep things going. I also feel however, that Captain Kirk, Major Talbot Ponsonby and I should be considered and that if I personally am willing to forgo my right and allow you to buy Thompson's share before our own that a definite date should be agreed on when you will buy ours – the end of the war is much too indefinite and as money appears to be forthcoming that date should be in the near future.

You will probably get along better on your own – Thompson and you never seemed to see eye to eye but if I may advise you I should certainly not lose the substance for the shadow. Thompson's routes are the substance that should be safeguarded at all costs – the right to run is the good-will and is worth much more than anything.

Yours sincerely,

Christopher Magnay.

In spite of the harsh terms of this letter, E.A.L. went ahead and at the Board meeting on 30 March 1943 the proposition that R.A.H. and myself should be appointed Directors was put but later withdrawn, as N.C.P.T. pointed out that R.A.H. had only been with us a short time. The second proposal was carried, and authorised R.A.H. to take control of the garage for a period of six months.

The Auditors remarked, to soften the blow to N.C.P.T.'s pride, that he occupied the position of Managing Director and should therefore not be worried with any of the small points with which he often had to deal.

Unfortunately, this effort at compromise did not work at all and the next few months were so horrible, so hurtful to all concerned, so ugly, that I

will draw a veil over the whole business and just record the final outcome of that hectic time.

On 15 July 1943 a meeting of the Company was held, with E.A.L. in the chair. A number of resolutions were proposed and carried, as a result of which N.C.P.T. relinquished his post as Managing Director to E.A.L.; R.A.H. and M.M.E.L. were elected Directors; and R.A.H. was appointed Company Secretary. N.C.P.T. retained his directorship but only for a year or so, after which his Premier connection ceased.

This was a very sad day for the founder of Harston and District Motor Services, caught up in a situation not of his own making, and all of us felt depressed and slightly defeated by events. It seemed to us, and still does, that N.C.P.T. had to pay too great a price for Premier Travel's sake, but we tended to believe and have always maintained that the Company must come first. So much so in fact, that even now in the eighties, when some problem is worrying the young Directors, the present Managing Director (F.N.M.) tells them, 'Ask yourself what is best for Premier, decide what it is, do it and it will prove to be best for you as well.' In 1943 the Company, like the country, was waging its own war of survival, and individuals were sacrificed. In times of peace, people came first. We were at war.

SECOND FRONT, 1943–46

From this traumatic Boardroom upheaval came a very great blessing for Premier. R.A.H. knew a well-known businessman in Cambridge, Mr W.F. Matthews, and, shortly after joining the Company, he talked to him about his concern for Premier's future and its need for substantial new capital. W.F.M. knew E.A.L. slightly from the days when the latter was up at St Catherine's College and had called there to ask him to display a UR poster. Later, he often told us that he had a nose for good people, consequently he had become very interested in the ex-undergraduate's new venture. It was at exactly this period that the personal difficulties between N.C.P.T. and R.A.H. were coming to a head, and so, after a re-introduction when E.A.L. was home on leave, W.F.M. offered to acquire a substantial shareholding in the Company, if consideration could be given to his joining the Board, to protect his investment. This resulted in his purchase of N.C.P.T.'s holding in March 1944.

A Board meeting followed on 20 July 1944, when the appointment of W.F.M. as Director was proposed by E.A.L., seconded by R.A.H. and carried.

The Minutes document this moment:

> Mr Lainson added that Mr Matthews would be a valuable addition to the Board, and, by virtue of his considerable business experience, his counsels would be very welcome.

At the same meeting, after reading a letter from N.C.P.T., E.A.L. proposed that the former's resignation from his office of Director be accepted and that N.C.P.T.'s great services to the Company be placed on record in the Minutes.

W.F.M.'s appointment to the Board was certainly the most fortunate thing that could have happened to Premier. He was older, wiser, stronger than we Lainsons, he was tolerant and calm, he gave confidence to people outside the Company, he backed his own judgements to the hilt. He wasn't the type we had known before, who could not withstand a summer squall, let alone the devastating storms that our Company had to meet from time to time. Having built up a thriving business with his own brothers, he had in mind the future of his five sons, three of whom were in the forces, and he saw Premier as a young Company, full of potential but sadly lacking capital and experience. W.F.M. had both, and the combination of the two families worked amazingly well from the beginning. In addition, W.F.M.'s directorship lifted the Company into a new era of authority and efficiency, and the weekly Board meetings of W.F.M., R.A.H. and myself brought the Company haltingly but successfully through the last days of the war. The prospect of peace in our little Company matched the progress in Europe and the world, and filled us all with hope for the future.

From March 1945, formal Minutes of deliberations were once again recorded regularly, a practice religiously adhered to ever since. Among the items of interest mentioned was the acquisition of 215–17 Newmarket Road for the purpose of erecting a garage and bus station, as soon as circumstances would permit. (They never did, because we had to sell the site later.) We ordered uniforms, we patted each other on the back at the great improvements in the garage set-up, we recorded our guarantee that 'Full wages, less Insurance Benefits, were to be paid during sickness.' This had been E.A.L.'s policy from the first days of the Company, and it has always been a source of pride to us that we were among the first to introduce sick pay, for up to one month, or longer in special cases.

We recorded a red-letter day for Premier when W.F.M. told the Board in March 1945 that he would like to make his son, Frank Neville Matthews, a shareholder and perhaps a future employee of the Company. On 24 May 1945 F.N.M. was himself present at the Board meeting, at the invitation of the Directors. From then on he worked for the Company during his leaves, or whenever able, until he was finally demobbed, still only twenty-two years old, after a distinguished Army career.

From March until May 1945, the Minutes record week by week the progress of negotiations for the purchase of the business of Mr F. E. Weeden of Chrishall. Finally, on the 24 May, we agreed to purchase, 'subject to transfer of Mr Weeden's existing Licences, all Mr Weeden's buses, garage, workshops, tools and equipment, stores, the bungalow and adjoining land in the possession of Mr Weeden for £17,000'.

E.A.L. recalls the history of this pioneer company:

'While I was stationed in Portsmouth, my wife and Mr Matthews phoned me to tell me they had purchased the Weeden business. I was extremely pleased and very happy because this was our first expansion scheme, after a period of about eight years.

'Mr Weeden had originally established his business in Heydon, near Royston, Hertfordshire, under the name "Heydon and District", and by the early 1930s he had transferred to Chrishall, where he built a bungalow and acquired about two acres of land. During the war he had also developed a busy route between Duxford Aerodrome and Cambridge. His services were numbered in the Premier series from 8 to 14.

When we acquired the business in 1945 we took over the big Dennis CVE 12, with two Albions, one a 26-seater, one a 20-seater, two or three Bedfords and a Gilford, WG 1284. In addition to the vehicles, Mr Weeden had a very good staff. Mr Bill Day, whom I had first met in the days of UR and who figures many times in our story, remained with us until his death; Mr H. Mardell became an exceptionally skilled body-builder but, alas, developed crippling arthritis and had to retire early; Mr Harry Law, one of three brothers who have enriched the Company, was in the top class of coach drivers until his retirement in 1976; Mr Alf Wisbey, a man of courage and skill, became and remains our first full-time storekeeper. Other members of Mr Weeden's staff only stayed a matter of years – twenty in one case, but not a lifetime as did the very loyal members of the family team.

'Mr Weeden died comparatively recently aged 80 after a long and interesting life.' RIP

Our steady progress through 1945 continued to be recorded on the Minutes. On 12 April, I prop-

CVE 12; Weeden's Dennis Lancet, 1945

osed and it was seconded by R.A.H. that all the Gilford coaches, except Mr Gifford's infamous HX 3464, be sold. Another sad day.

W.F.M.'s proposal to pay a £3 bonus to every full-time adult employee was carried unanimously. After several meetings and discussions, it was decided a dividend of six per cent for the year 1944 could be paid.

At no meeting in May, June or July 1945 was victory or the end of the war mentioned, but on 30 August it was suggested that the Company should take part in 'charity outings to celebrate victory'. E.A.L. commented that it would be better to hold them over until the end of the season.

The first post-war timetable, designed and printed by Index Publishers Ltd of Dunstable, was considered and agreed.

On 6 September we reported the final breakdown of HX 3464, owing to a cracked cylinder block. It was like saying farewell to an old friend. On 20 September HX was still on the agenda, since the Board had been offered £50 for it by a Mr Harris, a fairground showman. The offer was refused.

Chrishall garage extensions were discussed – the painting programme was behind; the bungalow at Chrishall was withdrawn from auction; it was agreed that no employee at Harston garage should work more than the flat 48 hours weekly. HX was soon back in the picture – a fish and chip vendor appeared interested in purchasing it for about £150 (still no decision). Regular excursions from Sawston and Saffron Walden to Newmarket Races were inaugurated in late September; new vehicles were proposed by W.F.M. for delivery the next year. On 4 October an investigation into the annual figures took place:

> It quickly became evident that a margin of profit exceeding that ever before earned by the Company had been achieved, largely due to the heavy volume of Private Hire. However, it was agreed that the Capital structure was most unsatisfactory.

Ever prudent, Mr Reeves, our Bank Manager, pointed out that the Company was trying to purchase far too much in too short a time.

Not a word anywhere about E.A.L.'s September 1945 demobilisation, so welcome, so longed for, so needed. He seemed just to reappear as though he had never been away.

Business was quickly getting back to normal. The first London services to be restored after the war were those of Grey Pullman and Mr Jennings of Ashen; Premier, and Drayton Motor Services restarted their London services in the same week, on 9 November 1945. The Directors were settling down and sometimes irritating each other – E.A.L.'s return to direct managerial control was necessarily at the expense of the free hand R.A.H. had enjoyed for a couple of years. W.F.M. called attention to these difficulties and favoured E.A.L., which was rather hard for R.A.H. However, we were all pushing forward, usually together.

In October, the first contact with Drayton Motor Services of Barley near Royston was reported in the Minutes, but in November 1945 it was suggested that the new Government's nationalisation programme made it doubtful whether the Company should continue its policy of expansion. E.A.L. replied that nationalisation of public transport was not included in the King's speech and he could see no reason why the Company should not continue negotiations with Drayton Motor Services, as, even if the Company was taken over in the near future, compensation would have to be paid.

As a result of this discussion, it was felt that the Company should add its full weight and influence to the opposition to the Government's proposals on this matter. W.F.M. therefore proposed that the Company join the Passenger Vehicle Operators Association as from 1945. This resolution was the first step in E.A.L.'s very close connection, on behalf of the Company, with the national affairs of the bus and coach industry.

Two further items of interest relevant to the future of the Company appear in the last Minutes of the first decade. On 3 January 1946, it was reported that a Mr Gill of Godmanchester had visited E.A.L. to discuss the purchase of his coach business in the Huntingdon area. At the same meeting we mentioned the possibility of having an arrangement with an American tourist company for tours in the British Isles, booked in America. It was turned down as 1946 was probably not the best time to consider the proposal. (Shades of things to come! In June 1981, thirty-five years later, the North American Department of Premier Travel Agency was opened in Rose Crescent and is flourishing greatly.)

E.A.L. signed these last minutes on 10 January 1946 and nowhere is there a reference to the anniversary of our first ten years. A pity, because, as we entered our second decade, the Company could have spared a little time for self-congratulation. Best of all, the war was over and won and no member of the Staff or Board had been killed, though F.N.M. was badly wounded in France on D-Day + 14. On demobilisation he joined Premier to become, with E.A.L., one of the chief architects of its success. The fleet was in better order than in 1940; we had the nucleus of a very loyal staff; all our services were expanding and increasing daily; and we had ended up with one large new acquisition under our belt, with two more en route. There was still a lamentable lack of capital in spite of W.F.M.'s investments. Otherwise we were all of us ready to go.

Support Independent Enterprise !

4

The Founding Members

In 1985 there are two founder members of Premier Travel Limited who have 'wintered and summered' it for 49 years. One is Edward Arthur Lainson, the other is Sidney Ernest Pennell. When Premier took over Harston and District Motor Services in 1936 there were eight people working for the firm, plus Mr Norman Thompson himself. One was his brother, Charlie Thompson, who was an immensely hard-working and uncomplaining driver cum conductor cum fitter who left us before the end of the war. All the rest drifted away, largely because of the war, but Syd Pennell came back after his service in the Suffolk Regiment and, luckily for us, has been with us ever since.

The excellent thing about him is that he can't be fooled, and nothing would ever stop him telling us exactly what was wrong with the Company, its Directors and its general strategy. When he was

A founding member: S.E. Pennell

made Staff Representative, we heard his sound views, his home truths, at official level. Later still came his public appearances at the Company dinners. He normally spoke last but one and he used to flay us alive, to the accompaniment of appreciative gusts of laughter. E.A.L. always, year by year, found the good things to say; the people to be congratulated; the achievements of individuals; his genuine pleasure at this or that success; and his total optimism for the future. Syd would come along with a catalogue of woe. He would stand up reluctantly and shyly and say something like:

> Well, I dunno! What do I say? The Guvnor here says we're doing fine . . . nearly out of the bloody wood. Well, what I say is, he ought to be driving my bus. No so and so brakes . . . no lights . . . 18 hours a day. You've got to be barmy to work for this firm . . . None of you lot know what's going on. Anyway, as Frankie says, its not all management . . . some of the men driving vehicles aren't worth a light . . . just steersmen. They haven't a clue what driving's about. I reckon we're all a lot of suckers to be with the Company but there you are . . . we've had a jolly good dinner thanks to the Directors and I dare say we'll be here next year . . .

We all loved it: it was, so to speak, 'family talk'. Added to the general euphoria of a company meal, Syd acted like a tonic, and when all was over the things we thought about were Syd's strictures, which needed remembering, and the fabulously funny stories F.N.M. would tell.

The annual dinner is now a very posh affair at the University Arms Hotel and at the top table sit the Directors and their wives. Syd doesn't usually speak nowadays but on the fortieth anniversary he did. To my horror, as at the Club 25 Dinner a month or two earlier, all attack had gone from him. He was full of very sincere praise for the Board's treatment of him now that arthritis in a vilely acute form prevented him from driving. I hated hearing him praise everyone; he even said the Company missed me. To all of us he'll always be the fighter, the strong individualist, the valuable friend and companion we've known nearly all our life. His wife is also an excellent example of how to work with a husband and not against him. Its the dickens of a life being a transport wife, because of the odd hours, now termed 'anti-social hours', the overnight stop-overs, the erratic calls upon overtime. No home plan is sacred where drivers are concerned, and Syd and his wife, being so able and willing, have suffered a lot from being used. Fortunately he knows that everyone in Premier loves and respects him and cares for him, however difficult it is to tell him so.

The following is his own story of his life with Premier.

LIFE WITH PREMIER

S.E. Pennell

I was born in 1915 in the West Country. We lived at Upper Minety and between 1901 and 1914 my father was local carrier between various villages like Hankerton and Upper Minety. I've often wondered what would have happened if he had lived . . . perhaps we'd have had a big transport company by now? But he died. He was killed in France on 27 November 1917 and he is buried in Louveral Cemetery. He was thirty-four years old and he'd only been out there a fortnight. The chap standing beside him was alright and he wrote to my mother and told her what had happened. I never have seen his grave. However, one day, not long ago, we were on holiday in the West and I said one morning, 'We'll go to Minety and have a look round today.' So we did. We wandered about the place but I couldn't find any traces of my father, so we went on to Hankerton. I found the church where I thought my father's name should be on the war memorial and there it was. It was the first time I had seen his name recorded anywhere.

After his death, my mother's family, who came from Harston, told her to come down and stay with them until we found a house, which we did, not far from Ron Bass. After a bit the owner, who was a nurse, wanted the house on her own, so got us out. We then moved to Hurrell's Row and we stayed there until I got married. God knows how my mother managed to bring us all up – Dad was only a corporal, so she didn't have much of a pension.

Why did I want to become a ruddy bus-driver? Well, it was a family connection, in a way, since Norman, my cousin, had five or six buses – Harston Motors, they were called. I joined them when I was sixteen and was too young to drive or conduct, but I very quickly learnt to start the buses up and shunt

them about the yard and I knew the services by heart.

I remember the first time I met E.A.L., though I had seen him about the place often enough. We had the first staff meeting one evening at the Marquis of Granby, Norman's pub. All of us were there: Harry Adams, Mrs Adams (who did the accounts for Harston Motors), Lance Northrop, Charlie Thompson, Chris Gatward, Buffer Gatward, Mick Fordham, Syd Neaves and myself. Mr Lainson was a typical 'grad' – bike clips over his heels, short trousers, good manners. He was only four years older than me, a bit taller, same fair hair. 'Mother' used to think we could be brothers. Anyway we drank our pints and smoked his De Reske cigarettes. He told us that he intended to build up, with our help, a network of express services covering the whole country. We sniggered slightly and got down to the real business of the meeting – money and wages.

Mr Lainson said, 'Your wages will be the same as hitherto.' Well I didn't agree with that, so we began to have a go at each other (not for the last time, either). Eventually, we settled for forty-five bob [£2.25] in the winter and £2 10s [£2.50] in the summer. Our normal week was about 60 hours and any overtime was a penny less an hour than ordinary time. Those were the days! Of course, what we earned we took home because there was no PAYE and our insurance stamp didn't amount to much.

Not long after Premier took over, they bought Empire Best's Express Service between Birmingham and Clacton and I remember vividly my first journey on Service 5. Harry Adams and Chris Gatward had been the regular drivers and I had to stand in one Friday for C.G. I had a bloody old Gilford and had never been to Birmingham in my life, so Harry told me how to go and I got there without a mistake. At that time I could get hold of a map and memorise it, which proved useful more than once. There wasn't much traffic on the road to Brum and I got there by 10 p.m. I needed a quick pint so it was quite some time before I went down the alleyway to the driver's lodgings. The landlord was waiting for me: 'Since Premier took over, this blankety bus has never been on time. You want to get some decent coaches . . . so and so old Gilfords . . . crawling up the hills . . . I want you here by eight o'clock or nine at the latest.' What a welcome on my first journey to Birmingham!

Actually I also did the last run on Service 5 before it was cancelled for the duration. It ran until the end of September 1939 and our last journey was made with side-lights or rather small slits across the blacked out lamps.

Although I was in a reserved occupation to begin with, I was called up to the RASC in 1941. Mother called up the stairs one day: 'Your papers are here!'

'Open them up then', I shouted back. 'Where for?'

'Bury St Edmunds', she called.

'Bugger!' I said, 'that means bloody infantry.'

Luckily I was put on buses, and had to take an instructor's course. When the OC asked me what I had learnt I had to tell him that I hadn't learnt anything. Which was quite true. I knew about buses before I got into the Army.

Then I had a spell in the Airborne and I hated that.

'If you don't jump, you'll be sent back to your unit and then overseas.'

'That'll suit me.'

'Aren't you going to jump?' asked the OC placatingly.

'No, Sir, I hate heights.'

So they made me Brigadier's Driver and we got sent to Gibraltar Barracks, Bury St Edmunds, to train with the 18th Division, which went to Singapore. However, the rule was that every man had to have had three months training before embarkation. I'd only been there six weeks and I was ordered off the draft. Perhaps it was lucky for me, but I was disappointed, as I had wanted to go very much. After various postings, I ended the war as Driver Instructor and was at Shrublands when Mr Frank Matthews was stationed there with the 8th Battalion. He was a captain by that time but we didn't meet each other then.

When I came back in 1946 I had seven weeks demob. leave due, but after a fortnight or so I made myself available for work and went up to the office and saw E.A.L. and Sailor Howard. They started me off as D.C. (driver–conductor) on Services 1 and 2. What impressed me most were the fiddlers who were about. None would do D.C. work. Well, I wasn't having that so I went up to the office again and put my bag and long rack of tickets on the counter and said, 'That's my lot!' E.A.L. agreed with me and I started again as a driver only.

I remember one incident shortly afterwards which had a bit to do with the war. I had a private hire to Oakington RAF Station, taking nurses to the officers' and sergeants' mess for a dance. While I was there a warrant officer looked at me and said: 'You!' I took no notice. 'You there. I'm talking to you. You do as I tell you on my camp.'

'Can you see a RAF uniform on me?' I asked. 'When I'm in the services, one thing. But I've had six years of types like you but not any more – not

any more.' I felt better. F.N.M. got a report about it but he didn't mention it until much later.

I always remember the first time I met Frankie (sorry, 'Mr Matthews' I should say, but we all called him Frank or Frankie – now of course he's Guvnor and E.A.L. is 'Father'!). Anyway, I was on service, coming through Harston and F.N.M. stood outside the garage and waved me down, I was driving the Albion.

'Where are you going? What's your name?' he asked.

'Pennell, I'm going to Fowlmere.'

'Well Pennell, why haven't you got Fowlmere up on your indicator?'

'Because I haven't got it up', I answered, and drove on. A day or so later, I met Mr W.F. Matthews.

'Ah,' he said, 'I want to see you about that destination roll. My son (Frank had only just joined so he wasn't a Director at the time) tells me you were showing Relief instead of Fowlmere.' Then he started getting a bit 'orty' and so did I: 'You have had these b . . . Weeden's buses I don't know how many months and you've done nothing about them at all. How the devil can I show Fowlmere when it's not on the roll?' Within three or four days, something was done.

Just to finish off my first ten years with Premier, when Service 5 to Birmingham started up after the war, they sent me up there in a car with Harry Law, Alf Wisbey and Gerry Good to teach them the route. We then did the service together for some time, driving alternative long and short weekends. Traffic was heavy and we were always overloaded with lots of reliefs to take care of. I drove an 'oiler' (i.e. diesel) coach, the Dennis 668, which went up the hills like hell. I'll never forget it. The vehicles on hire to us from Morley's Grey Coaches, AECs, were left standing and they would swear about the Dennis, partly because they were scared of losing me in the traffic.

'Keep going straight,' said I, 'then if I have to turn off, I'll wait for you.' And I did. One driver told another, who told me: 'One thing about old Pennell – he'll never leave you.' And he never did.

H. J. BIRD

Another Premier personality joined the Company in 1937. Herbert James Bird of Green Street, Royston was born in 1901 and, early in the twenties, had had the distinction of being one of the few drivers convicted of exceeding the 12 m.p.h. speed limit in a motor lorry. Later he had taken his PSV licence.

E.A.L. recalls the reasons for his employment by Premier: 'Mr Thompson and I purchased from Broadway Coaches of Hanslip a 20-seater Gilford coach, HX 3464, for the express purpose of out-stationing it at Royston to save dead mileage between Harston and Royston on Service 1. Birdie, as he became known to most of us, was taken on to do the 9.35 a.m. out of Royston, finishing his day at 7.10 p.m. at the Green Man, thus saving 16 miles a day. His commencing wage was £2 15s [£2.75] per week. He was a great success, proving one hundred per cent reliable, punctual to the minute, with the best handwriting ever seen in the Company. He was a law unto himself; he always wore a cloth cap, he would exchange it for no other; he hated any change of duty or upset in his routine and didn't hesitate to let us know his feelings.

'As an illustration of his "candour", he himself told me this story of an encounter he had with Sir Haviland Hiley, the Traffic Commissioner, and former General Manager of New Zealand State Railways.

'Apparently the latter was walking round Drummer Street one day and saw Birdie standing by his bus, so he spoke to him: "Where is this bus going?" In his dark-brown voice Birdie barked back:

"It's on the front." Then thinking he'd perhaps been a bit sharp, he added: "Where do you want to go anyway?"

"No-where, thanks very much," said Sir Haviland dryly, "I just wanted to know, as I am the Traffic Commissioner." Birdie was discomforted.

'Of course, his regulars revelled in this kind of gruff, down-to-earth, sardonic approach and he was much respected or feared by all of us, management, staff and passengers. My wife depended upon him as a senior driver in the war and, on more than one occasion, she went round to beg Birdie to do an extra journey for her or return a contract, in some emergency. He always said, "No! It'll do you no good because if I do change my duty, how will you cover for me and then where will you be? Buses all over the place, furious passengers and drivers out of position. You leave me as I am. You'll be glad later." She would go away frustrated and defeated but he was right and so taught her the hard lesson of traffic management, that each commitment should stand on its own.

One of his regular private hire commitments was for the University Department of Geography, who always asked that he should be their driver on their three- or four-day courses. On one occasion, he had a slight bump, coming out of a side road into a busy mainstream of traffic. On the face of it, it appeared to be his fault, but so convinced were the Company and Professor "X" that he was far too good a driver to make a mistake that the case was postponed twice so that the good Professor could appear personally in Birdie's defence. Needless to say, he was acquitted.

'When he retired from his full-time work at the age of 65, he continued to drive Service 4 from Cambridge to Yarmouth every Saturday for a number of years. We had a really heart-warming party for this man of integrity, who is still something of a legend in the Company's history, and his wife and daughter were there to see how greatly he was appreciated by all and sundry. RIP'

F. R. BARKER

The other new boy in 1937 was Frederick Robert Barker of Haslingfield. This young man was only twenty when he joined Premier, he left us again to go to war and returned to spend the remainder of his abruptly shortened life with us. During the war he was in the thick of trouble several times and was twice mentioned in dispatches, a very great honour in the Second World War. It was typical of Fred that no one in the Company seems to have known of these distinctions until after his death.

In fact, Fred was one of those salt-of-the-earth people who is not fully appreciated until it is too late. He was a quizzical type, who would do absolutely anything anyone asked him. Let a coach need a late night driver, let an early morning bus break down, let an excursion need covering on a Sunday, let a colleague need a lift home: Fred Barker was your man. His wife says he lived Premier; that such a man should think us a Company worth living for, must be our greatest pride. This is his speech made at his retirement party in November 1981:

Ladies and Gentlemen.

Those of you who know me are aware that I am not normally the person who leaps to his feet to make speeches – except of course after suitable alcoholic assistance. I have never needed to say too much – the wife usually says it for me!

Seriously, after 45 years with one company I think even I must break a habit. To say I am overwhelmed by what has happened today is too simple. I am obviously grateful for the tribute of this occasion, but really the pleasure of working for the company has been all mine.

When I joined the small company of Premier Travel at the Harston garage I could never have guessed what would happen all these years later.

We remember them well: (left to right) *F.R. Barker, E.W. Day, A.W. Hill*

Luxury coaches, travel companies and freight transport were unthinkable. I left the Company from 1940 and rejoined in 1946 after the war years, moving from garage-hand to conductor to driver. My old friend Jack Gifford, who has beaten us all as a Director, has, I am sure, some very fond memories of our time at Harston: the pit we built which filled up with water, the old buses we managed to keep on the road against all odds, and the weeks when we cleared away years of rubbish before moving to Chrishall garage. Lately we have moved to our new premises at Kilmaine Close, and all those memories are very much in the past. When I think of the old cold buses I used to drive I realise how much the Company has developed.

I would like to thank all the Directors, Mr Matthews, Mr and Mrs Lainson and all who I have worked with these past years. I have been happy working for the Company and pleased to see its development to its present state. I hope my small contribution has assisted in this respect and I look forward to a few more years before I am finally 'parked up' into retirement.

Thank you for giving me and my family a good living during these many years and I hope the Company continues to strengthen in the future. Thank you all.

We were all deeply shaken when, four months later, Fred had a violent heart attack, and then another, and it was all over. Three hundred people attended his funeral at Haslingfield parish church, including people who had worked with him thirty years earlier. A large funeral is not necessarily a sign of love and respect, but in Fred's case it certainly was. RIP

E. W. DAY

Bill Day and E.A.L. first met when the former was driving on regular commitments for UR. He was then, in the early thirties, working for Weeden's Motor Services and when Premier took the company over, Bill Day came too.

He was a lovely type of person. He became Depot Foreman at Chrishall but that did not mean he worked only in the garage. He turned into a driver at the drop of a hat, which, in transport terms, meant that in every emergency he would turn up anywhere in the Company's area, when and as required.

He was co-driver with Harry Law on the great expedition to Austria in 1956, and when they dropped me outside the refugee camp in Vienna he was so upset at leaving me alone that he pressed two fivers into my hand, in case I ran out of money in a strange land. Both of them embraced me in tearful farewells.

His first days of retirement went sour on him, as they do for many people, but then he started working again full-time and was one of the oldest men ever to drive a coach.

Premier will never forget the warmth, laughter and loyalty Bill Day and his wife and family brought to the daily life of the Company. RIP

5

Running the Show

FORWARD! 1946–49

From the beginning of Premier's second decade, the Company launched itself into a period of great expansion. An agreement to purchase Mr A. Gill's coach business in Godmanchester was signed and sealed on 14 January 1946 with a completion date in March. There is an interesting Minute about this new enterprise:

> The Company hoped and expected a considerable extension of business in this new locality, and that to obtain this, every assistance would be given to the manager of the depot in the way of publicity and vehicle provision. All the Directors expressed confidence in its possibilities, and also in the ability of the proposed manager, F.N. Matthews.

In the same month, the Company acquired the Excursion Licences of W. H. Thorne of Clacton, together with his Saturday service from Clacton to London.

During the next couple of years, the Company considered, investigated and finally opted out from purchasing or attempting to purchase a number of local operators who had approached it from time to time. It was a period of great political uncertainty for independent companies, since the fear of being swallowed up by nationalisation was in everyone's mind. There was also a sense that the great power of the National Bus Empire would be unassailable, even in the Traffic Courts, so many felt the moment had come to leave the profession. As the years went by, however, the alarms and anxieties quietened, the Commissioners proved that their justice was untarnished by the force of the bigger battalions, and so, many of the operators who contemplated selling out between 1945 and 1949 are still happily running buses and coaches throughout the region to this day.

By the end of January 1946 Premier was busily negotiating the purchase of Drayton's Motor Services of Barley and had got as far as seeing the legal representative. However, 'it was unanimously agreed that, for the time being, the Company's offer should remain in abeyance until such time as the ability to raise the necessary Capital should be apparent'. When long negotiations started again in October 1946, the financial position was still very murky and disagreement about the whole purchase position ruffled the harmony of the Board. However, all was finally and happily settled and on 4 September 1947 the Minutes record the completion of the Drayton purchase on 2 August and it was confirmed that the operation of the new vehicles and services and commenced on 23 August.

E.A.L. had come into contact with Mr Drayton early on in the days of Undergraduate Roadways. In fact, in the early thirties when UR took the Babraham Girl Guides to Walberswick for their annual camp, together with a lorry to carry their equipment, Drayton's Motor Services supplied the coach and Mr Drayton himself drove the lorry. E.A.L. went as passenger and assistant 'tent erector' when they got there. This same lorry, incidentally, was specifically left out of Premier's purchase terms, even though it had been fitted with benches for passengers. By the time Premier came into the picture, Mr Drayton was a fine patriarchal figure, surrounded by his wife and children, Will, Jim and Sis (Mrs Elizabeth Green), who all worked full-time for the firm. Indeed, Belle-Vue garage and bus depot was the modern heart of the ancient 'turnpike' village of Barley, near Royston, and the Draytons were not only engaged in transporting people by car, bus and coach (or even lorry) but they were extremely active in every aspect of village life.

Mrs Green was, and is, a remarkable person. She handled all the administration of this thriving Company, including Licensing and Traffic Court applications, even pleading their case in person. This could be quite an ordeal for anyone, especially in the Metropolitan area where discipline under Mr Gleeson-Robinson was strict. She and her brothers were full of fire and enthusiasm and had built an excellent business on the foundations of their father's enterprise. It seemed a great pity when they sold out to Premier, even though we gained greatly by the purchase, including some of the most beautiful bus routes in England. However, their loss of control did not sever their interest in passenger transport since they became shareholders in Premier as part of their purchase. Best of all, Jim Drayton's daughter, Janet, came to work at Head Office, where she was not only able and efficient but also the life and soul of the Company's daily gossip session. Everyone was delighted, especially the Matthews and Lainsons, when she and John Matthews were married in 1957. There has thus been hardly any interruption in the Drayton's interest in coach operations, even if Janet's work has been behind the scenes as the wife of the Traffic Director of Premier Travel Services.

In some ways the history of A. Drayton and his sons followed the pattern of F. Weeden and N.C.P.T., in that all three operators had set up in business shortly after the First World War and pioneered passenger transport in their particular areas. Indeed, so accurately had they gauged the needs of their local parishes, that whilst the original service frequencies have been reduced over the years, most of their rural routes are still operated on much the same timetables. This must be a tribute to their business acumen forty or fifty years ago.

Moreover, all these local operators promoted a much wider vision of the mobility that was to come by starting services to London from the most unlikely sources of traffic. Indeed, some of the pick-up points for Kings Cross were hamlets rather than villages, remote crossroads rather than community centres. The services criss-crossed Cambridgeshire, Essex and Hertfordshire, giving a facility new and rare to country people. Sometimes there was a profusion of alternative services as on Friday mornings, for example, when Mr Weeden and Mr Drayton passed each other near the village of Heydon, both going to London in different directions.

This seems a good moment to discuss what happened to these country services when they got to the great metropolis, a major problem for both independent and combine operators. The following brief and abbreviated history of Premier's difficulties, shared by many others, shows how hard it is to find or afford good premises in London. Perhaps the authorities should undertake this social service?

The Road Traffic Act of 1930 created a banned zone, in the area south of Euston Road and east of Edgware Road, for the setting down or picking up of passengers from scheduled coach services. As a result of this edict London Coastal Coaches was set up to develop Victoria Coach Station and a purpose-built coach station was opened for independent operators, in the basement of a building immediately opposite St Pancras Station. This was an ideal terminal for services from the North and East and was highly successful until 1939, when it was requisitioned by the General Post Office and has never been returned.

Since services into London were discontinued throughout the war, the problem had to be reconsidered in 1945, and when Premier first operated its newly acquired London licence, we joined the rest of the independents at Judd Street. This was an open-yard site near Euston and proved quite satisfactory for a number of years. Unfortunately its turn came for redevelopment and the services had to look elsewhere.

With the help of PSV Operators, a site was discovered in Pentonville Road, where the facilities were primitive in the extreme. F.N.M., who was, by this time, a Director of PSV, found and refurbished a coach-based 'caravan' to act as the ticket office for all services using the so-called station. Passengers were able to wait in their coaches – if the driver was around to unlock the doors. This sort of treatment is not good for anyone, let alone the profession of passenger transport. PSV tried again and the next move was to another, much better place, also in Pentonville Road. Here, British United Airlines' coaches and tours picked up and set down their passengers; consequently a good deal was done for their comfort, which also benefited ordinary London express services. A fairly spacious waiting-room, a reasonable buffet, lots of station announcements and a covered space for boarding the coaches made it a pleasant and satisfactory, if often overcrowded, terminal.

But yet again there was a change. The lease ended and the search resumed. This time it was British Coachways, established in the 1980s, who found a very short-term solution, on a vast area of derelict land, next door to St Pancras. Like an island in an ocean of asphalt, two caravans appeared, one as a waiting-room, one as a booking office. Sadly the brave attempt to inject a new spirit into Britain's coach services by independent operators only resulted in a vast increase in the national coach network, which rose to the challenge of competition, and suddenly cheap, fast, almost luxurious services were dashing backwards and forwards across the country to everyone's delight, except the pioneering independents the government was so anxious to set free.

Today, in 1984, the rural express services have resorted to street pick-ups, without 'facilities' or comfort, and the immense amount of work PSV Operators have done in lobbying the LCC, the GLC and private developers has come to nothing.

The Haverhill Contingent: (left to right, above) *R. Scrivener, R. Roope, R. Baker;* (below) *F. W. Smith, G. Sargent, J. Gogin*

In 1946, Sir Henry Pigott, the Metropolitan Traffic Commissioner, irritated by some police instructions on the London licence, asked E.A.L.: 'What does this mean? Pick up point with TS opp. SB.'

'May I suggest, Sir, it stands for "Tail stop opposite sand bin".' That is the sort of terminal the multiple operators of London express services still have to timetable for their passengers. All we really need is the return of the original Kings Cross Coach Station.

Our expansionist era continued throughout the late 40s. In January 1949, we successfully started negotiations for the purchase of Long's Coaches Ltd of West Wratting. On 24 February the Board made an important expedition to 'sus out' the whole Haverhill area, including the premises of G.F. Burgoin Ltd of Grey Pullman Coaches, Haverhill, and Long's Coaches. This was followed up by an extensive financial exercise in adding up, multiplying and dividing our limited resources and finally we went off to Lloyds Bank, our constant source of support and hope (though Mr Parry was not the easiest of Managers to convince that the interests of the Company and the bank were synonymous). Four months later the final outcome of all the ups and downs of negotiations were summarised in the Minutes of 9 June 1949, which recorded three vital meetings. One was on Thursday 20 May, when the outcome of a visit to Mr and Mrs Towse was a deposit cheque to assure the purchase of all the assets of Long's of West Wratting. The second was on Monday 23 May, when an exchange of views and figures with Mr Burgoin resulted in final agreement. The third meeting took place on Thursday 28 May, when we passed a deposit cheque to cover the purchase of G.F. Burgoin (Haverhill) Ltd (trading as Grey Pullman Coaches).

So in one full and exciting week, the size of Premier had almost doubled. From 3 depots we had risen to 5; from 30 coaches and buses to 48; from about 30 employees we had leapt to 50; from 34 stage and express services we were now operating 59. The only group that remained quite static was the Directors.

These purchases had two immediate results for the Company. On the positive side, the area of Premier's operations doubled overnight, including two express services to London and several monopoly stage services; the properties acquired were potentially very valuable, especially in a 'new' or 'overspill town', as Haverhill was scheduled to become; the staff were exceptionally attractive people, able, skilled, warm and not at all unwelcoming to the outsider company; the opportunities for integration and consequent savings were obvious to see.

On the other hand, the negative aspects were fairly daunting. Firstly, the influx of another assorted batch of vehicles, of which Grey Pullman had had both the best and worst, caused engineering headaches and expense for years to come. Secondly, Haverhill was to a certain extent out on a limb and it took time and quite a little acrimony to mould the staffs and services into an harmonious whole with Chrishall, Harston and Huntingdon depots. Thirdly, the worst feature by far was that the purchases were made on a *nil* capital basis. The Company cheerfully expanded on this very large, challenging scale, with borrowed funds. The consequent financial results were, as Chapter 8 reveals, expensive and painful.

However, the immediate tasks were administrative and organisational and at a Board meeting on 22 September 1949 a great redistribution of executives was discussed. The need to do this had arisen partly because of the new acquisitions but also because changes in those who were running the show had taken place in the previous years.

In December 1947, I had tendered my resignation from the Board, having come to the end of my useful period of service during the war. Luckily, the Board had already decided to ask F.N.M. to join them as soon as he had 'done' twelve months in his depot at Huntingdon. The invitation was then brought forward, so that Frank Matthews commenced his long directorship of the Company in January 1948. He nicely made it a condition that I stay on – which I did for a further twenty-eight years.

In 1948 R.A.H. had tendered his resignation as Director and Secretary of the Company, as from 20 November. His counsels, skill and energy during the war years had certainly been the prime factor in bringing Premier to a profitable state by 1946 and his efforts to achieve that success can never be too highly valued. In December 1948 F.N.M. had been appointed Company Secretary in succession to R.A.H.

Thus, for a brief eleven months, the Board consisted of five members. Then R.A.H.'s resignation reduced it to the two families only, and during the next eleven years, the four, W.F.M., F.N.M., E.A.L. and M.M.E.L., endured much, coped with much, learnt a lot, laughed a lot, and grew together in deep friendship and mutual respect. Therefore, by 1949 the Board was in a strong and confident position to cope with the problems of their expansive ambitions. But they also relied very heavily on the talents and energies of the team of management they had gradually acquired during the years immediately after the war.

Chief amongst them was R.C.H. Dodkin, who joined the Company, as his own account in Chapter 6 tells, in 1946 and whose history spans forty years. It was at the Board meeting of 22 September 1949 that it was decided to transfer Mr Dodkin to Head Office to be responsible to F.N.M. for the administration. Mr John Hibbs, a recent recruit, was to be designated Personal Assistant to E.A.L. Incidentally, in 1946 Mr Sandy Buchanan, who had shown enthusiastic interest in the Company for more than three years, whilst an undergraduate at Emmanuel College, had been appointed to be E.A.L.'s assistant on his discharge from the Army, but he had left us in 1948 for the wider opportunities of Grey Green Coaches and then ECOC.

Mr Frank Grice had worked his way up from a garage-boy at the age of fourteen in 1942 to being R.A.H.'s trainee office-boy at sixteen years old.

The Matthews family at play in the 1950s: Roger, F.N.M., W.F.M., Peter, J.A.M.

He then became Cambridge and District Traffic Manager when John Matthews left to do his national service. It was decided at this meeting to congratulate 'young Grice', as we affectionately called him, on his efforts in the summer period and to offer him the post of Depot Manager, Saffron Walden. Mr Leonard Backler, who had been 'acquired', so to speak, with the Grey Pullman take-over, held the twin position at Haverhill and between these two lovely types, the intermarrying of the two areas was put into practice with efficiency and a great deal of humour and laughter.

In overall command, under the Directors, was Mr Erskine MacPherson, one of the cleverest men ever employed by Premier Travel. He joined the company from ENOC and was appointed to manage the Chrishall/Saffron Walden area. He was a fanatical and knowledgeable 'bus buff' and set about putting his theories into practice in the Chrishall area, greatly to the improvement of local traffic in the early days. He was therefore the natural choice to co-ordinate the new acquisition

and was appointed Area Manager, Haverhill and Saffron Walden Districts.

The last directive of the Board Meeting of 22 September 1949 defined E.A.L.'s and F.N.M.'s new duties as 'overseeing more of the organisation and maintaining a closer contact with all the depots'.

All these appointments and promotions among the very young men involved was the exciting, exhilarating side of life that everyone in Premier enjoyed so much. Those still with the Company look back upon it as one of the most challenging times in its history.

There was a very great deal to be done and the organisation and direction of the multiple aspects of passenger transport was entirely the responsibility of E.A.L. and F.N.M. The other two on the Board at this particular period were 'Thursday meeting Directors' – absolutely invaluable as wise and indomitable people (says she!), especially W.F.M. – but limited in their time.

E.A.L.'s chief function, apart from being Chairman and Managing Director, i.e. the buck-stopping man, was to co-ordinate and revise, extend and develop the multiple services Premier had so rapidly acquired. During the next ten years, between 1949 and 1958, the rate of development increased enormously and he was constantly in and out of the Traffic Courts. The presentation of these applications was in itself a major exercise involving masses of schedules and timetables, and for quite a long time, before Mr Bray took over the job, E.A.L. did all the paperwork as well as presenting his case. (This could be an exaggeration because E.A.L. has never had any trouble finding helping hands, and he sometimes had half a dozen people, from R.C.H.D. down to the newest little clerk, not to mention his wife, working on his schedules.)

Incidentally, this method of acquiring Road Service Licences by application to the courts has been much criticised lately, and, since the so-called Freedom Act of 1980, has fallen into abeyance, market forces being considered a better criterion. In point of fact, the control exercised so impartially by the Commissioners ensured that enterprise and initiative could be rewarded by the granting of a secure Licence, not threatened by cowboy operators or the insidious blackmail of the large combines' power to offer the modern alternative of 'share or beware'. In the fifties and sixties, Premier was able to build up services on the basis of anticipating traffic demands, and E.A.L.'s constant appearances in the Traffic Courts of the Midlands, Eastern and Metropolitan areas brought much needed assets to the Company without considerable financial outlay – other than the experimental operations of the first year or two, which were sometimes loss-making. Nevertheless, an application for a Leeds to Clacton service and other important routes from Cambridge to Torquay and Nottingham to Clacton were not granted in the courts, so it was not always an easy way to expand.

It is worth recording at this point a section of the Minutes from the Board meeting of 5 April 1950.

> An agreement has been reached with Midland Red that no new agents would be appointed in their territory, without their consent, but it is clearly understood that all existing direct (i.e.: not Midland Red) agents should be retained. This places the Company in a very advantageous and almost unique position. Relations with Midland Red had been and would, no doubt, continue to be very cordial.

They even remained that way when, a year later, Midland Red asked for our rate of commission to them to be increased from 7½% to 10%!

In the mid-fifties Mr Geoffrey Bray joined E.A.L.'s operational team and began his work in the Midlands, building up the most excellent relationship with many Midland Agency managers, carrying Premier publicity throughout the area and greatly enhancing the Company's reputation and stature. G.B.'s own history in Chapter 6 tells more of the story.

One of E.A.L.'s other perennial preoccupations was the reduction of mileage and the increase of fares on stage carriage services, until, it was hoped, they would produce marginal profits. From this time on, he also built up his involvement with PVOA and took an active interest in the various other national interests of independent operators.

Meanwhile, F.N.M.'s life at this period was, if possible, even more strenuous than his colleague's, since he had to deal with the overall state of the fleet, vehicle sales and acquisitions, personnel problems, property, garages and MONEY. He set about professionalising the engineering department and by 1955 was able to report to the Board that 'Mr Wood of the Technical section of the Licensing Authority, and indeed the Chairman himself, had expressed renewed confidence in the Company's Engineering and Maintenance organisation.'

In 1948 he introduced a tyre maintenance scheme, still operated by Reginald Mumby, resulting in enormous efficiency and saving to Premier. He negotiated fuel rebates with the major companies, which resulted in Shell-Mex and BP becoming our chief suppliers; he was responsible for the development, from 1953 onwards, of the Pye contracts and supervised the quite extraordinary flow of labour from the Fens to the expanding Pye group; he conceived and planned deals that would reduce costs and produce profits.

Such were the tight spending controls on all departments, that he is reported as having 'asked the authorisation of the Board to spend £32 approximately for a second-hand lathe, because it would result in much greater efficiency in the garage'.

In addition to all this detailed work, he was Company Secretary, with all the legal and organisational responsibility that implies. It was a big job.

Together, E.A.L. and F.N.M. carried out the decisions of the Board – however trivial, momentous, painful, or exhilarating. They negotiated the purchase from Allenways Coaches of their service from Birmingham to Harwich for £220 (Service 67). Harston garage was rebuilt for £712; heaters were fitted in Bedford Vistas for the first time; they turned down the first quotation for 'wireless sets' in the coaches – £11 10s (£11.50) was considered too expensive. Later we were the first to have them installed, by Pye's of Cambridge. In 1951 W.F.M. challenged E.A.L., F.N.M. and the Company in general to intensify efforts to obtain new traffic. 'Even greater energy was needed.' 'Do it now' was made Premier's motto. Mr Fred (W.F.M.) was also responsible for our first staff dinner on 3 January 1955 at the Masonic Hall in Corn Exchange Street, under the auspices of Mr Jack Hall, chef and compère. Eighty members had a happy evening, as many will still remember well. These dinners have been an annual event ever since.

F.N.M. spent hours negotiating contract terms with the County Council and with Pye's. He and E.A.L. accompanied a delightful Pye staff outing to Boulogne. Mr Grice was promoted Traffic Manager in 1957; Mr Gower became the Depot Manager of Haverhill when Mr L. Backler left the Company. Television advertising was used in 1958 to promote Premier express services and the whole Board went to Norwich to watch the production, sharing the stage with a Buttered Kippered Fillet advert being made at the same time.

The two recommended bonuses to be paid to individual members of staff whenever any particularly good work merited praise: sometimes £2, sometimes £5; annual ones were only forgotten once, in 1952. In addition, farewell gifts were ordained to many, many people, especially the girl secretaries who almost inevitably come and go – usually to matrimony. Mr Backler, more exalted, had a presentation at the Company dinner, and a lunch was given at the University Arms for Mr MacPherson. Driver Syd Pennell was again first in his class in 1957 in BGV 719 at the Battersea Coach Rally, after being Coach Driver of the Year at Brighton in 1956.

In December 1957 Yelloway and Premier agreed the first step in their excellent joint operation by providing connectional facilities at Leicester.

Inspectors were created; some drivers disappeared for disciplinary reasons; as a result of a prolonged skirmish with Watches of Switzerland, Premier took over two floors of 15 Market Hill and were granted 47 square yards in the entrance lobby. This kiosk became our first PTA outlet in Cambridge. The happy solution of our accommodation problem was primarily the result of F.N.M.'s persistence and skill, combined with Mr Roger Coleby's expertise. The latter was awarded a bonus of fifteen guineas.

In the year of the Coronation, 1953, the Board opened wide its purse and responded to various pleas for help with Coronation arrangements:

Haverhill Urban District Council were given five guineas; Cowlinge received seats for a new bus shelter (from old utility vehicles); Cambridge Borough Council were provided with free transport for an old people's special tea; Harston Parish Council received two guineas; and Shelford Parish Council one guinea. An allocation of £5 was made for the decoration of Premier's own vehicles and offices, and we used it very effectively!

Premier was once found guilty of carrying an overload and was fined £1. On another occasion the Company was fined £10 for allowing Driver Jolly to drive more than the permitted number of hours.

In 1955 the Lord Chief Justice, Lord Goddard, quashed our conviction, ordered by the Bottisham magistrates, for emitting black smoke from a double-decker and allowed our appeal with costs. A telegram of congratulations was sent to Mr D. McIntyre QC who had taken our case and had proved that our servicing was efficient and up to date.

In 1955 a 7.00 a.m. departure on Service 5 from Clacton to Birmingham and a 2.30 p.m. Birmingham to Clacton run were granted. The Board received the news with enthusiasm as these new journeys provided connections from Colchester and Cambridge to North Wales. Service 4 was extended from Yarmouth to Caister and Hemsby.

An exciting happening took place in December 1956 when Premier sent a coach to Vienna as part of a convoy, organised by the United Nations Association, to take parcels of food, gifts and clothing to the Hungarian refugee camps in Austria and to return with refugees to this country. Bill Day and Harry Law drove HVE 36 there and back, accompanied on the outward journey by myself. I

HVE 36 with Bill Day and Harry Law, Vienna rescue, 1956

had the good fortune to be able to stay in Vienna and help distribute the generous parcels collected in Cambridgeshire. The Minutes record that 'our coach was 100% throughout and of the seven that were inspected by the Lord Mayor at the Mansion House on their return, only ours and one other had had a trouble-free, 3,000-mile trip. The 30 refugees brought back were taken on to a reception camp in Skipton, Yorkshire.' This journey, undertaken in harsh winter weather, was the first occasion a Premier coach had been driven on the Continent.

Yet another memorable occasion took place on Wednesday, 16 January 1957, when the Twenty-First Anniversary Dinner was held at the Masonic Hall. W.F.M. was in charge of the proceedings and for the first time we had a printed menu, incorporating the Company's badge. The toasts were proposed and replied to thus:

'The Company' proposed by Mr E.A. Lainson and responded to by Mr S.E. Pennell, senior member of the staff.

'The Staff' proposed by Mr W.F. Matthews and responded to by Mr R.C.H. Dodkin.

'Past and Present' proposed by Mr F.N. Matthews and responded to by Mr F. Grice.

'The Future' proposed by Mrs M.M.E. Lainson and responded to by Mr L. Backler.

It was a splendid celebration and marked not only Premier's first twenty-one years but also the feelings of survival and hope and enthusiasm which were stimulating everyone as the fifties progressed.

Sometimes the Board scratched its own back. In June 1955, for instance, they thanked F.N.M. for 'the efficient handling of the considerable Army traffic that arose from the rail strike, during which Premier operated 230 vehicle journeys, of which only 37 were run by hired coaches'. F.N.M. was awarded £50 and he, in turn, spoke of the 'unstinted co-operation he had received from Mr Grice, Mr Backler and Inspectors Blyth and Walker'. They also received practical acknowledgements, as did several drivers concerned.

Again, in January 1957, when a considerable programme of stage carriage mileage cuts had just been completed, E.A.L. paid high tribute to the work done by F.G. and by Mr Backler and his secretary, Mrs Burgess. The latter was awarded one week's extra salary and the others £10 each. When I suggested that E.A.L. and F.N.M., who had both done so much work, should also be recognised, F.N.M. stated that 'E.A.L. was certainly entitled to recognition for the continued and constant efforts he made to advance the prestige of the Company in the Industry'. The two 'Thursday Directors' voted each of them a welcome *douceur*

and we all purred with contentment that we had so much to celebrate.

Meanwhile, M.J.G. and the rest of the engineering staff had been having a difficult time, as his account explains.

NUTS AND BOLTS

M. J. Gifford

Returning to the Company in mid 1946 after Army service, some significant changes had taken place. In late 1943 a new Bedford, ECE 879, was bought, and in 1944 two more new Bedfords arrived, ECE 948 and EER 242. In 1945 the Company started to expand by purchasing Weeden's Motor Services of Chrishall, including seven vehicles, and also another new Bedford, EER 99. In early 1946 another operator, A. V. Gill of Godmanchester, was purchased with four vehicles, and also during this period four second-hand vehicles were added. The fleet thus consisted of 22 vehicles when I rejoined the Company, of which only three belonged to the original Premier fleet.

A lot of movement and changes had taken place, and the fleet was now more mixed. I thought that getting the original buses working had paid off. At this time nationalisation of road transport was taking place and it appeared that the bigger an undertaking was, the longer it was likely to remain independent, and so during this decade we con-

EER 570. First non-utility Bedford built in Britain, 1945

'County of Essex', luxury double-decker, with Charlie Jaggard, 1953

tinued to expand. In 1947 another new Bedford was bought, FER 241, and we purchased Drayton's Motor Services of Barley, together with eight vehicles.

1948 was a memorable year, as we took delivery of six new vehicles, GER 140, GCE 422, GCE 654, GCE 655, GER 422 and GER 217. Also in April of the same year we acquired our first double-decker, BU 7601, and later in the year two more double-deckers were purchased, DW 6942 and DW 6944.

The following year saw further expansion, with three new vehicles being bought, GER 141, GER 834 and GER 835, and one second-hand double-decker, JY 6739.

Towards the end of 1949 we purchased Long's Coaches of West Wratting, together with three double-deckers, and G.F. Burgoin's Grey Pullman Coaches of Haverhill together with thirteen vehicles.

The last new vehicles of Premier's second decade entered the fleet in 1950: HVE 36, HVE 242, HVE 401, HVE 403, HVE 402 and HVE 707; but between 1951 and 1955 we continued to bring in about nineteen second-hand vehicles.

As can be imagined, bringing in such a large number of vehicles, although spread over ten years, required a tremendous amount of main-

tenance work, but this was eased by the fact that we were now operating from five depots, Harston, Chrishall, Haverhill, West Wratting and Godmanchester, each with its own maintenance staff. The finding and purchasing of these second-hand vehicles was mainly done by F.N. Matthews and myself. I used to pick him up on Mitcham's Corner at 4 a.m. and we would set off for Yorkshire, and then over to Lancashire, and back via the Midlands, looking for vehicles that were a little better than the ones we had. We made marathon runs on this exercise, and not always in a Rolls Royce! Magical moves must surely have been made on the administration side as the time came round each month for bills to be paid. It was a case of those who made most noise, or whose eyeballs got a little whiter than white, being able to make a slight draw. I credit all the foregoing to F.N. Matthews. The ability to haggle and make a purchase with practically nothing was wizardry to me. This must have been the time when the phrase 'pound stretching' came into being, and we certainly had some super-elastic notes. Never was so much bought with so little: it was the tenth wonder of the world.

All this expansion during Premier's second decade was, perhaps unavoidably, a little too fast, and, coupled with the building up of the double-decker fleet, it involved handling 70 vehicles, 16 new and 54 second-hand. I imagine that a glance at the books during this period showed very little light at the end of the tunnel.

The cost of all the expansion between 1936 and 1955, including the purchase of twelve new vehicles between 1948 and 1950, and the continuous subsequent buying-in resulted in the finances lying very sparse on the polished bottom of the barrel, due to the continuous scraping thereof. So the well-known phrase, 'We're not out of the wood yet', became almost an every-other-week utterance. At Chrishall there were one or two artists, and when things were not going too well a drawing of a 'Woodland Scene' would be hung in the rest room, and if things smelt a little better, another drawing of the same 'Woodland Scene', but with the addition of a coach nosing it's way out through the trees, would be hung over the first drawing. Inevitably something would happen within a day or so, and we would be back in the wood again. This turned out to be a great morale booster.

From an engineering point of view, this influx of used vehicles made it essential for us to do the specialist repair and maintenance work ourselves, rather than putting it out. It was mainly related to fuel injection and electrical equipment. We had a

The engineers: (left to right, above) *A. Wisbey, M.J.G., L. South;* (below) *R. Moore, S.J. Law, R. Mumby*

very good source of supply for service-exchange fuel pumps, dynamos and starter motors, and these units cost around £54 each. Since all the second-hand buses we bought were about ten years old, this equipment was in need of repair. With the help of Mr Walno of CAV, Ipswich I worked out an estimate of between £750 and £800 for all the machinery needed to set up a pump room. After consultation with F.N. Matthews he agreed to go ahead with it, and we built a very good clinical pump room in the tunnel at Harston. We were able to buy all the necessary parts to recondition a fuel pump completely for £25; a bigger saving was also made in that on a lot of vehicles the pump required no more than recalibrating and phasing. This was in late 1952 and early 1953 when we were running at a fleet strength of 56 vehicles, 31 of which had diesel engines. At about this time too, we bought a second-hand lathe from Webb the Blacksmith, of Great Shelford, and this was also set up in the tunnel at Harston. With this we were able to carry out most of the repairs required to the dynamos and starter motors – a great step towards self-sufficiency. I estimate that the pump shop test equipment paid for itself in seven years. In addition we built a ceiling in the big barn building and set up our first spare part stores department, and some time later employed our first storekeeper, Mr Buttress. Another great asset.

Another good move made in this decade was the establishment of a Tyre Department. Our first tyre-fitter was Lance Northrop, after he had been on a course at the Firestone Tyre Co., and later on we were fortunate enough to get Reg Mumby to take on this most important job. He has kept at this heavy and not very glamorous job tirelessly right up to the present day. Since our fleet strength over the years has generally been above 50 vehicles, there have always been at least 300 tyres in contact with the road, and it takes a pretty conscientious man to cope with the task of orchestrating this number of tyres to get the maximum mileage per tyre. Most of the tyre manufacturers know Reg and consider him to be one of the best company tyre-fitters around. This is exemplified by an instance a few years back: I was invited to attend a meeting and discussion at Fort Dunlop, and when I was introduced as the representative of Premier Travel, the Dunlop chairman of the discussion came over to me and said: 'Is it your company I have heard employs an exceptional tyre-fitter?'

'It must be,' I replied, 'because we've got one.'
It was a boost to think that someone had been impressed enough to mention our set-up to these tyre people. Running our own Tyre Department saves us a lot of money per year and is therefore another asset.

Later in 1953 we carried out some improvements to the Harston depot by having a new garage building erected high enough to take in double-deckers. We ourselves built in the side walls and the back wall, and also put in two pits and concreted the floor. Large wooden folding doors were made and fitted by Unwins of Histon. Two people figured prominently in this work: F. Nixon, who did some building and repair work for us; and F. Barker, one of the Company's original drivers. This gave us a good workshop in which to carry out the ever increasing amount of maintenance work required, especially by second-hand vehicles, which were usually fairly well worn when they were bought. In 1955 we reconditioned some 25 engines, and in 1956 a further 20 engines of various makes such as AEC, Daimler, Leyland and Bedford. We also converted an Albion, CUR 921, from petrol to

diesel by fitting a Perkins P6 engine. The Ministry of Transport were now less lenient and required more work and chassis cleaning to be done. To overcome this problem and save many tedious hours of cleaning chassis by hand, we had a new ten ton twin post lift and a steam cleaner installed at Harston. Another unforeseen and costly setback was that the six new coaches and three new double-deckers bought between 1948 and 1950 were built by Wilkes Wood Construction with kiln-dried timber. Within five years the frame structure of all these vehicles had dried out like balsa wood. We had practically to rebuild all these bodies, but, thankfully, in H. Mardell we had the best and most efficient body-builder possible. Normally bodies go on for about ten years before they require major work, so it was very costly to keep these going for that period.

Another snag that cropped up with the introduction of the diesel-engined vehicles was that none of the Chrishall fitters had worked the necessary fuel injection equipment, and when this equipment gave trouble the vehicles were parked up, and soon there were several deckers out of service. F.N. Matthews came to Harston one day and asked me if I would go up to Chrishall for a month to get these vehicles going, and, as the depots were pretty hostile towards each other, I said I would go provided he and I went up there first to get them to agree to the idea, and to set up a plan of work, which we did. We arranged that S. Law, J. Jackson and C. Handscombe would work in the front workshop and S. Peel said he would work with me in the Romney workshop at the rear. This left R. Scarr in charge at Harston. We got all the deckers going again, but that 'month' turned out to be the longest in history, as it lasted until the end of 1974 when we moved out of Chrishall. It was towards the end of this decade that Mr Durran joined the Company as Chief Engineer. I believe he had come fresh from the Army to Eastern Counties for a short while and then to us. As is often the case with such men, they are going to change everything overnight, and show or tell everyone how it is done. Entirely the wrong approach. The only way we had been able to keep going was by cannibalising redundant vehicles.

Looking back to the early fifties I would agree that for those who had to juggle with the finances the odds against success must have looked pretty hopeless. All credit to those who stuck at it and kept us going through what was undoubtedly the worst period in the Company's history, because in my opinion it was also the turning point. The facilities put in on the engineering side, the Fuel

'County of West Suffolk', stripped and rebuilt by H. Mardell, 1959

Injection Department, the Electrical Department, the Tyre Department and the new workshop, started to feed the roots of the tree that was to grow to success.

In the 1956–65 decade, the tree grew vigorously and we had a very successful period. We handled some 85 vehicles during this time and we had laid on the means to carry out most of our own maintenance, repair and overhaul work, and as from 1959 we concentrated on the standardisation of the coach rolling stock to AEC, starting with UVE 333. From places as far apart as Darlington and Newquay we purchased 24 Burlingham 'Seagull-bodied' AEC Reliance coaches to replace our half-cab express vehicles. Then in 1964 we replaced the half-cab service saloons with thirteen ex-LPTB, AEC Regal MK IV saloons. In addition to this, in 1962 we had purchased ten Leyland deckers with full fronts and enclosed rear platform bodies to replace the half-cab, open rear platform, Guy vehicles. All these changes raised the fleet standard, improved our image, and matched the vehicles run by the opposition. (See Appendix 7.) This vehicle standardisation enabled us to equip the workshops to cater fully for AEC and Leyland repair, and this in turn made it easier to organise maintenance and repair programmes. We were also able to streamline the Spare Part Stores Department to carry parts for two rather than seven makes of vehicle. Also during this decade the OMO [one man operated] bus became popular, and double-deckers were losing popularity, so we decided to reduce the double-decker fleet: by 1964 we were running 25 double-deckers and 32 saloons, and by the end of 1966 the fleet consisted of 12 double-deckers and 40 AEC saloons.

Five White Ladies (ex-Ribble Leylands), 1962

The 'big bus company' look, 1961

A problem that cropped up in 1964 was that the new coach length of eleven metres meant we were unable to turn round in the yard at Harston, unless the yard was empty; consequently drivers had to reverse out across the road, and on two occasions the street-lamp opposite the garage entrance was knocked down. Then, in 1964 I think, we sold the Harston premises and moved all the works up to Chrishall. There we had the task of setting up once again all the departments, except the Traffic Department, which was already there. Up to this point we had been in the fortunate position of having separate sites for the Engineering Department (Harston) and the Traffic Department (first in Cambridge, later at Chrishall). Speaking from an engineering point of view, if any progress at all is to be made towards mechanical reliability, especially when running vintage vehicles as we were (even in the early sixties half the fleet of 52 were fourteen or fifteen years old), you cannot have the Traffic Department strapped to your back, like a baby, demanding more vehicles than you can safely provide and be responsible for in service. So for me this bit of 'no man's land' between us had been essential. We were better organised than at any time previously, and I began to feel an increasing sense of hope for the future; even the coach in the wood had been steadily creeping out and was almost clear of the trees. Moving up to Chrishall had its good points, because it centralised the main works, but it also created some problems. As our vehicles worked mainly in the Cambridge area all day, the repair of small defects, such as windscreen wipers failing, or brakes requiring adjustment (and there were many such instances), involved a round trip of some thirty miles to Chrishall and back. In these circumstances it was not long before we were running a considerable number of light miles to cover this work.

As expected, the inevitable age-old friction that will forever exist between Traffic and Engineering Departments became more pronounced when both were on the same premises. It wasn't long before Traffic were in and out of the workshops like yo-yos, wanting half-repaired vehicles to go on the road. Traffic should never be able to override the orders already given by the engineer, it undermines the fitting staff, and the standard of reliability which you have strived to achieve vanishes. Mr Durran had left the Company by this time, and I had taken on the responsibility for the maintenance and repair of the fleet and with it all responsibility for the safety and roadworthiness of vehicles. Determined, if I kept with the job, not to let the standard that had taken ten years to achieve fall

away in as many weeks, I stuck to my guns and survived, amidst a fair amount of friendly hostility. One is not liked very much in these circumstances, and work became very strained, but I did make one gain: I got twinned with one of the seven dwarfs and was known as 'Old Grumpy'.

During the latter part of this decade we improved the facilities at the Chrishall depot by building a tyre department and a battery charging shop onto the Romney building. Then we built a new paint shop at the rear of the Romney, long enough to take the twelve-metre long coach. In the old paint shop, which was at the rear of the front workshop, we put in a pit and converted the roof into a 'lantern rood', which gave us another workshop which could take in a double-decker. Very useful. We dug up the vehicle lift at Harston and transferred it to Chrishall. In 1965 we built the new office block alongside the store's Nissen hut, and concreted all the garden to make a good parking area. Bob Cage and his helpers did most of this work. Ever conscious of the light miles being logged against engineering, we were always looking for somewhere in the Cambridge area where we could set up a light facility to stem this drain of the life blood.

In January 1965 F. N. Matthews and I had a meeting at 15 Market Hill with Tom Gray, Chief Engineer of the Cambridge Co-op, to discuss the possibility of Premier hiring one of the pits and the servicing equipment at his Sleaford Street workshops, and we were able to come to an extremely favourable arrangement. We took in one vehicle a day and the Co-op servicing team carried out a servicing programme, and we put on Ginger Linsdell to supervise and carry out all the running repairs it was possible to handle. This was a great improvement and worked very well, and of course we hoped it would work forever. It went on until March 1966 when another engineer, Mr Renolds, took over the Co-op fleet, and our arrangements were not to his liking, so we had to move out. We tried to carry on the servicing at Herbert Robinson's garage, Newmarket Road, which is a subsidiary of the Co-op and under the same management, but it was difficult to get the coaches in, and the servicing costs had somehow got hooked on to a skyrocket so we took fright.

From then on anything that became available in Cambridge was checked out, including plots of land in Newmarket Road and Mercer Row. Both these sites were found to be unsuitable, because they had originally been rubbish tips. I also checked several garages that became vacant in Cambridge, just to get the use of fuel pumps, but as soon as you mentioned buses the discussion was closed. Another place we tried was the Tenison Road area where British Rail had cleared away all the sidings etc., leaving a large and useful building space, but they would only let it on a ten-year lease basis. This was no good for building a depot, so we were unable during this period to set up a replacement service facility in Cambridge.

FIRST PREMIER PUBLICATIONS

Premier began 1946 with a fine gesture of confidence – the publication on 1 January of its first wholly comprehensive timetable of stage carriage and express services, together with fare-tables, and conditions and regulations.

It was a really good timetable – the print was large and easy to understand; the detail was accurate and explicit; the layout clear and concise; the

index and the Company information, including a list of the Directors, was sensible and reassuring. Moreover, it used every inch of paper to publicise all the Premier potentials of those heady days of peace: coach cruises, inclusive holidays, private coach hire, excursions and tours, and travel. One of these hopeful invitations to the public read thus:

> Our Head Office, 15 Market Hill, Cambridge includes a Travel Agency for Bookings and Reservations by Coach Services, Steamships and Airways. As travel conditions improve we shall be able to offer an increasingly comprehensive travel service for all tastes and needs.

Once again, our farsighted founder anticipated by twenty years our first fully equipped IATA, ABTA travel agency in Cambridge. At the time, our one-room 'Head Office' could hardly cope with the day excursion bookings, and the air tickets, which

First route map, 1946

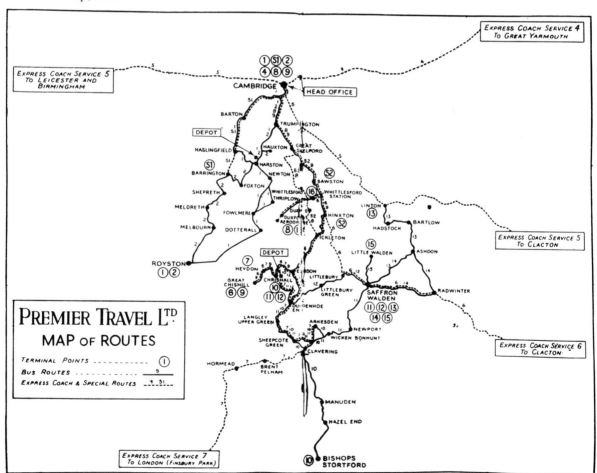

another young hopeful, the BEA representative, gave to E.A.L. 'to have a shot at selling', remained in an obscure drawer until they were withdrawn.

The centre spread was the first route map. Finally, this excellent example of the art of timetabling – largely the work of E.A.L. – ended with a concise summing up of the difficult road the Company was travelling, set out very attractively on the inside of the back cover, as follows:

> FROM WAR TO PEACE
>
> Many war-time problems still confront us:
>
> *Several of our Staff are still in the forces.
> *Spare parts are difficult to obtain.
> *We are still heavily engaged on special priority transport.
> *New luxury Coaches are not yet available.
>
> Please remember these points if our service is not always as we would wish it to be.

Inside the front cover, and again on the back, appears E.A.L.'s motto which we used for years and years:

Support Independent Enterprise!

Sometimes the slogan 'and help us to help you' was added. The publisher was Index Publishers Ltd, Dunstable; it was navy blue on white and the price for 28 pages was threepence [1½p]. No fewer than six large advertisements, mostly from well-known firms in Royston, including the Green Plunge swimming pool, helped pay for this proud production.

Several district timetables appeared as time went on, one included the following advertisement:

> NEW AND IMPROVED SERVICES
>
> In Cambs., Herts. & Essex, including services previously operated by Messrs Drayton Brothers, commencing MONDAY, SEPTEMBER 22, 1947.

This time the Queen of the Fleet, CCE 568, appears in full glory on the front cover, loaded with passengers and winding handle in place.

Another timetable printed on 1 January 1949 listed Premier services in 'Hunts, Beds and Northants including express services to and from the Midlands, the East Coast and Lincolnshire'. Also included was a complicated and detailed map which gave a somewhat distorted impression of the importance of an area so sparsely populated that, when one family left the village, the revenue on

Service 18 plunged by forty per cent. All Huntingdon stage carriage services were surrendered in 1974, only shortly before Huntingdon County Council gave a handsome subsidy to maintain rural services in their area.

In 1950 Mr MacPherson produced the famous, or infamous, depending on how you look at it, Windmill Timetable. This was an attempt to turn haphazard market services, in and out of the small towns around Chrishall, into frequent services, linking one town to another, using Chrishall as a Junction X.

The plan was fine on paper – good allocations, hardly any dead mileage, good timings, efficient use of men and machines. We all hailed it with excited pleasure. Unfortunately, country men and women will not change their habits because of a bus. The windmill said it all: no wind, motionless sails. You can't get people to travel from Saffron Walden to Hitchin just because the timetable says so. The result was extremely expensive in what was financially a bad time, so cuts in the services had to be made almost before they began. However, Mr MacPherson's general skill and enthusiasm, his expertise and his courage in adversity were so great that easily the worst result of the Company's financial crisis was the absolute necessity to say goodbye to him in August 1952. We were all devastated by his departure and felt his absence for a very long time. It was luckily a good move for him because he went to Canada with his young wife and family and earned rapid promotion in the world of transport there.

While on the subject of timetabling, we were faced with the dilemma that haunts many publicity departments – the choice that has to be made between a fully comprehensive printed statement of a company's services and activities and individual timetables to cover each service or group of services. The former is the most desirable method from the point of view of the company itself, its agents, the Traffic Commissioners and other authorities; it is easily the best tool for all those who issue tickets, including drivers and conductors. Unfortunately, however, it is extremely, outrageously expensive and so is fast becoming a very rare species indeed.

Incidentally, one of the most useful functions of the local authority transport departments has been to compile and issue wholly comprehensive stage carriage, express and rail timetables for their own areas. They are arguably better productions than any individual operator could possibly publish.

Windmill timetable with HVE 36

PREMIER TRAVEL
LTD

SUPPORT INDEPENDENT ENTERPRISE

COMPLETE

TIME - TABLE

of all

Stage & Express Services

from

Saturday, 10th June, 1950

PRICE NINEPENCE

6
The Senior Team

R.C.H. DODKIN

The second decade of Premier Travel brought a great wealth of new colleagues to the Company, as well as several who returned to us, older and wiser, after being demobbed. Twenty-one of the people who joined Premier between 1946 and 1954 have stayed with us twenty-five years or more, as did ten of those who belong to the first decade. No wonder we proudly call it a company of friends.

Amongst the newcomers was Robert Charles Harris Dodkin, who started on 1 August 1946, became Company Secretary in 1959, and a Director of PTS in 1976. His summary of his experiences as Chief Administrator illustrates the part back-room work played in our haul back to success. What it fails to convey is the valuable part he himself played in our affairs.

R.C.H.D. is a Pickwickian by nature and, to a certain degree, in appearance. He wears the look of a good-humoured, satisfied, sanguine man, and throughout thirty-five years with the Company he has continued to keep his cool, treating all the traumas and successes with an equal degree of quiet cynicism, as befits a wise and intelligent person.

The Board used him unmercifully. After a very short time he was put in to bat first on any sticky financial wicket that needed to be played. He would have to face the furious bowling of irate creditors and tetchy Bank Managers, and when his innings was over, the problem would either be solved, or greatly alleviated, before the two top dogs had to face the ordeal themselves. People

trusted him wholly. If he said the Company would pay such and such a sum, they believed him. The money people often told us how impressed they had been by 'your Mr Dodkin'. The day-by-day contacts he had with local business people were vital to the reputation of Premier, and anyone who dealt with him became confident of the future.

His air of solid, slightly resigned stoicism confirmed him as the rock of Premier's administration. Waves of disaster pounded us, and he was always there, unharried, unhurried, unmoved by the demands made by banks, creditors, hire purchase agreements, PAYE and insurance stamps. When we sailed into calmer waters and he became Company Secretary, his control over the legalities and liabilities, the Minutes and the responsibilities of the Board was careful, conscientious and controlled. He was a lovely man to work with.

Of course, part of his philosophical enjoyment of life came from his family. Three sons and three daughters came in quick succession and must have strained his personal finances to the limit. He once told us how many loaves of bread, pounds of potatoes, hundredweight of fruit his brood consumed – it made Lord Woolton's war-time job of feeding the nation pale into insignificance. The person who prevented both his Premier life and his family life becoming a burden was his wife, whose sense of humour, dead-pan and targeted at everyone and everything, illuminated his days – and very often Premier's, as the quips were retailed round the office in the mornings. Both of them remain incredibly buoyant and resilient in their retirement, surrounded by children and grandchildren, by laughter, warmth and intelligent delight in one hundred new pursuits.

Typically, in the following account, R.C.H.D. sums up the whole history of Premier in a few factual, no-nonsense pages. His contribution amounted to a great deal more.

The administrators: (left to right, above) *G.B., R.C.H.D.;* (below) *J. Gower, H. Bernardini*

SHORT ACCOUNT OF THE ADMINISTRATION OF PREMIER

R.C.H. Dodkin

The Company was ten years old when I joined in 1946 and I was thirty. Prior to that, between 1931 and 1933, I had spent six months in advertising and two years in non-marine insurance at the Head Office of the Anglo-Iranian Oil Co. Ltd, at Britannic House, Moorgate, London. Between 1933 and 1939 I worked for the merchant bankers, Erlangers Ltd, 4 Moorgate, London, and spent most of those six years in their Commercial Credits Department.

Having joined a territorial unit in 1937, I was at summer camp in 1939 when the War broke out. Eventually my unit was sent round the Cape of Good Hope to Egypt and then on to Crete in April 1941. Following the invasion of the island by the Germans in May, many of my unit were taken prisoner. Most of us were suffering from dysentery and on arrival at Luckenwald Camp I weighed 49 kilos. After two years in Berlin the Red Cross persuaded the Germans to move us to Saxony. At the end of April 1945, after liberation by the Americans, we were flown home via Brussels and I was eventually reunited with my wife five days after VE day. We had married on 31 August 1940 and we had not seen each other since December of that year. We had written to each other regularly, but, as letters took about three months to arrive, when one received the answer to a question it was often difficult to remember what the question had been. After eleven weeks accumulated leave, I reported back to the Army and worked in the orderly room until demobilisation in December 1945. I went back to Erlangers Ltd for two months. My wife was expecting our first baby and we were living in one room. As jobs were easier to get than homes, I gave up my job and bought a small clunch cottage at Burwell. For two months I worked at making the cottage habitable and then advertised myself as available for work. At Premier Travel the Cashier/ Book-keeper and Mr Lainson's secretary had left simultaneously. Mr R. A. Howard replied to my advertisement and on 29 July 1946 we met for an interview. Mr Howard then took me to Panton Street to obtain Mrs Lainson's approval, which was given. Three days later on 1 August I started work at 15 Market Hill, Cambridge. The office accommodation consisted of one room overlooking Market Square. The nearest toilet was on Market Square itself. Sharing the office were Mr E.A. Lainson (Managing Director) and Mr J.A. Buchanan (Traffic Manager). Essential letters were dictated by Mr Lainson to Mrs Handscombe (part-time typist) who, I believe, typed them at home. The other Directors were Mrs Lainson, who had her hands full coping with three young children, Mr W.F. Matthews, a wholesale tobacconist, and Mr R.A. Howard (Company Secretary), who worked at his home in Portugal Place with the help of his nephew. The fleet of twenty-three elderly coaches was based at Harston, Chrishall and Godmanchester.

Board meetings were usually held on Thursday afternoons at Panton Street, the Lainsons' home, because there was no office room available.

It was not until 1946 that the public in general was allowed to visit the seaside again, and most of the time there was a queue up the stairs to the office of people all wanting to book on excursions. Mr Lainson spent most of his time dealing with the public; our bus conductors jumped the queue and tipped out their bags on my desk in order that I might check the revenue collected against their waybills. I found money stuffed in desk drawers, which had accumulated since my predecessor had departed a fortnight before. I banked all this money without knowing where it had come from. The following winter I managed to account for it all except £15. As I had not had any previous experience in transport I spent the first three weeks learning what it was about and on 1 September 1946, just one month after starting, commenced the system of recording income and expenditure in a large analysis book. This system continued to be used for more than twenty years until Mr Peter Andrews adjusted it to suit his purposes. During September and October 1946 Joan Collins joined the staff to help with accounts and Angela Cash started her career as Mr Lainson's secretary. Together with Mr Lainson's Labrador, Sam, we were tightly packed in that one room.

Each week £300 was drawn from the bank and this covered all the wages and petty cash. A driver's basic pay was £5 1s 11d [£5.09½] for 60 hours spreadover time. Many of the drivers' timesheets claimed for more than 100 hours per week, for which they were paid between £8 and £9. Mr Lainson's salary was, I believe, £7 per week and mine was £6 10s [£6.50]. A docker's basic pay was £10 per week at this time. A five-and-a-half day week was standard in most offices until about 1963 when we changed to a five-day week. Hours of work for those of us who lived outside Cambridge depended a great deal on the time of the last bus home. In practice it seemed to allow us to work from 9 a.m. until 5.30–5.45 p.m. and a full lunch hour was seldom taken because of pressure of work.

A year to remember was 1947: the business of Drayton Motor Services of Barley was taken over; Mr F.N. Matthews was demobilised from the Army and was put in charge of the Godmanchester depot; the office at 65 St Andrews Street was opened giving us two rooms above the Phoenix Assurance Co.; Mr Lainson and Miss Cash were left to cover the Market Hill office and the rest of us moved to the new office, except Mr Buchanan who opened a new office at 14 Hill Street, Saffron Walden. New members of staff were Mr A.R. Darby, John Matthews and Miss Janet Drayton (now Mrs J.A. Matthews). Mr Darby, who was sixty, had taken early retirement from ECOC and I was pleased to hand over to him the duties of Cashier and Wages Clerk. He stayed with us for fifteen years and retired, reluctantly, at the age of seventy-five. I seem to remember that, for the first and possibly the second winter at the St Andrews Street office, the only form of heating was an open fire and the first job on arrival in the morning was to clean out the fireplaces and then to lay and light the fires. Mrs Lainson visited us about twice a week and we could always hear her singing loudly as she came up the stairs. We came to the conclusion that the singing was to warn us of her approach in order that we should not be found in the act of anything disorderly. We were too busy anyway. Mrs Lainson's arrival usually required most of us to stop whatever work we were on to complete the work she wanted done right away. This usually took about two hours and then Mrs Lainson would praise us extravagantly and depart, leaving us in disarray.

Financing the purchases of the various businesses and new venture services proved to be a heavy burden during the next eight years. Administrative staff was reduced to a minimum and the work shared by those of us who were left. The salaries of Directors and Staff reflected the difficulties of the Company. Fuel rationing during the Suez Crisis prompted the shedding of a good deal of unremunerative mileage and gradually from that time onward things began to improve. Mr G. Bray had been brought in to deal with Road Service Licensing, statistics, production of timetables and traffic promotion. During this time it had been essential to ensure that accounts were sent out promptly and payment received quickly. A good deal of my time was taken up doing just this, as well as keeping the creditors happy without paying

them too much. One of the difficulties involved in taking over the vehicles of the businesses we acquired was the mongrel fleet we had to keep spares for. This was an expensive business which together with the age of the vehicles meant a difficult task for the fitters.

At the end of 1959 we were saddened by the death of Mr W.F. Matthews, a kindly man.

About four months later I was appointed Secretary of the Company and the Directors were down to three.

Looking back on the fifties it seems that a good deal of time was spent in the Traffic Courts. Most coach operators defended any encroachment on their Road Service Licences by other operators and made applications which were seldom unopposed. I remember at least one day when Mr Lainson was representing the Company in the Eastern Area Court, Mr Frank Matthews in the West Midland Area Court and I was in the Metropolitan Area Court. Mr Lainson thoroughly enjoyed taking the cases but I believe he preferred not to go into the witness box. Frequently he would come to me at 10.45 a.m. saying that we were in court that morning and that he required me as the Company's expert witness. While we were walking to the court in Hobson Street he would tell me what it was I was supposed to be expert in and then quite happily put me into the witness box to be torn to shreds by the opposing counsel and the Traffic Commissioner. There were also the large set-piece hearings when we applied for permission to increase fares. Days were spent preparing schedules in support of the applications. The Commissioners seemed to delight in granting fare increases different from those applied for, so that all the fare tables would have to be amended yet again.

I believe it was about 1950 when we were first allowed to buy an adding machine, and the first mechanical decimal calculating machine about two years later. Previously all additions and cross agreements of totals were done in the head. The revenue earned on each service had to be brought to old pence and then, on scraps of paper, divided by the number of miles operated on that service, in order to obtain the pence per vehicle mile earned. About 1954 we bought our first duplicator. It was hand wound and running off 1,000 timesheets or more could be tiring. As we became more proficient we prepared three-colour publicity on the thing. I believe we had it for about eight years before it was replaced by a later model which was turned by an electric motor. The Directors spent a good deal of time discussing these purchases before authorisation. They were hard times, but even then local appeals for donations were always considered and seldom refused.

Mr Lainson frequently introduced me to visitors as an expert on all sorts of things. Actually I was a jack-of-all-trades. They gave me any job that no one else could cope with, such as designing waybills or agents' ticket books. Mr Bray tells the story of one Midlands agent who copied our design of ticket book and then complained because our next issue was better still.

John Linsdell joined our office staff at the age of sixteen in 1955. He remained with us for more than twenty years before joining ECOC.

In August 1960 Premier Airlines Ltd was formed jointly with Continental Air Transport Ltd. Within about twelve months Continental Air Transport Ltd went into liquidation and PAL became a wholly owned subsidiary of Premier Travel Ltd.

On 1 January 1964 Premier Travel Agency Ltd was duly incorporated and in that year had a turnover of £67,615 compared with £39,280 in the previous year. By 1970 PTA's turnover had reached £528,299. Whilst profits were modest during these early days, the cash flow was most beneficial, particularly during periods of high interest rates.

I believe it was in 1956 that Watches of Switzerland took over the 15 Market Hill property. We were asked to leave while considerable alterations were made. After some legal difficulties we were allowed to return and rent the first and second floors. Shortly after, the staff working at 65 St Andrews Street moved to the Market Hill office. Later, when United Dominions Trust moved from the third floor, we also rented that. When the leases expired in 1977 we had to move out after forty-one years of continuous occupation.

In the seventies the coach side of the business, under the care of Premier Travel Services Ltd, began to flourish. Now that the other subsidiary companies were self-sufficient, there was money to spend on the fleet which showed the flag with pride. The new garage at Kilmaine Close enabled the fitters to do their job really well. In fact, the Ministry Vehicle Examiners were full of praise for the standard of maintenance. Jack Gifford can take a great deal of the credit, as he worked closely with the architect in the design of the garage.

Looking back over my thirty-five years with the Company, I suppose the question must be asked, why did I stay with the Company, particularly through the long difficult period? Firstly, I believe it was the faith of the Directors in the future of the Company. Secondly, it was their attitude to the staff. We were made to feel needed. They were also unreasonable in defence of their staff against accusations made by the public. Thirdly, any member of the staff in any sort of trouble could rely on the help of the Board. I believe that the majority of the staff responded to being treated as human beings by putting that important little extra into their work and it is my impression that the newer Directors will continue to care for their staff in the same manner.

I thoroughly enjoyed my stay with the Company and I hope that all the Directors and staff enjoy theirs too.

FRANK GRICE, 'THE TRAFFIC'

Once upon a time we planned a game of Transport Happy Families and we named the Traffic Manager's family the Tearing-Hairs, because, as everyone engaged in passenger transport knows, traffic managing is the most pressurised, tense, exasperating, frustrating of all the jobs in the industry. 'There is nothing,' according to E.A.L., 'more perishable than a coach seat', and this immediacy and urgency dominates every traffic organisation.

The temperature probably rose more steeply in Premier than in most other companies, because we were a small, under-capitalised group running a large, extraordinarily wide-flung network of stage and express services. Additionally, in the early fifties and sixties, new services and extra departures on established routes were pumped into the rotas, one after the other, by E.A.L. and G.B.

Normally, 'Traffic' would expect a new service allocation to merit additional vehicles and staff but, because we were poor and needy, no extra resources were available, so the poor old Traffic Department would often have to redesign the greater part of the schedules. This involved long arguments with rest-day staff, robbing the engineers of vehicles in the middle of servicing or repair, rewriting orders, calculating legal limits, changing, altering, hiring and begging. Above all, working and working so that every service would be covered, approximately on time.

The man in Premier who did this job was Frank Grice. He was promoted to Traffic Manager at the age of twenty-seven when we said goodbye to Erskine MacPherson, whose assistant he had been, and for the greater part of the period between 1953 and 1975 Frank sat up at Chrishall depot and controlled the operation of all Premier's services and organised the immense amount of paperwork that is bound up with successful traffic management.

Of course, he was ably assisted by many people

over the years, notably John Gower, who ran the Haverhill depot traffic, plus express service charting, in the fifties. This work called for constant telephoning between the two areas, so John Gower transferred to Chrishall, so that the two young men could work more comfortably and efficiently together. When the 'all change' period of the sixties arrived, he could have chosen any one of about four avenues of promotion, so highly respected is he by the Board and so delightful and reliable a colleague has he been for thirty odd years. However, he chose to remain in the administrative department of traffic and now works at Kilmaine Close as Chief Admin. Officer. Heather Bernardini and Terry Knights are two of the other people who maintained the amazing work output of the 'powerhouse' of Premier.

But it was F.G.'s empire and it was from Chrishall that he summoned up the fleets of hired vehicles for weekend operations. N and S of Leicester, Whittle Coaches of Kidderminster, Nesbit of Somerby, Heads of Luton, Barnes of Clacton, Whippet's of Hilton, among many others, waited for F.G.'s call to confirm their Saturday duties on the Midland services. Thanks to them, and to our own road staff nursing ageing vehicles, F.G. could boast proudly that no stage or express service was missed from the orders during his period of office.

Nevertheless, there was no possibility of relying on even the most flexible rota: daily orders were seldom completed before the 4 p.m. deadline because hardly anyone carried out their rostered duty. Something almost always had to be changed – destination, route or timing. It was like one of those maddening jigsaws whose pieces fit in more than one place and you have to keep moving them round to achieve the best overall pattern.

All this applies to the fifties and early sixties. After that everything eased up. The fleet was transformed: pool services were introduced; reliability and punctuality – even comfort – became Premier's hallmarks. Courtesy had always been the characteristic of ninety per cent of the staff, as numerous letters of commendation, proudly displayed in crew rooms, bore witness; and in good times and bad times Frank Grice's patience, dedication and sense of humour prevailed.

F.G. thrived on our expansive improvements and helped greatly to achieve the steady progress of the sixties. Unfortunately, perhaps because he had held this most important position of Traffic Manager, with all its manifold responsibilities, from such a very early age, his own progress seemed to him to have slowed down and reached a dead end. Nevertheless, it was a great blow to Premier when Frank Grice left in 1975. Aged 14 when he joined Premier in 1942, Traffic Manager at 27, and, as E.A.L. pointed out, the last person who will ever do 25 years service before they are 40, because you cannot leave school until you are 16 nowadays, he had worked 33 years with the Company. He left because suddenly it seemed to him that he had no future in Premier. It was the reverse side of the coin of change and nothing anyone could say would alter this sensitive man's outlook.

The Minute of 19 May 1975 mentions, among other tributes, 'his ability to handle the road staff with sympathy and consideration', and goes on: 'The Board were deeply saddened that he should choose to make a clean break after so many years.'

This sadness persists – no one who knew him ever forgets; at Premier functions someone will say, 'We miss Gricey', and they speak for us all, especially the Board.

FIRST RUNGS OF THE LADDER

G. Bray

My first connection with Premier Travel was in October 1949. In those days it was the practice at Premier's Chrishall garage to have two people taking charge alternately of the morning and the late night shift. I seem to remember the second period was from 3 p.m. until midnight, so the duty staff, often back from acting as school attendant, would have the place to himself after six o'clock. If anything went wrong there was no one else to refer to, yet it was part of the duty to deal with any trouble. The rest of the job was basically a question of seeing the vehicles in, sweeping them out and parking them ready for the next morning.

Chrishall was controlled by an office in Saffron Walden, where Mr Dodkin was in charge during my first few months. He was followed by Mr Grice. The orders for the following day used to come up on the 4.30 p.m. bus and I was amazed to find that the first thing to do on their arrival was to alter them, due to lack of communication between Saffron Walden and Chrishall. It happened, perhaps, that a big end had gone, so the vehicle had to be changed or, worse still, a crew that had finished at midday would not know that their duty had been altered, and it was part of your job to go and see them at home and tell them what had happened. You can imagine the reception you got sometimes. I remember being bewildered that this was how a bus company worked, but by and large it did.

A short time later Mr Durran became Chief Engineer and, in my opinion, he did put things on a more professional basis. Admittedly he introduced a great deal more paperwork but a method or machinery was introduced that simplified and regularised procedures. Actually, one of his innovations was the cause of the only strike in Premier's history. He put up an instruction that staff cars were to be parked in front of the garage in an orderly manner and not left all over the place, as had been the custom. This unfortunately caused so much bitterness that everyone downed tools and went into the rest room, until Mr Lainson and the Board came up to see what it was all about. A compromise was soon reached and things went back to normal. [Three or four hours on strike during fifty years operation is not a bad record.]

I first took driving tests in the early fifties, as I wanted to get on the road. I was successful with the saloon test and subsequently passed the full 'decker' test as well, so I joined the Chrishall stage carriage rota.

About this time two things happened: the Company started on its big expansion of stage carriage mileage and Mr MacPherson appeared on the scene as Area Manager. He was preparing what became known as the Windmill timetable for the Saffron Walden printers. It so happened that, although I was quite a new boy, I had been asked to write a letter to the Directors about a slight dispute the staff had on one occasion about Sunday services. The letter didn't have the slightest effect but soon after that I found myself Drivers' Representative. When proof copies of the changes appeared at the depot we said, 'What's going on? What's going to happen to our rotas? We'll be working twenty-four hours a day unless we sort this lot out.' Mr MacPherson wisely saw that there was going to be trouble if he didn't involve us in his plan, so in order to iron out any objections he asked me to spend my lay-by times in Saffron Walden, at his house called 'Cluny', which sounded quite appropriate I thought! So I spent many happy hours proof-reading with him and putting the staff point of view.

I remember coming across Service 41 in the new timetable: 'Service 41, where the blazes is this one going to? Therfield to Buntingford? Whoever's going to travel on that?' But it was felt it might be a heavily used service. It so happened that I was on the first day of its operation, with Mr Pennell at the wheel. There were two journeys, one in the morning and one in the afternoon, and we didn't pick up a single passenger. Mr Pennell, bored to tears, didn't know how to drive slowly enough so as not to get ahead of time. He came to a halt in Kelshall and said to me, 'For heaven's sake ring that ruddy bell and get out and get in again!'

Many additional journeys had been added on most of our routes, and one in particular was Service 26, Royston to Bishop's Stortford via East Hertfordshire and into Essex. Prior to the Windmill timetable it had been a weekly service; it now became daily, with goodness knows how many journeys, and on Saturdays it needed three vehicles to cover it.

Dear old Mrs Wilson, the landlady of The Fox in Measden, where certain services terminated, was astounded when we went in for our usual cheese sandwiches and a drink on the first Saturday of the new timetable.

'Whatever's going on? I've never seen so many buses in my life – look, here comes another one!' Certainly they were up and down that route like yo-yos, but it all provided quite a good number of extra hours for the staff, so we, at least, benefited.

As Drivers' Representatives, we had started to prepare the rotas. After discussion amongst ourselves, we went to the management who altered a bit here and there and we ended up with agreed rotas and no difficulties. Because ninety per cent of the Company's mileage was at that time scheduled stage carriage, this system enabled us to have a rota that, all things being equal, made daily orders unnecessary, except to cover holidays or sickness, and for a couple of years or more the duty rotas ticked over successfully.

Another major step forward, in my opinion, was the introduction of Set-Right ticket machines in about 1951. We had previously been using the old Bell Punch system and since the denomination of the tickets did not match the slowly increasing fares we often had to 'marry up' tickets – a slow and laborious business, sometimes involving three tickets per passenger.

We were carrying very heavy standing loads at this time, especially on market days and on the evening cinema journeys, so the insert-type Set-Rights enabled us to cope much more easily. These same machines have only recently gone out of service and I daresay the new roll-on type of ticketing is even better, but we were all very satisfied in 1951.

This was also the period when the Company became more publicity minded. Apart from the Windmill timetable, which had incorporated what little express mileage we operated, very little else had been done to publicise the long-distance express services, so it was decided that more effort was to be put into publicity. It happened that

Clacton UDC had decided on a policy of promoting coach travel, and after a meeting with the Board, it was agreed to have a joint venture in the Midlands during the winter period. HVE 36 was fitted up with big display boards, designed and painted by Mr Wisbey at Chrishall; the interior was turned into a cinema, with curtains and screen, and Mr Harry Thompson of the Clacton Publicity Department and Mr Harry Law of Premier went off on the first tour of the West Midlands and Black Country. I succeeded Harry Law as driver on subsequent tours when we visited Leicester, Derby, Coventry, Birmingham and Northampton. We had to find as good a spot as possible to park the coach, either near the town centre or in factory yards, if we could get permission. Then Mr Thompson would show his film, called 'Back to the Sun', and special leaflets designed for each area by Mrs Lainson were handed out to people as they left the coach. This was certainly Premier's first attempt at comprehensive publicity and it worked for two or three years.

During these visits to the Midlands, I made many contacts with various travel agents, told them what we were doing and gave them follow-up supplies of leaflets, on the basis of 'if you spread enough mud, some of it will stick', and it did. Even after the cinema tours had ended, I continued to represent Premier by regular visits not only to agencies but also to operators, especially to Midland Red, whose people were very interested in the initiative shown by Premier. This reinforced the unique relationship between Midland Red and our company which began in 1937 when Service 5 from Birmingham to Clacton first picked up at Midland Red's Digbeth Coach Station. Moreover, a number of restrictive practices that had developed between the nationalised sector and the independents were altered or removed, partly as the result of the good relationship between the two companies.

These publicity drives were, in my opinion, the start of the huge summer Saturday loadings from the Midlands in the early fifties. Most cities had adopted a scheme for holiday weeks or fortnights, very much on the lines of the Lancashire Wakes Weeks, and this almost total exodus from the towns meant that we sometimes had up to thirty coaches or nearly 1,000 passengers from one destination on one departure time. It was really quite something. In those days in Leicester, for instance, we had to pick up at the kerbside in Red Cross Street and, with no coach station to go to, the queues would stretch in both directions, searching for the right coach; police would move us on and, one way or another, it could be rather an ordeal for all concerned!

Since we knew that these vast extra numbers of passengers must have been influenced by our publicity efforts, the money spent on it was obviously justified and from then on publicity was treated much more seriously by the Company and continues to be so.

A short diversion from our normal work occurred in 1955, when there was a total rail strike for about three weeks. Premier was asked to supply eleven vehicles for War Office transport, of which five were based at Wellington Barracks in London and six at Harwich, on the East Coast. I reverted to being a driver, as it was a case of all hands to the pump, and I spent one week at Wellington Barracks and the rest at Harwich. It was a most enjoyable, amusing and, I suspect, quite profitable time for the Company. One incident I remember well.

There were six of us down at Harwich and a Major Thompson was in charge of the transport arrangements. He was only too pleased to have someone in charge of our vehicles and, because of my experience, I was elected to be foreman, as it were, to report to Major Thompson each evening to find out what he wanted us to do next day. A lot of the work was to and from London, with some journeys to Lichfield, but on one evening he asked for two coaches to be ready for a VIP job the next day. He knew nothing else about it and it sounded so intriguing that I knew who one of the drivers would be. The other chappie was a very good old friend of mine, Mr Cater. He was driving the old Dennis, the Ant, as we knew her.

Anyway, the next morning we paraded on the square but no details had come through, so we were told to stand by. Eventually the orders arrived and to our surprise the VIPs turned out to be the Ivy Benson Girls Band, who had been on the Continent entertaining the BAOR and had returned to Harwich to find, of course, no trains. They had a huge load of instruments, dresses and hampers, plus some chaperones, and we loaded up everything except the double-bass and the drums. We more or less commandeered a small 15 cwt truck with its Army driver to take them to London. It was all great fun and the girls treated it as a great joke – a charabanc ride to the City.

In 1955 I had started to drive long-distance express services. We used to alternate long and short weekends: the long weekend involved driving up from Clacton on Fridays, then backwards and forwards until Monday, when we returned the 9 a.m. from Birmingham to Clacton; the short weekend ran in opposite directions on Saturdays and Sundays. The two service drivers at that particular time were Harry Law and Mack King and, as the traffic developed, a permanent relief had to be supplied. The same drivers were allocated each week, so that it kept the same two men together, which all made for very efficient operation. [One man, one coach, one service has worked as the very best programme for efficiency and, more valuable still, job satisfaction.] I was fortunate enough to be permanent relief driver to Harry Law. He mothered me, shepherded me and after a few weeks told me I could do the service and he'd be the relief, which was his way of passing me out.

During this period, Mr L. came to both of us and asked if we knew of any passengers who had originated in Worcester, as he was contemplating a direct Worcester–Clacton service. It so happened that there was a regular passenger who was always concerned about onward connections, so I was detailed to get his reactions next time I saw him. They were favourable, which pleased Mr L., so he asked me to come off the road for about a fortnight and take a little Austin car to Worcester to see what I could do to get people interested in the enquiry.

I remember arriving in Worcester for the first time in my life, one winter's evening. I had been recommended by a Midland Red inspector to stay at the Bridge Hotel, which I did for the best part of a week. I got to know mine host, Mr Jeavons, fairly well and liked him, so when he asked one day how I was getting on I replied: 'Not particularly well.'

'Can I help?'

'I don't suppose so, unless you want a coach service to Clacton.'

'Wherever's that?' So I told him and explained what we were trying to do. He said he would be ready to help us in any way he could, even though he didn't know Premier Travel.

The difficulty was that although loads of people came into his pub, they all went to Weston-super-Mare and didn't want to go anywhere else. So I thought up a new angle of approach: even if they had wanted a change, it was a job to get anywhere else from Worcester. I suggested to Mr Jeavons, 'Bert', that this should be the basis of his evidence before the Traffic Court and he agreed to appear for us. He requested that Henry, a friend of his who kept a pub in the Shambles, should also be asked to join us. Henry's response was: 'Yes, I'll come and have a day out with you. I didn't know there was such a thing as a Traffic Court . . . let's have a go!'

The day of the hearing arrived and I chartered a large vehicle locally, picked up the two friends and

various other witnesses I had obtained and went off to Birmingham. There we met up with Mr L. who had travelled up from Cambridge and had arrived, as usual, ten minutes late, so I had no chance to introduce him to anyone prior to the start, so we just sat down and waited.

It was all new to me of course so I was very interested but, after the first hour or so of listening to another case, Bert and Henry got bored with the whole thing and told me they were going across the road to have a drink. I was to fetch them when they were needed. However, the case went on the whole morning and it wasn't until we adjourned for the lunch break that I went out to find them and took them and all the other witnesses to lunch. Bert and Henry had had a few by this time and after a glass or two of wine they were in a good mood.

We went back to the courtroom and as we came down the corridor Henry said: 'What's this place we're supposed to be going to?'

I was sweating blood, but when at last our case was called and it was time for Bert to give evidence he thumped the table and said to the Commissioner, 'If you were in the bar all day, you'd know what people want – they want this service.'

Indeed, after hearing all the authentic witnesses, the Court decided to grant our application and we ran the service for many years.

In the same year, an application was lodged to extend Service 5 to Walsall and Lichfield and I was again fortunate in being given the job of finding witnesses to support the new service, though I made myself unpopular with my fellow-drivers for trying to extend our long-distance routes even further. However, there was a competing application and ours was refused.

During 1955–56 Premier also became more serious, if that is the right word, about statistics, a department which had become much more important as the Company expanded. I was asked to assist in compiling the passenger-revenue figures during my layover periods, still usually in Saffron Walden, and I found the work very interesting, though it often showed up some alarmingly unremunerative services.

At the beginning of this period I was still driving on an on-and-off basis but it was an unsatisfactory arrangement because every time I was called to do some special duty it threw the rota into disarray. Not only were other members of the staff on the rota rather aggrieved about the whole position but it also presented a personal difficulty for me. I had followed up the original publicity effort and my visits to the Midlands became more frequent. From one or two trips a year, it became a more or less continual thing and expanded to cover East Anglia, Essex, and North Hertfordshire, and thus it had become an almost full-time job. But I was still officially on the drivers' rota so that sometimes I went round as a representative, visiting agents and seeing the boss man, probably having lunch with him or a drink and so on; then next time I saw him I was driving the coach on the road. Human nature being what it is, it was a little awkward to say the least.

So gradually I came off the road and only drove on odd days, usually on summer Saturdays. By 1957 I had stopped driving coaches altogether and I became more and more involved in office work and publicity. Soon after that I was introduced to Road Service Licensing, of which I knew nothing, and I was again bewildered and confused. 'All these forms and all these timetables and route maps and what have you.' However, I shared it all with Mrs L. for a few months and eventually took over responsibility for it. Luckily I did have an enormous amount of help from the Eastern Area Traffic Commissioners where Miss Jacklin, Derek Chilvers and Herbie Blows were very, very helpful to me and explained the difference between a variation and a modification and all the kerfuffle that went on. Thus by the end of 1957, the extent of my duties covered Road Service Licensing, coupled with the preparation of applications for new licences.

The competing applications by Associated Motorways and Premier Travel constituted another major event of 1957. Associated Motorways proposed a service between Cheltenham and Felixstowe and Premier proposed a service between Oxford and Clacton. We had a two-day hearing at Bristol before the Western Area Traffic Commissioners, followed by a joint sitting in Oxford before the East Midland, Metropolitan and Eastern Traffic Commissioners. It occupied three sessions of two days apiece – a total of eight days devoted to the case, the longest hearing in our history. Premier judged it to be of such importance that we engaged counsel to represent us. The usual drill was for Mr Lainson to present the facts of any application and then put either Mr Dodkin or myself in the witness box for cross-examination. The combine or nationalised companies almost invariably used counsel.

As a preliminary I was sent to the Temple, with a young solicitor's clerk, to meet our advocate, Mr Grant. I was amazed to find that he didn't know the first thing about the case, so I set about explaining the main details of our application and finally he appeared for us at the mammoth sitting in Oxford.

The application by Associated Motorways was granted in the Western Area but the other three areas refused pick-up points. The effect of the decision was, therefore, that Associated Motorways could carry passengers only between the Western Area – effectively Cheltenham – to Ipswich and Felixstowe, so they did not take up their licence and the Premier application was refused.

Another application was for Service 72, Cambridge to Bournemouth, which was applied for in the Eastern Traffic Area. It was one of the easier ones and we were able to fill the court with witnesses and consequently we were successful and were granted a licence, restricted initially to main summer Saturdays. But it was again an occasion of 'Dear oh dear, all this bumbledom' – one witness was asked how far he lived from the bus stop. Whatever did it matter? I couldn't help feeling that there was something wrong in the idea that there's got to be a huge unsatisfied demand before the industry can do anything about it, because the industry had no means of catering for the unsatisfied demand before a licence is granted. I couldn't and still can't understand the system but that's how it worked in those days.

The same thing happened in 1959 when we made application for Service 73, Bedford to Cromer. It was basically a replacement service for the old M and GN, but again we had to come back to finding witnesses to prove an unsatisfied demand. Well, there really weren't any, there really weren't! I went beyond Bedford, to Luton, to see if people would get on a stage carriage bus to come to Bedford and join our service but there was no evidence at all, other than some witnesses I was able to get from Cromer. The local authorities there and at Sheringham and the Runtons supported us and that was enough to get the grant.

And in this way the background work of our expansion went on until the sixties, when the pace quickened even more. But that is another story.

61

7

'It's All About People' I

Another great 'character' to whom Premier owes a very great deal was Albert Warren Hill of Dalorin, Elmdon. (Dalorin celebrated his three children, Daphne, Lorna and Colin, who were a lively part of the Premier family until their own top-dog professions took them away from us.) Mr Hill, who became Uncle Bert to ninety per cent of his contacts, joined us as a middle-aged man and immediately took a very personalised interest in the passengers and in the Company. He always relayed complaints, suggestions, funny, exaggerated stories to E.A.L. or F.N.M. or to F.G. He was not a thin man and sometimes, as he grew older, he would glow with righteous indignation or almost burst with the force of his eloquence. Day and night he involved himself with Premier.

Unfortunately, he died shortly after contributing his recollections. Just re-reading them brings back some of the wild improbabilities of his stories as well as the very real worth and warmth of this excellent man. In July 1982, in Elmdon Church, Inspector Hill was presented with a silver salver, given by the whole village. The inscription read:

> Presented to Albert Warren Hill, for many years a worshipper in Saint Nicholas, Elmdon and a devoted worker for the church.
>
> CHURCHWARDEN
> Elmdom with Wendon Lofts,
> 1970–1982

He died in 1983 and was buried at this same church. RIP

EARLY DAYS AS A CONDUCTOR

A.W. Hill

On Saturday 1 June 1951 I reported to Chrishall depot to start my days as a conductor. My driver was Geoff Bray, and he alone had been told that I was to start! As no one had been expecting me, there was no kit available. Geoff found a ticket rack and board, a bell punch and a waybill. Then we proceeded to Little Hadham for Service 27. As I issued my first ticket, the bell punch disintegrated, so for the next month I just tore a piece out of each ticket as required, until someone repaired my punch. The last run on Service 27 on my first day was Cambridge to Little Hadham via Barkway and Nuthampstead. Geoff said that the crew always stopped at The Woodman, Nuthamstead, to inform the passengers that their bus had arrived. As always, there was a pint ready for the crew! When we returned to the bus, it was full of bikes. I turned to the passengers and said: 'You can't do this. This isn't allowed!'

The passengers just turned to Geoff Bray and said: 'He must be new!'

The following Saturday I was given a double duty to do with a part-time driver from Haverhill. He didn't know any of the routes either but we struggled along until the 4.00 p.m. Bishop's Stortford to Royston. Someone asked if the bus went to Washall Green. I looked at my driver and we both said, 'Never heard of it'. Another passenger offered to act as our guide but the driver misunderstood part of the instructions and we ended up on a dung heap in a farmyard. Later on we had a thirty-minute wait at Sandon for the return journey and the fee for our guide was three gins.

I remember one of my first journeys to Cambridge, conducting Albert Reeves on a double-decker. We stopped at the bus point in Lensfield Road where an elderly lady with three young daughters started to load her suitcases onto the bus. One of the daughters said: 'Mama, surely this old bus isn't going to take us to Clacton?'

The mother was heard to reply, 'Get on, because you never know what kind of bus *Primitive* Travel will send.' This time she was wrong and I told her to wait for Service 5.

I was travelling to Sandon one Saturday with Harry Walters in one of the old utility buses. On

Three men and a bus: A. Reeves (right), *K. Andrews* (centre)

the way we saw a group of huntsmen and hounds in full cry. On our return journey shortly afterwards we saw a fox by the roadside, gasping for breath and obviously tired out by the chase. Harry stopped the bus, I opened the door and said, 'Come on mate, in you get'. The fox got up and climbed into the bus. I had just shut the door and we were preparing to move off, when we were surrounded by the hounds, horses and huntsmen. The hounds could smell the fox – who was lying quietly on the floor – but of course the huntsmen never thought a fox would be in a bus, so they whipped up the hounds and eventually went away, and we continued our journey. Just outside Kelshall I opened the door, the fox calmly got out and I said to him, 'Don't get into trouble like that again, we might not be around next time'.

We did not just carry passengers in those days. Occasionally people gave us parcels to deliver, some were regular deliveries but if you were new to the job you didn't always know about the parcels in time. One day, unbeknown to me, a parcel of special fish had been put on my bus at midday, to be delivered as usual. At 5.30 p.m. an irate Curly MacPherson, the Traffic Manager, demanded to know what I had done with the fish. By that time I knew it was on the bus by the pong.

No one could say that Premier Travel did not look after its passengers. One New Year's Eve I was doing the final Service 26 run from Bishop's Stortford to Barkway at 10.45 p.m. with Driver Ron Gray. There must have been 120 people on a 56-seater double-decker. As usual we stopped at the pub in Berden in order to collect any waiting passengers. We rushed in and shouted, 'Come on, we must get going!' The landlady replied, 'You'll have a job!' I looked back and all the passengers were off the bus and had joined me inside the pub, and a queue had formed to pass drinks to the driver. It took one and a half hours to get them all onto the bus in order to resume our journey!

The Essex Show one year was held in Chestnut Avenue, Littlebury. When the show was on Harry Readman and I took a double-decker to Audley

'Tally ho! Tally ho! Off by bus I'll go'

End railway station to pick up passengers for the showground. On our first run all the top deck windows were broken by the low branches in Chestnut Avenue. The last day of the show was 'Dog Day'. At the station there were thirty passengers and thirty dogs waiting for the bus. I had just managed to get everyone on, when another lady appeared with an Afghan hound. The dog was simply enormous. When I told her we were full up she burst into tears, whereupon all the other passengers insisted that she travelled somehow; so I asked all who were standing, plus one passenger from the front seat, to get off the bus. Then I took the dog to the front, made him put his front paws on the seat, until his head touched the ceiling of the bus. I kept him there until everyone managed to pack in again and we got to the show. When I got home that night, my family, who had visited the show that day, claimed that they had seen the biggest dog ever.

'Yes,' I said, 'I had that b . . . dog on my bus with thirty others!' But they took some convincing.

What do you do when a passenger dies on your bus? One morning I was doing the 10.15 a.m. Cambridge to Royston run with Sam Law. At Foxton a man ran to catch the bus, got on, sat down and died. Sam stopped at a telephone box and I phoned Royston hospital to ask for an ambulance to meet the bus at Melbourn. I moved all the passengers to the top deck. The ambulance met the bus but the crew refused to take the man, claiming that he was dead. I lifted the man carefully out of the bus onto the pavement and said that he had not been certified as dead, therefore he was not officially dead. The men still refused to take the body as they knew a stiff when they saw one. A passing policeman came over to help. I told him my tale and he took my part and asked the ambulance men to take the man to hospital. I was on the bus in a flash, rang the bell and we continued on our way.

One evening on the last bus out of Bishop's Stortford when Broody Flack was driving, several passengers wanted to attend the wants of nature. I rang the bell to stop the bus at a suitable place and invited the passengers to do what they wished to do. They were reluctant to leave the bus so I said that I would go with them and I informed the driver of the delay. Unfortunately someone rang the bell before we returned, so the bus moved away without us. However, fortune smiles on those who help others, for I found we were at Blacksmith's Corner, where the bus makes a detour. We all ran very quickly and arrived at the return corner just as the bus came to the stop. Broody Flack's face was a study when he saw his conductor waiting for the bus.

Service 1, 8.45 p.m. Cambridge to Royston: I was again with Broody Flack on a double-decker bus, with the door at the front. Passengers came down to complain that a man on the top deck had a knife and was threatening people. I went upstairs and spoke to the man in question. Yes, he had a knife, but he was not threatening anyone. Everyone kept calm and there were no other incidents. By the time we reached Fowlmere everyone else had left the bus and I told Broody to drive straight to Royston, not to stop for anything until he reached the police station. Meanwhile, the man had come down the stairs and cornered me at the back of the bus. He threw the knife, which stuck in the wood to one side of me. I wound my set-right around my hand and managed to get him in the corner. Broody was driving so fast that he went over a roundabout, flower beds and all, and drove the wrong way up a one-way street before screeching to a halt outside the police station. He ran inside and fetched a policeman who took charge of the man and the knife. Then he took our statements. After a short while the constable explained that the man was only having a joke with us, so he was allowed to go free, with his knife. Broody Flack and I didn't enjoy the joke at all.

When Jim Baker died four of us were asked to

A. 'Broody' Flack with ex-Drayton Bedford, 1948

bear his coffin at the funeral. Sid Pennell, Harold Lee, Maurice Scripps and myself travelled with the coffin to church. When we got to Barley I asked the driver of the hearse to stop outside The Fox and Hounds. He did so. I touched the coffin and said, 'Jim, we're at the Fox and Hounds!' Not receiving an answer we all agreed that he must be well and truly dead, as he had never passed that pub before without going in.

These are some of the incidents of the lighter side of conducting, but there was the other side, when the running services and the state of the buses left a lot to be desired. The staff went out of their way to be helpful to passengers who, in return, were some of the best people to take about; I always had a good relationship with the passengers. Later on when my wife and I organised private hires and outings, our contacts meant there was never any difficulty in filling the seats on several coaches. I still have all the records of the many private hires that Premier ran from the entire Chrishall–Walden–Stortford area.

FIRST DAYS AS AN INSPECTOR

A.W. Hill

It is never easy being promoted within a company, and with Premier Travel it was no exception. My whole life changed overnight. Suddenly my mates regarded me as someone to be avoided. My loyalty to the firm was such that, in spite of this instant change of attitude amongst my friends, I set about this new venture giving it all I had. It was not easy. I often found when checking the buses that my plans for getting on and doing my work were frustrated. Drivers would speed along the road, having possibly spotted my van. Thus I would not have the time to check the bus correctly, or, if I did, I would have a very long walk back to the van. It seemed that certain people could do no wrong – even if I found that they could!

The checking and loading of the Service 5 passengers played a large part in the summer seasons. It was a nightmare at first. I used to get up at 3.30 a.m. and go to Haverhill to check all the Yelloway coaches. Then I rode with them to Clacton and loaded all their passengers while the drivers had breakfast. The chaos there had to be seen to be believed: tempers were very easily roused; some drivers preferred certain passengers or certain routes and objected to being organised; very often the number of passengers did not tally with the number of coaches available, so I used to hire anything available to get them all away. If the passengers were going on holiday they were in a mood to be pleased and rarely got upset, but if they were returning home they wanted to get there with the minimum amount of fuss. I remember having fifteen passengers left at Coventry, the coaches having been loaded at Birmingham. They were going to have to wait for a later coach and travel in the afternoon although their tickets stated a morning departure time. 'Give them some lunch' said Mr Matthews and promptly left. I had Hubert Mardell with me and it took all our money to keep them happy. All went well until we ourselves needed something to eat and smoke. I travelled on the bus from Coventry to Birmingham and Smudger Smith took me to the men's canteen in Birmingham and bought me a meal and some cigarettes, while the Midland Red drivers hooted with glee to see a driver buy an inspector a meal.

As the season progressed I managed to get things organised as I wanted, both at Clacton and Birmingham, and Mr Lainson was heard to remark that his complaint basket *re* Clacton departures had dwindled to almost nothing; that was the best news I could have had.

One incident that I always recall with great pleasure was the day that Pye's held a great party at Newmarket for all their agents in Britain. This should have been an ordinary day for me as an inspector, but from the minute I arrived at Cambridge Airport things started to hot up. Mr Jones, who worked for Premier Airlines, should have taken charge of the whole operation. Unfortunately one of the Premier Airlines planes had been forced to land on the South Coast – and so he had more than enough to deal with at the time. The planes with the Pye agents started to come in; the Premier Travel coaches were lined up ready to take the passengers on to Newmarket. They arrived exactly on schedule, thanks to a little detour along the way. A Pye official informed me that 1,000 bottles of champagne and 1,000 bottles of wine had been ordered for this party, so I knew that the return trip would be fun and games, and it was! As the coaches arrived from Newmarket we had to help each passenger onto the plane and strap them in. The air hostesses did not have to be told that these passengers would not be doing much on this journey. They were all taken safely aboard so quickly and with so little fuss that, as the aircraft took off, Mr Lainson said that they looked like a swarm of bees flying into the dark. I received a very nice letter from Pye's, thanking me for the smooth organisation.

Acrow's of Saffron Walden were having their annual outing to London for dinner and a theatre visit. I had booked the dinner for all the passengers in the same restaurant but there were separate theatre visits. Altogether there were six coach loads of people. The London police observed, with interest, the unloading and shepherding into the restaurant of these six coaches, and asked where and when I intended reloading them. I replied that it would be in Cambridge Circus at 11 p.m. and was told in no uncertain terms that this would not be allowed. I then spent the next part of the evening visiting police station after police station, talking to this inspector and that sergeant, explaining my case. Eventually someone telephoned Scotland Yard. I was told to wait at a police station just off Picadilly. At last, a call came from the highest authority: Inspector Hill could have fifteen minutes only to load his coaches in Cambridge Circus, between 11 and 11.15 p.m.; all constables were informed of this by radio. Everything went according to plan and the coaches were away within the time limit. Just another day's work for one inspector of Premier Travel.

WIN WITH WYNN

Another of the bright people who, in these days of free advanced education, will never again enrich small businesses with their brain and acumen was Harry Wynn. He came to us in 1946 as a bus driver at Godmanchester depot. He had been a taxi driver in London from his earliest possible birthday and continued to be so throughout the war. However, he had evacuated his wife and family to Huntingdonshire and at the end of the war decided to leave the smoke and come into the country himself.

He often spoke of his first day with us and expressed the sort of bewildered amusement that many of our staff felt for the set-up. It somehow captivated their imaginations, so that they stayed on to see what might happen. Later he was made Manager of our Huntingdon concern and actually began the Premier Travel agency in a miserable and clammy office off the High Street.

In 1962 he transferred to Head Office to do the job of Chief Cashier, until he retired in 1972. During his time there, he lightened every day with his Cockney quick wit – very dry, very solemn and totally tension breaking.

The wages man is in the very centre of any company's affairs but in our case, because of our close involvement with one another, the cash drawer was the solution to all immediate worries: E.A.L. used to put in very exact IOUs at night when he wanted a couple of quid; F.N.M. and I had running accounts, from which our Harry would add or subtract and carry forward. Very, very occasionally he would say to us, 'Would you like a decco?', which meant we were going a bit beyond ourselves and we'd be very careful for about a month and then start again. The days of reckoning always came in the end but we were so short of money, having cut our salaries at bad moments, that we all three thought it proper, not to say vital, to mortgage our future. Harry also did this kind of 'personal service' for other members of the staff, but it was easier to get them out of debt by deducting the cash from their weekly or monthly wages.

Harry Wynn was a most meticulous and efficient worker. He arrived at the office about 8.15 a.m. and was always at his place until the day was done at 5.00 p.m. When the wage cheque was not forthcoming or, as happened on several occasions, he got to the bank and was told to wait until the Manager had been consulted, he would fidget slightly; and back at the office his desk would be unnaturally tidy, ready for operation 'Fill 'em up'. Sometimes we were so late getting wages through

that all of us had to go and fill with him, list by list, pounds, shillings and pence. You felt pretty silly when, after filling about forty envelopes, you were 2s 6d (12½p) over. This wasn't good enough for Harry who prided himself on total accuracy on his cash dealings. I remember well his achievement one year in the late sixties when he handled just under half a million pounds of cash and found himself 1½d (½p) out. Job satisfaction was very high in the old days of cash balances and analysed books with their neat additions, copy-book writing and final red lines.

In 1964 he undertook to do the new Agency income and expenditure books and immediately the financial ground seemed more solid and safe. He took over from a young girl who didn't have much of a clue. 'Figures,' he said with scorn, 'the only figures she knows anything about are 36 – 26 – 36. You give her to me and I'll teach her a thing or two about her figure. But don't let her near my books.' And so he made us laugh whilst getting on with yet another job.

It almost goes without saying, for the catalogue of human behaviour often combines humour and courage, that Harry, during his fifties and early sixties, was seldom out of pain, with horrors like open ulcers and running sores affecting his legs.

'Good old Harry', as everybody knew him, retired on his 65th birthday and we all deeply regret that he didn't have a good retirement. He gave up his council work in Godmanchester the year before he should have become Mayor (his slogan was 'Win with Wynn') and he dropped out of Premier's world. He just stayed at home and watched television and drove his dear wife Rosie to despair. It all seemed such a waste and perhaps he should have stayed on and done part-time work, but the new order has computerised wages and no one uses any cash nowadays and IOUs and advances and cash discrepancies are all things of the past, quite taboo.

He died in 1982 leaving his wife Rosie and three daughters, who guarded both of them and still do. RIP

THE GOOD OLD DAYS

W.J. Aldous

I was demobilised from the Army early in 1948 after serving in Palestine. After I had taken all my leave, I met Herbert Bird in the public house which we both used. I asked him if there was a chance of a job with Premier. He said he would find out. He

Ace drivers of Chrishall: (left to right) *H. Lee, H. Law, J. Aldous*

did so and told me that I would have to go and have an interview with Mr Howard, the Company Secretary.

I then had this interview and he asked me if I could drive. When I told him that I had been in the RASC armoured division, driving tank transporters, he gave me the job but said that Mr Bird would have to take me out for a trial run that night. Then we came to pay: £5 2s 6d [£5.12½p] for sixty hours and 2s 6d [12½p] overtime. I took the job.

I started on the following Monday, conducting Service 1, 7.40 a.m. from Royston to Cambridge, with Herbert Bird driving. One week I was driving and the other conducting. Also based at Royston was Fred Dumelow, and working with us were Mrs Kit Hitch and Mrs Cooper. These were what I call the good old days. We had one depot at Harston and the other at Chrishall and we were all mates together and we would help one and all. I remember what the fares were from Royston to Cambridge: 2s [10p] return; 1s 9d [8p] return from Fowlmere; 1s [5p] Thriplow; 1s 2d [6p] Newton; 11d [4½p] Harston and Haslingfield and 8d [3½p] return from Barton.

One Sunday I was on with Fred Dumelow. We left Cambridge at 6 o'clock in the evening. I was courting my wife at the time, so when we got to Fowlmere, we picked her up and went on to Royston, where we all had a drink. When we got to Thriplow on the way back I had to go to the toilet. I went into the Green Man and when I came out

the bus had gone. I rang Harston garage and they came out and picked me up.

When we arrived at Cambridge, there was Fred talking to my wife. We had a few words and I found out they had not missed me until they got to Barton. It was then that my wife went upstairs, thinking I was talking to some other girl, but there was no one up there. She rang the bell and told Fred I was not on the bus. At the time I was wild but we have laughed about it since.

In the 1950s and part of the 60s we used to have a lot of social events, such as football matches against the Eastern National, the Police and others in the Sunday League; darts matches; and a lot of theatre outings. We had a very good Welfare Club. Goodness know's what happened to that.

The buses we used to drive then were Bedfords with wooden seats and half-cabs. I remember one day I took TF on service to Birmingham and every five miles the bonnet fell off and by the time I got to Birmingham I looked more like a chimney sweep than a coach driver.

I cannot speak too highly of our Traffic Manager, Mr Frank Grice. When he left it was a great loss to the Company, and all who knew him wish that he was still here.

As for today, things have changed: I who am the senior driver in the Company have one of the oldest coaches on the road and I know hardly any of the other drivers. So my honest opinion is give me the days when we were all mates.

'THE WELFARE'

A. Cash, Welfare Club Secretary, 1947–55

In the early spring of 1947 a very 'young and green' girl, straight out of secretarial school, joined Premier Travel at Rose Crescent. From the start, it was clear this was no ordinary commercially minded company and that, in the Premier world, people would always come first. With such views it wasn't very long before the idea of a Welfare and Social Club was born. The early meetings usually began in the office, then adjourned to The Red Cow across Market Square. Broadly, the aims of the Club were to foster good fellowship and raise cash by social functions to provide treats and outings for staff and children and to help in times of need.

Memories flood back of the fun it was helping to organise the dances, outings and Christmas parties. The first dances were held in Village Halls at Newton, Harston and Foxton and, to make the occasions authentic, Mr A. Wisbey constructed a cut-out model of one of the coaches, complete with flashing headlights, as a frontispiece to the stage. More ambitious dances followed at Haverhill and Huntingdon Town Halls. Grandly, it was agreed ever larger halls could be filled and the Rex Ballroom in Cambridge was booked. This was owned by a great character, one George Webb, resplendent with fat cigar and an American Cadillac with green tinted windows. Powers of business negotiation didn't quite stand up on this occasion and the young girl felt even greener.

The darts and football teams thrived, but whilst the warmth and *bonhomie* of the local village pubs was most attractive (not to mention the opportunity of learning songs one never knew existed), chilly football pitches on a wet Sunday morning didn't have quite the same appeal.

The children's summer outings to places like London Zoo were feats of organisation, but perhaps best of all were the Christmas parties, when Father Christmas (alias E.A.L.) arrived in

Spot your child! We've found our three (Ed.), 1948–49

splendid style in a sledge, once again made by enthusiastic staff, and drawn along by Sam, the immortal black Labrador.

The years between 1947 and 1955 linger in my memory as times of fun, warmth and humour, working with people who had the great gift of making other people feel important and necessary to the Company. As time passes it becomes ever more clear how rare this is in the world today.

BRIGHTON COACH RALLY, 1956

S.E. Pennell

One day 'Gricey' said to me, 'They want you to enter for the rally in 719 (Bedford Vista) and Stan Bradman will enter in the double-decker class.

What we're going to do is send you by car to go over the route and then it is up to you.' Premier's usual compulsory volunteering routine.

Anyway, Roland Scrivener, Willy Day and we two drivers went off to Brighton and got the feel of the place. The rally started on the Saturday, and from the beginning I didn't think I had a chance. Half-way through the blooming route tests, where you have to do a certain mileage in a certain time, a tractor came out of a field and stopped us dead. I'd got Mr Lainson and Willy Day as passengers: Mr Lainson said I'd have to cover so far in so many minutes; and Willy said I'd have to 'open up a bit'. But I kept going my way and completed the section not too badly. Then came the driving tests – well, blimey. I'd been a driver more than a couple of months and if I couldn't handle a so and so Bedford, I ought to be shot. But a lot of other real drivers were there – not just 'steersmen' like some I

Our hero. Syd Pennell, Coach Driver of the Year, 1956

could name, so I wasn't very confident. When it was over we met up with Stan, who hadn't had a bad day either, and he said to me: 'Where are they putting us for the night, boy?'

'I think it's the Grand.'

'Bugger, they're lashing out a bit, aren't they', he said.

'Yes,' I said, 'they always do!' So we parked up and Frank Matthews got hold of a taxi.

'I can't take six', the driver said.

'Get in', said Mr Lainson.

We did. I've never had a ride like it in my life, all of us a bit drunk with excitement and the long, long day. When we'd cleaned up, we met in the hall of the Grand.

'Now I want the best piece of steak in Brighton', said Frank Matthews and I reckon we found it. I still think it was the best steak I've ever had in my life. Then we had a few drinks and got to the Coach Rally Dance a bit on the late side. I remember as we went into the crowded hall, I heard a voice saying, 'Ladies and Gentlemen, we are now about to announce the winners of the Coach Driver of the Year competition. This year, Number 38 has not only won it but won it by a mile.' Of course, I took no notice. Number 38 meant nothing to me.

'That's you, you b . . . fool', said Willy Day.

'Don't talk so b . . . silly, don't', I said. But of course it was me and I had to go up on the platform. To add to our delight, Stan Bradman won a pair of driving gauntlets as second in his class. Well, we celebrated that night! We got back to the hotel long after midnight and Mr Lainson ordered six coffees – wouldn't listen to the porter's complaints.

'Six coffees now!' and we got to bed at 3 a.m.

We were called at seven o'clock and after breakfast went round to our coaches to get them cleaned up. A reporter bloke came up to me and asked me what sort of a rally I had had.

'Ask that bloke over there', I answered. Stan told him what was what and he soon slung his hook.

The loud-speakers were calling out the number of each coach, in the order they were to proceed to the promenade. We all got quite worried when Number 38 didn't come up. Suddenly a police motor bike roared up to me, 'Come on! They've been calling you for 10 minutes.' So I got a police escort to the rostrum to receive my cup from the Mayor!

What a journey home we had that day. I phoned my wife, told her to take a taxi to The Shah at Nuthampstead.

'I've got no money', she said.

'Call at the Draytons,' I answered, 'they'll look after you.'

Sure enough when we all eventually arrived – we'd collected a whole coach load by this time – 'Mother' was inside drinking a gin and orange. Everyone was blotto by the end of the evening. The last thing I remember was Jack Robert's saying, 'Go on, Syd, have another brandy, mate.' Next thing I was asleep, bolt upright in my chair at home, and it was morning. I reckon it was one of the best weekends in my life.

I know one thing too, Premier hadn't got much money when I won the cup – Frank Matthews told me afterwards that we had had a job to get home.

8

Grim Reality

Behind all the pleasure, excitement and activity of our expansionist period lay the grim reality of finance, or, in our case, the lack of it. Indeed, the worst chore for E.A.L. and F.N.M. when they were running the Company together was the regular Thursday morning call to Lloyds. F.N.M. would take up the phone and, with E.A.L. sitting opposite him, would contact the Bank Manager to negotiate the payment of wages.

It was a tense and moving scene: R.C.H.D. would bring in the figures showing how the account stood that morning – what cheques were in transit, what cash was available to pay in, etc.; and then he would stand by F.N.M.'s shoulder as play commenced. Sometimes it was very sticky going, in which case the phone would be passed to E.A.L., who would put a different angle on the manipulations, and, one way or another, the ordeal would end and wages would be secured for another week.

W.F.M.

This situation arose because we had purchased five businesses, plus new vehicles, within the space of five years, without raising more than a fraction of the purchase price from additional invested capital, so we had piled up for ourselves an enormous hire-purchase and bank-loan debt. During this period W.F.M. constantly backed his own assessment of the potential of the Company by coming to its immediate help on many urgent occasions. Again and again the Minutes spell out the gratitude and appreciation of the Board for his constant and ungrudging assistance, especially when over the years he made each member of his family in turn a shareholder of Premier. This show of confidence by the senior and most respected member of the Board, who without blame or criticism continued to support the active Directors, E.A.L. and F.N.M., made all the difference to their morale and gave them an extra sense of energetic determination needed in the bad times.

E.A.L.'s mother also contributed greatly at a time of heavy pressure, but it cost her a good deal of anxiety and worry. This gave her family a sense of guilt to add to the loan. It was almost our worst moment.

Indeed, as the fifties progressed and the AGMs told their story of heavy losses, heavy commitments, failure of dividends, a log-jam in cash flow, it seemed sometimes that we were involving everyone in sight in our distress. Week after week, the Minutes record HP difficulties, insurance stamp difficulties, creditor difficulties; they record the sad inevitability of our forced farewell to Erskine Mac-Pherson, another of our worst moments. We also said goodbye in 1952 to John Hibbs. At the same time all the Directors cut their own salaries considerably – not an easy thing to do but good for the soul. There was no staff bonus in 1952. Mr Durran, Chief Engineer, left in 1953, with our good wishes for his success elsewhere. Worst of all John Matthews decided in February 1953 that he ought to leave Premier, to everyone's regret. He was sincerely thanked for his past services, and returned safely to the Company in 1969.

This dependence on other people continued throughout the fifties, but out of these experiences grew the unwritten code of Premier Travel's Board. Briefly summarised it is as follows:

Ten Commandments for Small Firms in Difficulty

1 Hold on!
2 Rearrange your HP agreements, extend your bank loans, talk – even grovel – to your Bank Managers, your finance companies, but keep confident. Remember they have to be on your side.
3 Attempt, at all costs, to keep the reduced payments flowing.
4 Forget your rich relatives and friends. Although they may help, they may not love you anymore.
5 Always go to the professional money men and keep faith with them.
6 Settle your small and medium creditors – it is from them the fatal writs tend to come.
7 Make arrangements with the large creditors and pay even one per cent of your debt with absolute regularity. They, too, have to be on your side, if only out of self interest.
8 Above all, ask the help of your staff and reward their trust and faith when times change.
9 Avoid redundancies like the plague. They are an insult to your previous business acumen.
10 Never seek a truce amid the traumatic anxieties by sacrificing the life of your firm.

Partly as a result of keeping, more or less, the above tenets of business behaviour, we were able to record the help we received so generously from many quarters in the bad times. One marvellous tyre supplier, Abbey Tyre Co., allowed us to pay off £50 a week on a five-figure bill; R. Burleigh of Eastern Counties Lubricants exercised the patience of Job with our account; E.F. Lindsey of Shell Mex, Jim Truelove of Cambridge Battery Service and Jack Moore of Moore's Engineering were the most outstandingly kind of our many suppliers. Our debt of gratitude remains. On one occasion, we gave our finance company 291 cheques, the first dated 9.3.51 and the last dated 15.1.56 and all written out by R.C.H.D.

We collected immediately every penny owing to us. On the last day of each month R.C.H.D. would present the contract account to Pye's. On the very next day, they would have the cheque ready for him to collect, almost before the ink was dry on the signatures.

Nearly everyone seemed to be backing us, putting confidence in our future, safeguarding their money but letting us have it. That was the inspiring aspect of the battle. When your bank, as worried as you are by ill-secured overdrafts, acts as guarantor, by recommendation, to your finance company (even if not in writing) you have reason to be grateful.

There was a time when ECOC came to see us on operational matters and having presumably heard whispers of our predicament suggested we sell our stage carriage interests to the British Transport Commission. This was a very tempting way out of our difficulties and E.A.L. and F.N.M. were pressurised into agreeing to consider it. We then made the sum required so enormous that it was quite clear we had no real intention of selling anything. Incidentally, this fairly open contact with ECOC started such a flood of rumours that we had to spend a lot of time contradicting the stories that were circulating. The force of our denials again convinced us that in no way would we ever be defeated.

In 1953 one of the people most closely connected with our financial position died, Mr Coates, Managing Director of North Central Waggon Company Ltd. As recorded in the Minutes, 'the Board commented that Mr Coates and his Company had been very real friends of Premier Travel and his death would mean a great loss to North Central and to the business world as a whole. Mr Lainson was asked to send a message of sympathy to the General Manager of the Company.' Now Mr Coates was an astute, rather terrifying businessman, and though we had to be grateful to him for the firmness of his control over our debt, it must have amazed his colleagues that Premier, one of their least satisfactory financial contacts, should offer such genuine sympathy.

Luckily for Premier, during these traumatic years of anxiety, loss and constant financial pressure, E.A.L. and F.N.M. convinced themselves and nearly all the Company's creditors, especially Lloyds and NCWC, that all was fundamentally well, that all would be well and no one would lose from trusting Premier. Indeed, that is exactly how it has turned out, and the present Chairman and the Managing Director have the total satisfaction of reaping the reward of those harsh days.

Their success was a matter of character and attitude. E.A.L. is a living example of British sang-froid (it seems funny that we have to use a French term to describe a typically Anglo-Saxon attitude). He remained completely unflapped by either failure or success; he was unconvinced by the reality of bad figures or prognostications of doom. He daily exhibited to all and sundry the strange aspect of utter solidity and confidence that has

'Queen of the Fleet', UVE 333, at Harston with Bill Day

F.N.M. in the hot-seat, Market Hill, 1948–75

proved the most murderous war weapon of the English. A refusal to surrender when there is clearly no hope whatsoever of coming out alive demoralises and worries the enemy. He thinks, 'this lot must have a secret weapon over the wall – we'd better take care', and he withdraws and the English breathe again. That is how E.A.L. helped break the back of near financial disaster; how he dealt with angry shareholders, impossibly bad figures, his wife's nagging desire to do the sensible thing and sell out, in part at least. His refusal to be beaten in the thirties, forties and fifties is the reason why Premier survives to tell the tale.

The second pillar of the Company was the young Director, Frank Matthews. He is, by any standards, an exceptionally intelligent man, full of insight and sensitivity. He plunged into the challenges of this small Company, even though he was still only in his twenties during the darkest days. He guided, schemed, planned, directed Premier through the morass, like any wartime general. Again and again he saved money by brilliant negotiation. He demanded high standards from the staff, but produced a pension scheme, which we could hardly afford, for their future. He played the

Company's cards like a professional, and after working full out went off to play with the same total dedication. His father commented that, on social occasions, often after a distressing Board meeting, F.N.M. would behave as a young man without a care in the world. It impressed his father, so you can imagine the effect on others.

Both he and E.A.L. have in common an unsinkable sense of humour and total business integrity, and the combination of enthusiasm and enjoyment, scheming and worrying together, has produced a partnership that has become a legend in Premier's world.

Of course, another reason for the long-term confidence of the money men was Premier's continuing expansion, its increased earning capacity and the gradual signs of improvement that crept into the accounts year by year. For instance, a net loss of £3,069 in 1954 had turned in 1955 into a profit of £169. In 1956 the results were good enough for the payment of the first preference dividend for five years – a very special occasion in the life of the Company – and for its preference shareholders!

From then on the tide started to turn and in April 1959, as a result of a good profit in 1958, we were able to purchase one AEC Reliance chassis mounted with a Mark VII Seagull body by H.V. Burlingham Ltd, of Blackpool: UVE 333, with yellow and grey decor chosen by Doreen Matthews and me, was our first new vehicle for ten years. What a boost for morale that vehicle proved to be and how excellent it was that W.F.M. shared in its

acquisition and so knew that the Company he had invested in so heavily and generously, with little financial reward, had pulled through. Thanks to his guidance, his son's efficiency and intelligence, E.A.L.'s dedication and obstinacy and the most outstanding staff, it was en route to success.

Sadly he didn't live to see more than the promise of a successful future for, after months of increasing ill health, he died at the Royal Masonic Hospital in London on 27 December 1959. This was an immensely hard blow for his family and for everyone in Premier, but for the Board, who depended on his advice and strength, it was pretty overwhelming. The Minutes state starkly our sense of loss.

> The Directors wish to record their deep sense of grief at the death, on December 27th 1959, of their Co-Director Mr W.F. Matthews.
> Mr Matthews joined us in 1943 and was largely instrumental in the growth and development of the Company to its present position.
> Mr Matthews was much beloved and respected by members of the staff who valued his high qualities, kindliness and sincerity.
> His unfailing support and loyalty during difficult times showed his courage and strength of purpose and enabled the Company successfully to surmount its problems.
> He was unfailingly cheerful and optimistic.
> His passing leaves a great gap and we shall miss him very deeply.
> His spirit will live on in the Company.

9
Success in Sight

CHANGES, 1960

The death of W.F.M. obviously had a profound effect on the direction of the Company and on each of the three survivors; E.A.L., F.N.M. and M.M.E.L. had to adapt to the new circumstances. Our sense of responsibility and determination was strengthened, but the lack of our part-time Director coming to the Board meetings to criticise, applaud, advise, or stimulate progress was greatly missed by all of us. Moreover, no one had the heart to introduce strangers into the tight little group at this time, so another solution was found in March 1960:

> It was felt that the duties of the Secretary should be divorced from the Directorial functions and that it would be advantageous to the Company if Mr Dodkin, who had occupied a position of trust since 1946, should undertake the duties of Secretary in succession to F.N.M., who would be released for the added responsibilities now falling upon the Directors.

R.C.H.D. was then called to the meeting and was offered the appointment at a salary of £900 per annum, which he accepted with pleasure.

F.N.M. was awarded an honorarium of £50 as a small memento of his twelve years' work as Company Secretary.

This appointment off-loaded an ever-present 'nag' of administrative and legal work onto R.C.H.D.'s broad shoulders and was extremely effective until he retired in 1981.

Thus, the day-by-day business of Premier was again left to the energies of F.N.M. and E.A.L., but we began the sixties in a state of flexibility and enthusiasm, in spite of the sadness.

It turned out that the 1959 profit was around £6,500, which caused general glee – so much so that the Directors felt able to change the old faithful Wolseley car, HYA 206, which had been used by the Lainsons and Matthews for ten years. Another plush-looking Wolseley, SVE 3, was bought instead. It's worth noting here that F.N.M. and E.A.L. shared happily and without irritation or

division first a van and then the Company cars for about twenty-five years – in fact, until 1973, when E.A.L. moved to the country and had to have his own. This remarkable record of amity on such a sensitive matter as 'use of car' partly arose because the Lainson garage was occupied by a pet tramp, known locally as Jock, and also because E.A.L. always walked to the office with one of his dogs. F.N.M., on the other hand, really loved driving but always made certain no one else needed the precious vehicle more. A good record.

PREMIER DOGS

This is a good moment to interrupt progress to celebrate the canines in our history. Husband has been accompanied by one dog or another throughout our married life and our dogs have become as much part of the Company's coporate memory as any other personality.

Our first 'Premier dog' was a large black Labrador who attached himself to Husband when straying in the Market Place and although we took him to the police station he was not claimed and so became ours.

This splendid dog did a lot for us and for the harmony of the Company. It made Husband feel secure and complete to have the handsome animal always with him. It made serious meetings more relaxed when there was a dog to sit at the feet of the opposition, or the money men, asking to be fondled. Staff meetings, during which old Sam would make the rounds, lost some of their antipathies, and visitations by the Board, when the first out of the car was a bouncing black dog, were robbed of all false formality.

Actually, Sam himself behaved a bit like visiting royalty and we never felt we possessed him. It was he who had graciously chosen us and we felt slightly privileged to have him around, and we would not have been surprised if he had decided to leave in the same dignified way he had come. In fact, he did make a mistake one day that might well have removed him from us for ever, and was probably a repetition of the manner in which he

'His master's voice'; Tom gets his orders by phone

was originally lost. Husband had coffee almost every day at a small place near the town centre. Sam would wander from table to table seeing what he could scrounge from the customers and one day he wandered up to the proprietor's wife, who had just come in on a visit. Unheard by either Husband or her husband, she said to Sam, 'Good Lord, you shouldn't be here! Come along home at once', and, thinking him her own Labrador, she took him by the collar, bundled him into the back of her car and drove off into the country where they lived.

When she turned into the drive of her house, she was appalled to see her own Labrador coming to greet her. Quick as a flash and much embarrassed, she turned round and drove back to the café, where she released Sam and reported to her husband. The next day the story was relayed to Husband, and Sam was congratulated on yet another escapade, the idiot dog.

Sam died in 1956, aged about twelve. Our next dog was Toby, born to our children's bitch, Suki. We gave him to the Matthews but he turned out to be one of those rogue animals that occur in the best of families, so they gave him back. He bit seven people in his time, chased motor-bikes, brought men, women and children off their push-bikes and fought every dog in Cambridge. So he was confined to a lead, which E.A.L. hated. One day Husband took him from the office to lunch and the lead was loose by his side, so that Toby was able suddenly to leap out and nip a passing male's trouser leg. Husband, as on previous occasions, offered to pay for the damage and gave the victim 10s (50p) to cover the cost of repair. On the way back from lunch, Toby, once again on loose and nonchalant lead, leapt again and stripped off a piece of grey flannel trouser. This time, Husband, having paid for lunch and one repair, was not well off, so he proffered only 3s 6d (17½p) with which the poor innocuous pedestrian was appeased.

We celebrated our twenty-fifth wedding anniversary by sharing a splendid Labrador puppy called Tom. He was extremely intelligent, even for his breed of knowledgeable canines, and showed remarkable understanding.

One day Husband and I had come home without revisiting the office, where earlier on we had left our coats. When evening came, P.S.A. and Alison, the secretary, wanted to go home but they found they could not shift the huge resisting solidity of Tom, so they rang us up to come and help. 'Better still,' I said, 'let's try putting the phone near his ear and I'll try and talk him into coming home by himself.' This they did and in my most determined, resonant voice I spoke to him: 'Tom, what are you doing down there? Come home at once. Good dog. Come home.' What an example of HMV. Apparently, he at once started down the passage, scented a bit around the stairs, went out into Rose Crescent, sniffed around again and then made off at full speed in the direction of our house, a mile away. He burst open the door about ten minutes later, where we greeted him as a hero.

Tom, who died on a visit to our Ware office in the Summer of 1976, was perhaps one of the very last dogs to be allowed to move freely about the town or country on his own business.

And so we return to more human happenings.

AFTER THE SILVER JUBILEE, 1961–66

The history of Premier divided from 1960 onwards into its new constituent parts, Premier Airlines Limited, Air Plan Holidays and Premier Travel Agency, whose various individual stories appear elsewhere in this book. In Premier Travel itself, the financial difficulties still reared up from time to time but were no longer hair-raising.

By 16 January 1961 it was time to hold the Staff Dinner to celebrate the Company's Silver Jubilee. The staff subscribed for a presentation wallet for E.A.L., which was presented by S.P. Similarly, E.A.L. presented our Syd with an identical wallet on behalf of the Company. With the £3 19s 9d (£3.99) oversubscribed for E.A.L.'s present, it was decided to purchase a suitable plaque, which evolved later into the Long Service Membership Board, a source of pride to us all.

Thus began the custom, which has persevered ever since, of presenting each member of the staff with an identical, initialled wallet on completing

twenty-five years service. In the sixties it was impossible to fill them with five crisp fivers but when this was eventually afforded in 1971, all previously presented wallets had the long delayed lining supplied. Wives, nowadays, also receive a wallet-purse for their valuable part in keeping our staff so loyal and true. (The only person in the whole Premier fiefdom who has never had a wallet, as worker or wife, is your poor old editor. Boo hoo!)

We celebrated again in April 1961 when the Silver Jubilee Dinner was held at the University Arms and eighty-two guests were present. The Company's health was proposed by W.P.S. Ormond MA, M.Inst.T., Chairman of the Traffic Commissioners, Eastern Area, which was a great honour for the Company. Mr W.G. Hall MBE, Assistant General Manager of ECOC and Mr F.J. Speight, M.Inst.T., Chairman of the PSV Operators, also spoke of Premier in suitably flattering terms, for which the two Company speakers, E.A.L. and F.N.M., were duly grateful. It was reported by Mr Hall that E.A.L. spoke for 43½ minutes!

In 1961 our existing Staff Pension Scheme was wound up and a much higher Staff Life Assurance replaced it. Members were entitled to a return of the premium and the distribution of contributions took place on 25 May 1961, 'and was obviously greeted with pleasure and surprise by the staff', especially the older ones, one or two of whom received over £300 – a fairly handsome sum at the time. The executives were introduced into a tailor-made Endowment Policy, which was itself overtaken in the seventies by a high-flying Executive Pension Scheme.

Mr Arthur Darby indicated in 1962 that he did not intend to work after his 75th birthday in October. He was heartily congratulated on the good work he had done as Chief Cashier for the Company since he left ECOC when he was just 60.

Another disrupting event took place in 1963. The surveyor's department of the Cambridge City Council had its office in the Guildhall, directly across the Market Place from Rose Crescent and 15 Market Hill. One day they looked out of their window during a lull in their busy work and were astonished to see our former building gently leaning out of line. The Borough Surveyor ordered Watches of Switzerland, our landlord, to evacuate the building immediately and then stabilise it with hefty building work. So Premier had to move to Regent Street for the month of August and when we came back we took over two floors instead of one, and eventually we added the third floor as

PREMIER TRAVEL GROUP LONG SERVICE MEMBERS	
E. A. LAINSON	1936
S. E. PENNELL	1936 - 1980
F. R. BARKER	1937 - 1982
H. J. BIRD	1937 - 1970
Mrs. M. M. E. LAINSON	1939
M. J. GIFFORD	1941
F. A. GRICE	1942 - 1975
E. W. DAY	1945 - 1980
H. J. LAW	1945 - 1977
A. J. WISBEY	1945
R. C. H. DODKIN	1946 - 1981
H. F. W. WYNN	1946 - 1972
Mrs. M. M. FRANCIS	1947
E. P. LAW	1947 - 1973
S. J. LAW	1947
H. W. LEE	1947
F. N. MATTHEWS	1947
A. W. REEVES	1947 - 1975
W. J. ALDOUS	1948
G. BRAY	1949 - 1982
J. B. GOWER	1949
J. C. JAGGARD	1949 - 1978
R. R. ROOPE	1949
W. E. RUFFLE	1949 - 1980
R. E. SCARR	1949
R. R. SCRIVENER	1949
R. R. MUMBY	1951
A. W. HILL	1951 - 1981
R. BAKER	1953
N. L. BELL	1953
H. J. IMPEY	1954 - 1981
L. C. SOUTH	1956
Mrs. H. BERNARDINI	1957

The Honours Board

well. Many people earned a guinea or two for their extra and practical work involved in the two moves.

In November 1964 we finally left Harston for Chrishall, as M.J.G. describes in Chapter 5.

On 7 January 1966 married men were accompanied by their wives at the Annual Dinner. Progress was dynamic!

On Thursday 23 June 1966 'the Company was honoured by the appointment of Mr E.A. Lainson as Chairman of the Passenger Vehicle Operators Association'. During the post-war years E.A.L.

had been most active on behalf of the independent operators as a committee member. A luncheon attended by the Directors and executives of the Company was held on Monday 27 June to mark the occasion and E.A.L. expressed his gratitude for all the nice things said. F.N.M. proposed and it was agreed that the Company should be responsible for all out of pocket expenses incurred as a result of E.A.L.'s chairmanship of the PVOA.

On 6 February 1967 E.A.L. had another honour: he was elected a Member of the Institute of Transport.

10
Diversion for the Chairman

RETROSPECT

E.A. Lainson

With the passing of the Road Traffic Act 1930, and the appointment of Traffic Commissioners, the economics and administration of the bus and coach industry were completely changed.

A red letter day was 1 January 1931, as it marked a transformation in the Eastern Traffic Area. The first Chairman was Sir Haviland Hiley, who had been General Manager of the New Zealand State Railways.

The Panel Commissioners, drawn from County Councils and other local authorities, usually two in number at public sittings, played a very important part in the work of the Traffic Courts.

I was present at some of the very early sittings and was greatly impressed by the patience and good humour with which the hearings were conducted. The scope of the problem was extremely large and diverse. The twin purposes of the Act were: (1) to determine the existence of public need, proved in evidence; (2) to prevent unreasonable abstraction of traffic from established operators. From the earliest days much of the contention arose on the frequent and heavily used services.

A good example of this was the operation of Hillman's Saloon Coaches, who were running about 103 vehicles on the East Anglian trunk routes between London and Colchester, Clacton, Ipswich, Southwold, Norwich and Yarmouth. From their inception in the late 1920s these services were specifically devised to carry all types of traffic and consequently posed a considerable threat to the various local stage services. The fast running Gilford vehicles (there was one AEC on the London–Yarmouth route) proved very popular and caused great concern to the local operators (both combine and independent) on services such as Chelmsford–Colchester and Colchester–Clacton. Several independents – Empire Best, Sutton, Batten and Monty – operated on the London–Clacton service, with many additional seasonal services.

Fare levels were an important feature. Prior to the Traffic Act there was a day return fare of only 2s [10p] (2s 6d [12½p] by Varsity and Westminster) between Cambridge and London. The Commissioners, wisely in my opinion, authorised a minimum cheap day return fare of 4s [20p] to Varsity and Westminster on Thursdays, as they considered this to be in the public interest.

When new services were introduced, for example by Grey Pullman between Haverhill and Bury in the early 1930s, restrictions were placed on the competitive sections, and some such restrictions exist to this day. In point of fact, many operators of long stage services were content with these restrictions, as the handling of fairly local traffic remote from their depot would have caused difficulties in providing uneconomic reliefs over short distances.

An important feature in East Anglia were the limited-stop services, jointly operated by Ortona Motor Co. and Eastern Counties Road Car between Cambridge and Felixstowe, and by United Automobile Services and Eastern Counties between Norwich and Ipswich and Yarmouth and Ipswich.

An interesting service of Eastern Counties was a Felixstowe–Yarmouth route which was a partial replacement for the Belle Steamer service. This enabled the steamer people (New Medway Steam Packet Co.) to curtail their service at Felixstowe. Previously passengers from/to Yarmouth, Lowestoft, and Southwold used the steamers for many purposes, including holiday access. The Southwold Railway had also closed in 1929, largely due to bus and coach competition.

Even after the Second World War, coach and steamer services were both complementary and competitive. Premier Travel, for example, operated a single-journey only service on summer Saturdays. The goodwill was acquired from Mr W.H. Thorne of Clacton between Clacton and London. The evidence for the transfer was hotly contested before the Traffic Commissioners by several Clacton–London operators. Premier operated on a three-part allocation: Service 5, 09.00 Birmingham–Clacton; Service 35, 14.00 Clacton–Kings Cross; Service 38, 18.15 Kings Cross–

Haverhill. This was a demanding duty for our road staff but worked surprisingly well. In the early post-war years as many as 4,000 passenger journeys were made on Service 5 on peak summer Saturdays.

Much 'dead' mileage was avoided by 'swinging', whereby passengers transferred to Linton and Horseheath, using lay-over vehicles from Clacton and Midland-based coaches from Birmingham, Coventry, and Leicester. On occasion we used other lay-over cars, as when F.N.M. telephoned me at Linton, saying that a United vehicle was to swing there. I was surprised to see a United Automobile Services bus with two drivers, as I had expected a United Counties car. The control of summer Saturday allocations was very arduous and we were still in the office at 11.00 on some Friday evenings. It would be difficult – almost impossible – to operate on this basis today, but the swing was a logical, economic and efficient method of moving two groups of people travelling west to east or vice versa, in more or less the same numbers. It involved the maximum utilisation not only of our own vehicles and staff but those of other operators as well. Indeed, the swing was the precursor of the interchange system of the eighties.

With the end of the War the future pattern of express fares became a matter of great importance. A meeting of the Central Fares Committee under the chairmanship of Mr Alfred Baynton, Joint General Manager of East Kent Road Car Co., was held in London towards the end of 1945.

Mr Briggs, of Standerwick, pointed out that his company was very concerned at the prospect of rail electrification to Blackpool (still unrealised in 1985) and Mr Jennings said that his own fares were too high. Mr Baynton to Mr Hall (convenor of the Number 6 Committee, East Anglia): 'Is he one of yours, Mr Hall?'

Premier proposed that express fares be 40% above pre-war. This found no favour and a resolution was passed that all operators apply for an increase of 16.66%.

In my opinion many of the difficulties which arose later when the industry was forced to apply for successive increases, against a pattern of falling traffic, could have been avoided, if we had had what W.G. Hall, a great pioneer of the industry and sometimes called the Transport King of Norwich, would have described as 'the Big Bite'. Equally, the Traffic Commissioners, as guardians of the public, would have been unlikely to agree an increase of this magnitude.

The Directors of Premier Travel decided, soon after the foundation of the Company, not to seek membership in either the Motor Hirers and Coach Services Association (MHCSA) or in the Commercial Motor Users Association (CMUA). They intimated, however, that they would wish to join a body which would merge the interests of these Associations. Their attitude was governed, at least in part, by the experiences of the companies from which Premier Travel Ltd takes its name, Premier Omnibus Co. Ltd and its offshoot Premier Hire Ltd. These companies were compulsorily acquired by the London Passenger Transport Board (LPTB). Our first Chairman, Sir Christopher Magnay, Bt, had been active in Premier Omnibus since 1924 and in the later development of Premier Hire Ltd, and served as a member of the committee formed to protect the interests of LPTB Stockholders. Our attitude then, as now, was to play a full part in the industry, whilst acting in the interests of professional unity.

In 1944, largely due to the efforts of John M. Birch and Frederick J. Speight, helped by independent operators nationwide, PVOA was formed and Premier Travel joined in 1945. Mr F.A. Walker, a pioneer operator in Mayfield Transport (London and Blackpool, later London and Leicester) and thereafter Secretary of MHCSA, became Secretary of PVOA and continued in office until his death in 1966.

Mr W.H. Webb, who started his career as a boy in the CMUA, is still very active in the industry, currently as Personal Assistant to Mr Dennis Quin, Director General of the Bus and Coach Council.

Premier's main interest and involvement was, of course, first of all, in PVOA. Many problems faced the industry. In 1952 a heavy tax was placed on fuel and this was further increased in 1953. The industry, being very heavily affected by the tax, formed the Joint Fuel Tax Committee representing MPTA, PTA, PVOA and the Scottish Association. It was not until 1966 that James Callaghan, then Chancellor of the Exchequer, gave a partial remission of fuel tax.

Following the death of F.A. Walker, the committee of PVOA, consisting of the National Chairman; two Vice Chairmen, John Birch and Freddy Speight; Frank Bloomfield, the Treasurer; and myself, as senior Vice Chairman, considered the appointment of his successor. The correspondence was handled by Freddy Speight, who announced that he had received a late application from Mr D.R. Quin, the Assistant Secretary of the Dairymen's Federation. Mr Quin was appointed and this proved an excellent choice. Following the merger of the four national associations into the Federation of British Road Passenger Transport, now the Bus and Coach Council, Mr Quin, who is its Director General, has been a tower of strength to the industry, through its many vicissitudes.

The first major battle to be undertaken was against the proposal to nationalise passenger transport. The Tilling group of companies under Sir Frederick Heaton accepted the Government's offer to acquire its assets, but the British Electric Traction Company (BET) solidly opposed the takeover of their large and profitable undertaking. The industry set up an organisation known as VOICE, the Vehicle Operators Independent Committee, largely due to the efforts of Peter Yorke, a senior figure in BET and a Director of Midland Red Omnibus Company Ltd. In early years, Peter Yorke had served as a solicitor and was expert in handling parliamentary questions. VOICE did a great deal to promote the opposition to nationalisation and it was a great sorrow to us and many others when the BET companies were sold.

At about the same period the Government announced that they were setting up a so-called Area Scheme to take over bus undertakings. The first was in the North Eastern Area and Frank Matthews and myself drove in an elderly van to Newcastle to attend the first meeting. We were welcomed by Bob Bailey, then with the Northern General, a BET company, whom I had first met when he was Superintendent Express Services, UCOC, Northampton, in 1937. Bob Bailey and I have met often over the years and he is one of the very few people in the industry who has served in all its sections. At the meeting in Newcastle, Frank Matthews and I found that we were really interlopers, for the large meeting consisted mainly of Town Clerks and other civic dignitaries of the North of England, whose understanding of the transport industry was rather limited.

In 1960, PVOA elected three Vice Chairmen, who were to serve for two years each. I was the junior of these three and ultimately assumed office in 1966. This was an arduous period with many meetings in different parts of the country and my wife and I were guests of the other three National Associations on a number of occasions. This gave us great pleasure and helped to knit together my view of the industry, through its many component parts. I look back with pleasure on the many pleasant people whom we met during this period. In 1968 I was President of the Omnibus Society and this also gave me great pleasure as I had been a member since the early 1930s. Transport is a fascinating industry and so much depends on the individual man or woman engaged in it.

Premier was one of the few independents who were appointed as members of the PTA. This was a signal honour which all of us in Premier greatly appreciated. We were able to meet the leaders of the industry in other sectors and the cross-fertilisation of ideas was both pleasant and very helpful.

PVOA and its recent successor, CIBS, have been tremendously important to the well-being of the independent bus and coach industry in Britain.

PREMIER'S STAFF RELATIONS
'You work with us, not for us'

From the beginning, the Company's staff relations have rested on close and frequent contacts between the Board and freely elected Staff Representatives. At first the numbers were so small that it was more or less a matter of individual agreements. However, the first staff meeting, described by S.P. in Chapter 4, was followed by others, usually in pubs, even during the War. People would tell E.A.L. what they thought of their conditions of work, their wages (not much) and the desperate condition of the fleet. He and N.C.P.T. would listen and make conciliatory noises but no one was in a position to do much more. These informal gatherings gave way in the forties and fifties to Boardroom battles held each year round about Whitsuntide.

Representatives of the stage and express drivers, the conductors and driver–conductors would engage in the numbers game with the Directors. They were always immensely well informed and put their case so strongly that it needed all F.N.M.'s nous and R.C.H.D.'s skill with his magic decimal calculator to get the figures agreed. The expenses were always a source of much bargaining: in a meeting in 1946 E.A.L. wondered aloud whether 2s 6d (12½p) wasn't far too much for lunch; however, he agreed that 11s (55p) was a reasonable allowance for bed and breakfast! When the road staff had agreed their annual rate increase and the engineers had done likewise, we all drank sherry together – the Board because inevitably we felt weak and the staff because, even if never enough, they had won something from the fairly bare cupboard.

This annual friendly confrontation has continued throughout our fifty years and the ability of successive representatives to fight their members' corner and obtain, on the basis of fair play and an intimate knowledge of their work, satisfactory wages and conditions, seems to underline the lack of need for a third party, i.e. trade-union negotiators.

Our staff have proved consistently that they have

numerous people among them who can represent their views fluently and reasonably, negotiate the very best of conditions available in both bad and good times, stand by their members in disciplinary matters, argue every case lucidly and, finally, demonstrate ferociously to the Directors any inefficiency or injustice that might have crept in. These are the people who have been the strength of Premier.

Every year the Minutes record the same pattern of results from these meetings: shorter hours, increased rates, higher expenses at all levels – all to be balanced by increased fares and tighter economies. Increased costs were seldom off-set in Premier by redundancies, but in winter, hours were nearly always reduced to the basic week, which often meant some discomfort, if not hardship.

A brief running commentary from our records will demonstrate how the problems and attitudes remain constant, even though the rates and conditions have changed out of all recognition in Premier's first fifty years.

Apart from E.A.L.'s first decision in 1936 to pay sick-pay, some of the first recorded Minutes are as follows:

> In April 1946, Premier agreed to continue paying £6 per week for Unemployment and Health contributions for its employees, until the new Compulsory Insurance Scheme was introduced.

> [In 1947] Mr King [Drivers' Representative] drew the attention of the Directors to the Company's policy regarding payment to Leading Drivers. He said there appeared to be no systematic consideration in choosing them. Long service and absence of complaint against a driver had been ignored in selecting the original ones. Specifically, Driver King mentioned Driver Pennell, who was the oldest employee and possibly the best driver but his services were not recognised. Mr Lainson suggested that more satisfactory results might be obtained if the staff themselves elected Leading Drivers, but that if this was not possible perhaps it would be best if all the drivers went back to the old flat rates. Mr King agreed to this proposal and said it would overcome the present resentment of drivers being ordered to do work that Leading Drivers had refused to do. Mr Lainson asked Driver King to suggest ways and means of rewarding long service. Mr King's reply was that 'If the employer is a good employer, the worker will stay with his employer without any further inducement. If the employer is not good, then obviously the worker would leave and find other employment.' It was finally resolved to obtain the view of other drivers.

Unfortunately Mr King himself left the Company perhaps because he was tempted by enormous night-shift wages.

In November 1947 F.N.M. said that if the drivers were more interested in their work, we could pay 2s 4d (11½p) per hour for working in garages, but he had seen so much slacking he hesitated to recommend this. Mr King replied that if there were any slackers, they should be discharged. He added that it was unsatisfactory for a man not to know if he was on clean or dirty work and he suggested overalls should be provided for garage work. He then referred to the possibility of a five-day week. E.A.L. agreed with the proposal for the winter months but said it could not be entertained in the summer.

In December 1947 Mr Howard raised the question of a staff bonus for the year 1947. It was agreed that bonus should be awarded as follows:

> For twelve months service, each employee to receive £1 and pro-rata for each completed three months, with a minimum of 5s [25p]. For executive officers of the Company, it was agreed Mr F.N. Matthews and Mr J. Buchanan should receive 80 £1 Preference Shares, Mr W. Day 25 £1 Preference Shares and Mr W. Long 20 £1 Preference Shares for the year 1947.

This was Premier's first attempt at profit sharing and creating employee shareholders.

In 1949, the Board had an interview with the Pension Manager of Scottish Union Insurance Company concerning the introduction of a Staff Pension Scheme. E.A.L. suggested the cost to the Company should be in the region of £1,000 a year or about five per cent of the Company's wage expenditure. W.F.M. proposed a system of a flat pension, say 30s [£1.50] per week, for all personnel at the retiring age of sixty, irrespective of their position in the Company at that moment.

In the same year E.A.L. reported that representatives of the staff had requested him to pass on their view that an increase in the basic wage should be considered, to meet the cost of living. Apart from this factor the conditions of the combine companies had improved and the staff had furnished him with certain comparative figures and ECOC's conditions of service. These showed that ECOC's were superior in some respects. W.F.M. said that he wished the Company staff to be at least as well off as Eastern Counties and felt the Directors should aim to make their conditions superior.

In 1950, F.N.M. reported that the five-day working week was in operation, he stated that overtime throughout the Company was costing an average of

£85 per week and that Haverhill depot was responsible for the largest proportion of it.

On 24 May 1951, it was decided to invite volunteers from the staff to be regular express service drivers on Services 3, 4, 34, 36, 37, 39 and 40. It was further agreed that an additional payment of 2s 6d (12½p) per day would be made to the driver while operating his service. (Service 5 had already been allocated to Drivers Sydney Pennell and Harry Law.) This was a second attempt to reward senior staff.

In March 1952 all Harston staff were allocated one vehicle each, which only they would drive. Their work was to consist mainly of private hire and contract, with weekend express services:

> There were obvious disadvantages to the scheme, particularly regarding allocation of vehicles between depots and on stage work, but it was agreed that savings in wages, in maintenance of vehicles and in light mileage would result.

This decision of the Board formalised one of the most satisfactory solutions to the problem of promotion and ladder climbing for road staff that Premier has ever devised. It enabled the Traffic Department to allocate the vehicles to the people it recognised as skilled and responsible, who were also dedicated coachmen. The latter are a class apart. They are to be found in every coach company, large or small, and their characteristics are skill, good humour, courtesy and infinite patience. Premier had, and have, a large preponderance of these Ace drivers. Another of the consequences of this co-operation in the one-man, one-coach system, was that our fleet lasted without a new vehicle for ten years, from 1949 to 1959.

A Minute of 6 May 1954 illustrates vividly how our staff stood by us in the awful early fifties:

> The Secretary reported on an interview last Tuesday with the Drivers' Representatives of Chrishall and Harston. They requested an increase in wages amounting to 15s [75p] per week. The Board agreed that some increase was necessary and appreciated the restraint shown by the staff in not coming forward before. It was two years since the last award of 2s [10p] per week was made. After discussion and bearing in mind overtime rates, sickness benefits, our Pension Scheme and the rates paid by other operators, it was agreed to offer to increase wages and salaries by 10s [50p], if acceptable.

The staff came to our rescue yet again in the fifties by agreeing to a reduction in their pension benefits, so recently awarded. In May 1952 the Board had to decide what to do about an expenditure it couldn't possibly afford:

> As part of the general economy drive now in progress, serious consideration was given to the possibility of reducing the benefits under the Staff Pension Scheme and thereby the cost of premiums that now amounted to £1,000 approx. It was agreed that the £300 Life Assurance incorporated in the scheme should if possible remain unaltered. The Secretary was instructed to ask Mr Berkeley, the Life Superintendent of the Scottish Union Co., to call and acquaint the Board with all details.

The staff meetings referred to above were some of many that punctuated the progress of Premier's continually improving wages and conditions of service, but it would be quite misleading to omit the function of the Transport and General Workers' Union (TGWU) in probing into our affairs if we happened to be behind the National Agreement on Wages that has always been the measuring stick in the industry.

As early as 1948, an approach by one member of our staff to the Union resulted in a meeting at the Ministry of Labour offices between ourselves and the TGWU representatives, with the man from the Ministry acting as umpire. There was a lively clash of personalities and outlooks, during which I was castigated by Mr Cherry of the Union: 'Come off it, sister. Don't tell me you in Premier are running a Benevolent Society.'

F.N.M., when querying one aspect of the National Agreement, was also rebuked, mainly for being too young: 'You don't understand. You weren't in at the drafting.'

The outcome was that the guaranteed working week was reduced, in principle, from 50 hours to 48 hours. Two points were not agreed: one was the payment of overtime after 44 hours at time and a quarter; the second was our refusal to be allied in any way to the principles of the TGWU organisation: 'The Board agreed and again unanimously resolved that under no circumstances should our present form of representation by employees be subject to the interference of a third party.'

On another occasion, in February 1949, E.A.L. informed the Board that a meeting with Mr Airy of the Ministry of Labour and Mr Cherry of the TGWU had been arranged to discuss the six-hour guaranteed day, plus time and a half on Sundays. On 3 March 1949 E.A.L. reported that these revisions had been agreed, except that Sunday pay would be time and a quarter and that the TGWU had been satisfied, 'although Mr Cherry tried very hard to draw up a whole lot of conditions in the form of an agreement between the Company and the TGWU. The Chairman made it clear to Mr Cherry that the Company's conditions of service were made primarily with the staff and not Mr Cherry's organisation.'

In June of the same year the Minutes recorded that the Board of Directors were unanimous in agreeing that the Company's conditions had now become 'far superior to those offered under the National Agreement and were pleased that finality had been reached'.

Another meeting between representatives of the TGWU and the Board of Directors took place on 24 May 1951. E.A.L. informed those present of the recent revisions to the Company's conditions of service and it was noted that time and a half was to be paid for all Sunday work. Mr Bagwell, representing the Union, stated that the only point still under discussion was the question of rates of overtime. Mr Bagwell was prepared to accept a standard 48-hour week for £6 10s (£6.50) and 2s 8d (13p) per hour. It was pointed out by E.A.L. that our men were definitely working under more favourable conditions of service than those working under the conditions as laid down in the National Agreement and, furthermore, the operating procedures of this Company could not be compared with those of the combine. On the proposition of F.N.M., 'it was resolved to ask Mr Bagwell to forward his proposals in writing, together with up to date copies of the National Agreement and on receipt of same the Directors would take legal advice and decide whether or not it would be correct policy to invite Mr Bagwell to arrange for the question to be settled by arbitration.'

Further correspondence ensued and E.A.L. wrote to say that the Directors would meet the staff and ascertain their views. Mr Bagwell replied 'that he was not interested in the proposed meetings, as he only concerned himself with making the terms and conditions embodied in the National Agreement effective throughout his area'. Having sent a fairly devastating reply to this letter, the Board went ahead with its staff meetings, and the one that took place in Haverhill is worthy of the following long quotation from the Minutes.

A report on the Meeting held on 7 June 1951 at Haverhill was presented to the Board. The Directors met the whole Haverhill staff and between 7.30 p.m. and 9 p.m. various domestic problems were discussed and satisfactorily resolved. At 9.30 p.m. a further Meeting was held, not on the Company's premises, at which Mr Soames of the TGWU was invited to be present. At this Meeting, Mr Lainson,

the Chairman, first asked Mr Soames to explain to the Staff the conditions contained in the National Agreement and more particularly those conditions at present being worked by the Staff of Eastern Counties Omnibus Co. Ltd. His lengthy explanation was followed by Mr Lainson's outline of this Company's conditions of service as at present being worked, and in conclusion members of the staff were asked to put any questions they liked to the Meeting. Much discussion ensued, particularly with regard to the payment by ECOC on Private Hire standing-time. No definite conclusions were reached by the time the Meeting was finally concluded at 1 a.m.

These meetings were followed up by a secret ballot (Premier as always in the vanguard of reform) and the outcome was as follows:

	For the Company	*Against the Company*
Chrishall	21	11
Haverhill	9	20
Harston	15	1
Huntingdon	5	0
Total	50	32

Incidentally, another ballot was conducted for basically the same reasons in 1984. The letter that J.A.M. and F.N.M. sent out to every member of the road staff is worth quoting in full.

PREMIER TRAVEL SERVICES LTD

August, 1984

To: All Full Time Road Staff

STAFF REPRESENTATION

The Directors have been advised by the Local Branch of the Transport and General Workers Union that a recent secret postal ballot of their 31 members indicated that 23 were in favour of being represented by the TGWU.

At the present time Premier Travel Service Ltd. have 53 full-time P.S.V. Drivers and your Staff Representatives have requested that another secret ballot be taken which on this occasion should include every member of the Road Staff. Accordingly we would ask each and every one to complete the enclosed ballot paper and return it to Mr B.V. Burnett, Company Secretary, in the stamped addressed envelope provided. The envelopes will be opened on Monday, 10th September, 1984 by your Representatives.

The Directors hope that the following points may be helpful:

1. For nearly 40 years Premier Staff Wages and

Conditions of Service have been negotiated direct with the Board by Staff Representatives elected by the majority of Road Staff. During this time several approaches by the TGWU to change this policy have been resisted by the staff.

2. It is anticipated that representation by the TGWU will mean Premier adopting the so-called National Agreement which, to the best of our knowledge does not include:
   a. Long Service Entitlements.
   b. £2000 Death Benefits. (Non-contributory.)
   c. Discretionary Personal Loans. (Interest Free.)
   d. Temporary Parking Concessions.
   e. Refreshment Allowance.
   f. Hospital Appointments.
   g. Occasional loan of Company Car.
   h. Retirement Award.
   i. Profit Sharing.
   j. The flexibility needed for the special 'Premier' operations.

3. Comparable annual wage settlements over the past 3 years in percentage terms are as follows:

	National Agreement	*Premier*
1982	6%	10.25%
1983	5%	8%
1984	4.9%	6.5%
Compound difference over three years.	16.75%	26.83%

Many thanks.
F. N. Matthews, Managing Director.

The votes of this secret ballot were counted on 10 September 1984 by the Staff Representatives and the results were as follows:

For the National Agreement	8
For Premier Travel	36
No votes cast	8
Total	52

Everyone, bar eight, in Premier felt very elated at this reconfirmation of our mutual trust.

Another sensible if far-reaching step forward in staff relations was taken at the end of 1962 when it was decided to call regular quarterly meetings of Executives, of Engineering Representatives and of Staff Representatives. They were spaced to provide one meeting a month for the Directors to attend and

R.C.H.D. as Secretary was asked to attend all the meetings and prepare their Minutes.

A few months later, the Board was worried by the standard of staff recruitment and suggested they should see the short-listed applicants. They also revised a long-standing rule that employees who had left could not be re-employed. Now they could be, if their applications were unanimously supported by the Staff Representatives.

In June 1966, the first Merit Money was paid for the 1965 summer season on the basis of 4s (20p) per qualifying day. The highest number of days was 100. Each driver was awarded his marks out of 20 by F.G. and the Directors, and most scored between 14 and 19. Had each driver obtained maximum marks, the total Merit Money would have been £251. The actual amount paid was £207, which shows just how high the standard was.

In the mid-seventies, a brand new plan was brought into operation. It was called the Premier Travel Group Profit-Sharing Scheme and this extract from a letter, signed by F.N.M., which was part of the 1984 statement of account, will give some idea of the Board's attempt to acknowledge their debt to the staff.

The splendid result for 1984 is the more remarkable as the national trend last year was one of increased competition and tighter profit margins generally. Further, we made a substantial investment from profits in Premier's own Tour Operations thereby ensuring the ultimate success of this prestigious programme now being marketed nationwide.

We congratulate all members of the team who have dedicated themselves throughout 1984 to the overall Premier cause and thank in particular the Staff in all sections of the Group who have at times performed far beyond the normal call of duty.

Accordingly the Directors are delighted to recognise these efforts by a significant increase in the sum allocated to Staff Profit Sharing which, for the year under review, will be based upon the following formula:

1. The unit upon which the Profit Sharing Scheme is based will be one full week's basic pay (at the rate current in December, 1984)

   AND

2. A special bonus will be paid to all eligible staff amounting to 65% of one week's basic pay at December, 1984 level.

The Chairman takes it easy, 1969

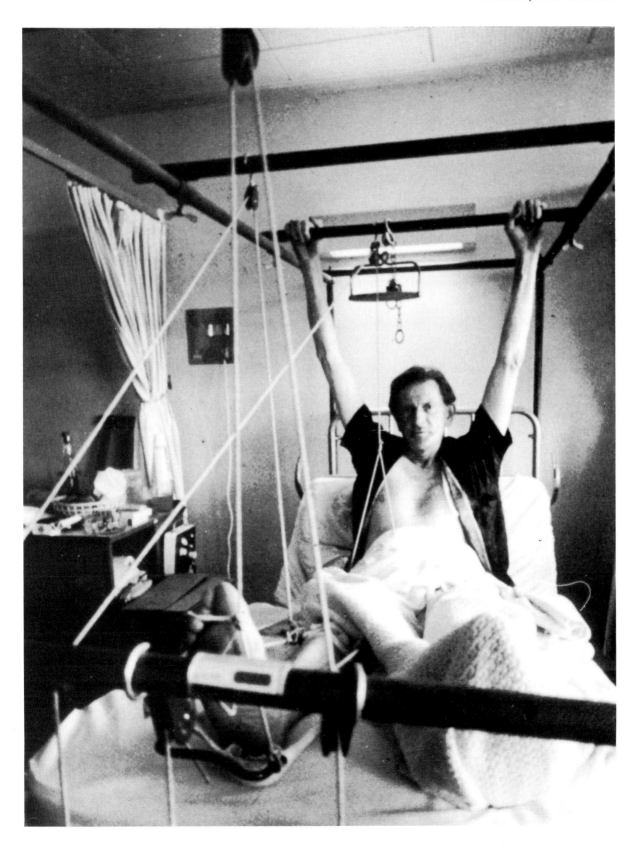

EXTRACTS FROM PREMIER BULLETINS

September 4th 1969. 10A. From M.M.E.L.

You will be sorry to hear that Husband had last night a rotten accident which resulted in his thigh bone being broken just above the knee-cap. It happened on Coe Fen when he was exercising our dog, Tom, and he approached, as is his normal custom, a grazing horse, to fondle it. Unfortunately, because of some nettles, he stepped too close to its hind quarters and was immediately kicked hard enough to break the bone instantly. He fell down and might easily have lain there for some time but luckily it was near Fen Causeway and a friend saw him and called us to assist.

New Addenbrookes diagnosed the trouble very quickly and ordered him to be treated by the 'traction' method, involving weights attached to a steel pin inserted below his knee. The worst feature is that he will have to be in hospital about three months, so he will need a lot of support from all of you, please and thank you at the same time.

September 1969. From E.A.L.

Very many thanks for your letter of sympathy on my fractured thigh. Your kind thought does much to cheer me up. The way in which so many of my friends have rallied round is a great comfort – and really helps.

The forecast is that I shall be here for fifteen weeks – ten weeks traction and five weeks on crutches. The Casualty Surgeon, Mr Illingworth, pinned the leg in the small hours, and has, I believe, and hope, done a good job. Being pretty familiar with horses I find it hard to explain my stupidity in getting within range of this beast's hooves. Twenty minutes in a bed of nettles did not help me. The Addenbrookes people had an unpleasant job, one being a part-time PT Staff Member.

[Almost every member of the staff visited E.A.L. in hospital. Not counting F.N.M. who went almost daily, he had over one hundred visitors – mostly on a rota basis.]

11

Premier Airlines Ltd

FACTS AND FIGURES

B.V. Burnett

The Airline Company was incorporated as a limited company on 8 August 1960, the original concept being to form a unit capable of operating as an aircraft handling agent and as an extension of the parent Company's activities.

The first airline to operate through Cambridge Airport for which Premier Airlines was the general sales agent was Derby Airways, later to be known as British Midland Airways (BMA), who operated scheduled services to the Channel Islands and, in the early years, a limited service to Ostend. At the end of the summer season 1969, BMA decided to concentrate their efforts in other fields and areas of operations.

In 1971 Intra Airways were persuaded to apply for the BMA licence on the Cambridge route to the Channel Islands and their successful application was to lead to a more extensive operation to the Channel Islands. Indeed, in 1979, it saw, for the first time in the airport's history, a passenger user figure in excess of 30,000. The original equipment used on the route by Intra was the Douglas DC 3, which even in 1971 was perhaps more suited to an aircraft museum than to operating a scheduled route, but they proved very successful and reliable before they were replaced by Viscount aircraft in 1975. In 1979 Intra Airways was bought out by Express Air Freight Ltd, and operated for the 1979/1980 season as Jersey European Airways, before a change in policy once again left Cambridge without a service.

However, during the winter of 1980 Guernsey Airlines/Alidair successfully applied for the licence and they operated the service until 1983, when they were taken over by British Air Ferries (BAF). Agreement was reached with BAF for Premier to have the franchise for the route in 1984 under the licence of Guernsey Airlines, which has proved most successful to date.

Passenger flights over the years have concentrated mainly on the Channel Island route. Abortive attempts have been made at varying times to persuade operators to offer other destinations, but pilot programmes have not been sufficiently supported to warrant the operation of any extensive programme.

Incoming passenger flights from European cities have continued to increase annually through the charter flight programme of ICI, using the larger jet aircraft of operators such as Lufthansa, Condor, K.L.M, Trans European and British Airways, and many other national and charter operators – a far cry from the DC 4 used by Lloyd International for the movement of ships' crews, which had been undertaken through the airport as far back as 1962. The aircraft used by the present-day charter operators include Boeing 727, Boeing 737 and BAC 1–11 aircraft.

The movement of bloodstock by air through Cambridge Airport has featured high in the workload of the Company over the years, but with the general decline in recent years of the bloodstock business, shipment by air has been one of the areas of economy. During the period 1967–76 many of the leading names in the horseracing world, such as Sir Ivor, Nijinsky and Parktop, were frequent visitors through the airport and some came so frequently that they seemed to be 'commuting' between Cambridge and France. Aircraft used as 'flying horse-boxes' include Bristol Freighter, Ambassador, DC 4, DC 6, DC 7, Argosy, Carvair, Britannia and CL 44.

An area of recent expansion has been in the executive aircraft charter brokerage and handling with local companies making more use of the services offered by PAL.

It is hoped that in the future the continued integration and pooling of resources with the fast-developing tour operating company will lead to other destinations being served from Cambridge Airport.

Behind these simple straightforward facts about PAL lies the involvement of many people, good and bad, and a long pilgrimage of losses and disappointments, before the Company, with B.V.B. as Airport Superintendent and then Director, won through to its present satisfactory position.

Premier Airlines on parade: S. Dartford and Tanya Baker

It all started in 1958 when it was decided to pursue a completely new line of activity – the operation of direct flights, under licence from the Air Traffic Licensing Board, for Air Plan Holidays to Ostend and Luxembourg, from Luton and Cambridge, during the 1959 season.

Unfortunately, the original airline, Pegasus Airways, who were based at Luton Airport, were unable to carry out their contract to be our carriers, so a panic search started for an alternative. Continental Air Services were found and they undertook the operation of a limited programme of flights from Cambridge Airport to Ostend in July and August.

To everyone's surprise, this shortened schedule of holidays didn't result in a loss, nor indeed in a profit. But we did break even, which demonstrated a potential of great promise.

Cheered by this result, the Board went ahead with planning a further batch of flights and holidays for 1960. It soon became apparent that it was essential to any development that customs facilities were available at the airport, so in consultation and collaboration with Sir Arthur Marshall, owner of Cambridge Airport, and Squadron Leader Worsdell, the Airport Manager, plus the co-operation of Cambridge City Council, the authorities were pursuaded to grant custom facilities on 14 April 1960. So it was that Cambridge became the proud possessor of an international airport.

Premier owes a great debt to Sir Arthur and everyone involved at the airport for their enthusiastic support and encouragement in setting up this important new development; also for the welcoming way in which they made available office space, landing facilities, etc. Enormous improvements

ally found and an exhausted party arrived back in Cambridge around 4 a.m. No 'dead-heads' who made the whole flight will ever forget one moment of it.

A very ambitious set of licences were granted in January 1961 for Santander, Pisa, Turin, Nice, Ostend and Zagreb (Paris, Zurich, Palma, and Rimini were refused). Unfortunately most flights, other than the easy Ostend departures, had to be cancelled for lack of passengers. Perhaps PAL was simply too far ahead of the great travel boom that has since occurred.

This lack of support virtually ended the Air Plan programme, but gradually other enterprises took its place, notably the Channel Island services which have grown year by year, reaching a seventy-two per cent load factor over the whole season in 1984.

SYD PENNELL AT CAMBRIDGE AIRPORT

Mr Matthews said to me 'I've got a proposition for you. We are starting air freight from Cambridge and we'll need a lot of collecting and delivering and driving to London Airport. We've ordered a special van and we want you to do the job for us. Will you do it?' I told him I didn't much want to be based at the airport, but I went, and I stayed until, in the end, I got rid of Mr X, the Superintendent.

It was like this. Mr X sent me to Bury to pick up a load. When I got back to Cambridge he said: 'I want you to unload these things here.' I was surprised because at this period all our freight was going via London Airport – we guaranteed express air services via London. When I asked him where they were going he told me they were to be taken on a local plane. Next day they'd gone. I asked around. No one knew of any plane. One of the blokes asked me what had happened last night.

'What do you mean?' I asked.

'Well what was that other truck doing loading up from yours?'

I immediately phoned Mr Matthews. Next day it was all over: no more Mr X.

Then we had one more Superintendent and then Mr Burnett came. Soon freight came to an end, because the prices were too low. If your price was profitable you lost the work. So Premier Freight had to go into cold storage.

During the peak period I used to go up to Witchingham, Bernard Matthews' (no connection with ours) turkey farm, at all hours of the day and night. I usually picked up at 5 a.m., and had my breakfast on the way back. My van was specially

have taken place since those early days and now Cambridge could without further ado become London's fourth airport. However, it is not at present on the cards, so let no one panic.

Immediately following this success it was decided to set up a new joint company, and Premier Airlines Limited was born. It was to act as general sales and aircraft handling agent, including the operation of Air Plan Holidays. F.N.M. was appointed Managing Director and was responsible for its promotion, expansion and ultimate success.

In June 1960, a number of adventurous flights by Continental Air Services took place, quite apart from the weekly departures to Ostend. One very memorable circular trip, Cambridge–Nice–Santander–Cambridge, picking up or dropping Air Plan Holiday-makers at each point, ended up in Southend at about midnight. A coach was eventu-

equipped for livestock and I used to take anything – from up to a thousand day-old chicks to boxes of young rabbits – to London Airport and off-load them in the airlines freight depot. They had one contract for Italy and another for the Middle East. The rabbits were a real menace to carry as they used to eat their way out of the cardboard boxes, if they had time.

Once when I had two loads in one day, I found my morning delivery still in depot. I reckoned they'd all be dead, a thousand turkey chicks, if I left them, so I phoned Witchingham, who told me to take them back to Langham Airfield. There the fog had come down and there I was, in the middle of the night, crouching down on my haunches in front of my van, trying to find my way – that's the kind of day you don't forget!

A.W. HILL AT CAMBRIDGE AIRPORT

There were two interesting trips organised by Premier Airlines and Premier Travel to Ostend. The first trip was arranged by D.W.R. with the majority of the passengers coming from the Perkins factory at Peterborough. Our flight started on a Viking aircraft which just managed to land at Ostend before finishing its flying career altogether! D.W.R. informed Marshalls Airport then went off to Germany, leaving me in charge. Imagine my surprise when Mr Matthews phoned to ask how many passengers there were to be brought home. He nearly had a fit when I told him, as there were twice as many as he had expected. He then wanted me to find out the weight of each passenger as Marshalls would be sending Rapide aircraft for the return journey. Now I ask you, how do you get top business men, on a business trip, to weigh themselves without telling them why? Well, I did it. The day for the return journey arrived. I had all the passengers through the customs and eyeing the waiting planes, wondering which they would be going on. Then the little Rapides started to drop in from the sky. Well, when the passengers realised what was about to happen, there was almost a riot. Some said that they would rather b . . . swim than go in one of those things. I had the task of sorting out five to a plane according to their weight. The pilots chased each other over the Channel, but we still arrived back to tell the tale!

The second trip was Christmas in Ostend with a group of staff from the Cambridge colleges. We did not know when we left Cambridge that there was a general strike in Ostend, so we arrived to find overfull dustbins, post-boxes which had not been emptied and strike meetings going on everywhere. On arrival at Hotel Plymouth we found another group from London who had been left to their own devices, so I asked them to join our Premier party on Christmas Eve. I settled them with drinks then went to the Treble Eight Hotel where the band was playing, but the staff were having a strike meeting. I spoke to the staff and persuaded some to come back to open the bar and serve the people. I bought the band some wine then collected my group and we danced Christmas Eve out and Christmas Day in. A good time was had by all. On Christmas Day I persuaded the Plymouth staff to set out long tables where we sat down together to traditional Christmas fare. Meanwhile phone calls were coming in from England, from parents who had read about the strikes and assumed that chaos reigned supreme! We had a good laugh because we were having an excellent time. The next day I managed to get a coach to take us to Bruges. When we arrived at the square, a terrific fight was going on between the strikers and the gendarmerie. I managed to tell one gendarme that we were a party of British tourists and that we wanted to look round the square. The gendarme blew his whistle and the fighting ceased. Using a loudspeaker he explained who we were and what we wanted to do. The men sat down, smoked and talked while we walked around, taking photographs etc. I thanked the Belgians, using their loudspeaker, and they cheered us to our coach. But as soon as we were on the move, fighting broke out again. The Ostend hoteliers could hardly believe it, another triumph for Premier Travel!

12
'It's All About People' II

This chapter has been compiled from the contributions of many different people in Premier and we are extremely grateful for the effort, humour, and, we hope, the historical accuracy of their stories. What is disappointing is that there is not enough room to celebrate all the people both in Club 25 and among those who have been in the Company from five to ten to twenty years.

It would have been good to have a long bit about Norman 'Dinga' Bell, Pyeman Extraordinary, who has been largely responsible over the last thirty years for the punctuality and reliability of the Pye contracts in the Fens. He is the longest serving member of a strong, individualistic group of Fenmen, including the ever-efficient and smart W. Dickerson, the ebullient G. Sparrow and Don Hull.

We should also have celebrated Roland Scrivener, Depot Controller at Haverhill, champion gardener and tap-dancer; 'Senator' R. Roope, quiet, harmonious, regular as clockwork on Service 44; A. Ruffle, 6ft 7ins, full of country lore. Was he gamekeeper or poacher during the many years he was running the Haverhill fleet? Add young R. Baker, who hasn't changed since he joined in 1953, conscientious, gentle and courageous; add Mrs Brennan, who started, developed and brought to success the Haverhill Travel Agency in each of its three locations; add George Sargent, sanguine and smiling; add all the Haverhill Depot and you still won't have the total of effort.

There should have been a hymn of praise to A. Wisbey, so skilful, efficient and artistic – many will remember his bathing beauties on the balcony of Market Hill; also to Roy Scarr, the dedicated perfectionist, always dissatisfied but able and skilled; to L. South, another Fred Barker, ready to

Modern Fenmen, 1984: (left to right) *B. Gillett, N. 'Dinga' Bell, D. Hull, C. Malkin*

A. Ruffle. Passenger transport, 1922–80

Mrs Mary Law

We lived through hard times in the fifties, the period of 'make do and mend'. The tyres were run to the last ounce of rubber, they were never finished until we saw the canvas. A 1000 × 20 coach tyre then cost £30, now, in 1985, £190. Through progress in every way, today the radial tyre does double the mileage of thirty years ago, when it was called the cross-ply. It would be interesting to know the number of tyres I've fitted in thirty-three years, let alone the cost.

The same year I passed my PSV test, which was handy for extra weekend earnings with a bit of stage driving and a few tours. You could count our luxury coaches on one hand – 2 Dennis Lancets, 2 Leyland PSIs, 1 Bedford 29-seater, and of course the Regal. The latter ended up on her back, sliding off icy Stretham Bridge and knocking half a house down. HVE 707, a Dennis Lancet, was the coach which opened the Cheddar Gorge day tour. Mack King, the driver, with me as co-driver, followed Mr Lainson's scenic route and arrived at the top of the Gorge to find we were not allowed down with a coach, only up. So we set off across country for Cheddar village. Mack was map reading, giving me instructions through the pigeon-hole of the half cab. We landed up in a farmyard and had to turn the coach round. Mack was saying to the passengers, 'It's alright! He used to be a tractor driver.' His quick joke broke the bewildered silence at the rear. I shook my fist at him, but we eventually found the bottom of the Gorge.

Looking back over the years, in the fifties and sixties we lived a steadier trend. With the establishment of the Premier Welfare Club there were seaside outings for wives and children in the summer and a Christmas party every year. Also the Premier Football Club – we played in the Thursday league, not that we often won, but the sportsmanship was wonderful. Today the firm seems so big, the family spirit harder to find.

help anyone at any time; to Smudger Smith, friend to passengers and colleagues alike and another Ace driver. Then we need to pay tribute to Mary Law, still working in DSO, even though it is her time sheet in Appendix 9 that records 80 hours work in 1948. She and her husband, S.J. Law, must between them have nearly as many years with Premier as Mr and Mrs Jack Gifford (Mrs Maisie Francis, that was, until 1984), who together have contributed eighty-four years to their Company.

The list of friends in the Company seems endless and those whose involvement is not formally acknowledged in full must blame time, space and the Editor.

TYRE TYCOON

R. Mumby

I joined Premier Travel in 1952 as Tyre-Fitter, recommended by Laurie Fuller, a good friend already with the firm. After a short course at the Firestone factory, I settled down to looking after the wheels.

MY LIFE AS A COACH DRIVER

H. Law

I started working for PT in September 1945. Let me tell you a little about my thirty-two years with the firm.

There was laughter, excitement and much frustration. At the start I was driving vehicles with no heaters, no starters and all manual steering. As time went by things improved – luxury coaches with power-assisted steering and all facilities for drivers and passengers. I did most of my driving on the Company's express services, private hire and all their British Tours. Also I was driving on PT Continental Tours.

My most frustrating journey was to Vienna: we drove through the night so were not able to change our clothes for three days and nights until we arrived in Salzburg, Austria; we were then able to relax for about twelve hours, having good food and a bath and change of clothes; the next day we journeyed on to Vienna where we unloaded all our gifts for the Hungarian refugees. Returning to England, we had a full load of refugees; we arrived home on Christmas Day at 5 a.m. after spending three weeks away. The coach we travelled in was a Dennis, HVE 36.

As I look back I also remember a ten-hour journey through thick fog from Manchester to Upwood RAF, with the windscreen open wide all the way. When I arrived home my wife told me I looked like a chimney sweep, my face was so black and dirty. I had not realised until I glanced in the mirror, then I just had to laugh at myself.

In 1976, the year of the heatwave, I had a very busy year. I enjoyed it very much. On one journey I was with Harold Lee. We were walking along when a man rushed across to shake hands with me; I asked the man if he knew Harold. He replied, 'Of course I do', shaking hands with Harold. He went on his way. When Harold asked me who he was, I replied, 'I don't know, I thought you did.' What Harold said was nobody's business.

Having remembered all this, I would like to thank the Directors of Premier Travel for all my years with the firm.

HAROLD LEE REMEMBERS

H. Lee

My adventures with Premier Travel began thirty-seven years ago at an interview with Mr Lainson in Market Hill, Cambridge. Invited to sit down, I had my first encounter with a wooden bus seat, which was much lower than Mr Lainson's desk, and my main view was of a heap of papers, and quite a number of Senior Service cigarette packets. From there I was referred to Mr Buchanan of the Saffron Walden office.

After passing my PSV test, I was to be working from Drayton Bros garage in Barley – they had just been bought out by PT. From there I was moved up to the Chrishall depot. However, before going up to Chrishall, my first run out was to drive on Service 26 to Bishop's Stortford, and here again, in EER 99, a Bedford Utility, the wooden seats turned up. I am not very proud to say that the passengers did not

Man working. H. Lee polishes while H. Law and W. Dickerson watch

enjoy it much because I went too fast round those bends. So what with my driving and the seats my passengers were, I think, quite pleased to get to their journey's end. However, I did my best to improve my driving over the years. EER 99 was heard of many times, because on orders one day a driver was instructed 'to pick up 99 and run fast'.

During my first four years I became a conductor and also a driver–conductor, and I had one or two disasters. One such incident occurred during my conducting days. We used to be issued with a very thick and heavy uniform, plus a heavy raincoat, bell punch, money bag and an eighteen-inch long ticket rack. With all this it was very hard to move down a vehicle in motion, and as I started to collect fares, the rack under my arm, I got it caught in a lady's hair. On trying to retrieve same, I finished with a hair-net as well.

Another disaster was when I was DC on Service 2 to Royston with 422, a vehicle with leather seats. On this particular day I had a very large lady on the seat behind me – at least that was where she was until I took a bend too fast and the poor woman slid from her seat to the centre gangway, getting wedged between the rows of seats. I told the lady how sorry I was and much to my relief she gave one heck of a laugh and said she would remain like that until we reached Royston.

As the years went by I was doing stage service work, excursion and express service relief, until I was promoted to be an express service driver on Service 5, Clacton to Birmingham. This brought me to the overnight stays at Birmingham and Barney Sharp's. 'Oh dear!' Now the backroom at Barney's contained two double and two single beds, which became rather tricky when at times we had six or eight or us staying over. The indoor toilet was just a white enamel bucket placed inside the bedroom. The only heating was the feather mattress, and the sheets had been slept in many times before, not only by Premier drivers. Nevertheless, we used to get one heck of a laugh and still talk about our days at Barney's of Hurst Street.

Very often I found luggage space would create rather a problem. One particular incident stands out in my mind: it was the time I arrived in Drummer Street almost full up. I was still trying hard to get all the luggage in when a lady arrived with birdcage and stand, Hoover, several parcels and a large suitcase, and while I was trying to juggle it all into the already full boot she apologised and said that she was leaving Cambridge. Without thinking I replied, 'You could have fooled me, Madam. I thought you were taking it with you.' I thought that had torn it, but everyone waiting saw the funny side and all finished with a good laugh.

I well remember the occasion when Harry Readman and myself were Drivers' Reps and during the time we were fighting for a pay rise, Mr Lainson got himself put into hospital – the result of walking round the wrong end of a horse. We both went in to see him and during our visit Mrs Lainson and Vicky arrived. At the end of visiting time Vicky went home ahead and we offered Mrs L. a lift. Once we were in the car, I told her we were going to kidnap her and hold her to ransome until Mr L. paid the penny an hour we were after. The only reply was a loud burst of laughter, 'You know what Husband would say to that, "Keep her, I will never pay up." '

Now, looking at the present day, I am very pleased that I served my years with Premier Travel when I did. Coaching is not coaching as I knew it. Look after your coach, look after your passengers, then the luggage boot will look after you.

NO TIME FOR SNAKES

J. Gogin

Mr Joe Gogin will have just managed to join Club 25 by the time this goes to print, as he started in Premier's Haverhill depot in 1961. Yet it seems difficult to remember a time when Joe was not Haverhill's Staff Representative, was not in charge of Service 71 Haverhill–Cambridge–Bournemouth every summer Saturday, and was not haring up and down to London every weekday on Service 38. His dead-pan humour and his negotiating skill have been a great asset to all of us, both sides of the table. Joe shares some of his memories with us here.

In the very early days I used to drive HOM 677 and one day, during the half-way break at Bagshot, a passenger walked round the bus and said to me, 'This old thing will never get to Bournemouth', but it did – with ten minutes to spare. I'm glad to say that when I drove to Bournemouth and back in a day, my timekeeping was so accurate that passengers who knew me would book their taxis in advance, knowing that I would get there on time. Never broke the speed limit – of course not!

One morning some time ago, when I was driving a Pye contract, I was amazed to see a huge snake curled up on the road in front of the bus. I managed to avoid it but I didn't stop to discover where it came from; I regularly saw a beautiful deer on the Blackbush route, before the motorway was constructed – he seemed to watch out for my coach.

The goodwill that existed between myself and my passengers, and the loyalty between drivers and the Company was of a very high standard – it needed to be. We encountered so many difficulties. In my early days money was so scarce that I often had to wait at Drummer Street while my conductor, Karl Wuebbelmann, paid in his takings to the inspector, so that we could be paid!

However, it has been a great pleasure to work for Premier and we wish it every success in the coming years – especially in 1986, the fiftieth anniversary.

DRIVING FOR PREMIER

C. Sadler

I started work for Premier Travel on the 20 January 1960. Since then I've travelled several thousands of miles for the Company, and I've met a lot of people. On one occasion I was bringing some people from Rhyl in North Wales and I happened to ask the couple sitting behind me, 'Where are you off to for your holiday?' They replied,

'We're going to Horringer, a village just outside Bury St Edmunds.'

'Well,' I said, 'you'll be surprised to hear that's where I live.' It turned out that they were going to stay with a lady who lived next door to my mother.

Once when I was coming from Rhyl, an elderly lady on the bus was taken very ill, so, as I was near Northampton Hospital, I drove the bus right up to the front entrance, and the staff were quickly out to help her off the bus.

The greatest improvement that I've seen has been in the buses themselves. When I first started with the Company, I drove a 29-seater petrol driven Vista and now, in 1984, I've driven a 53-seater Highliner.

The most amusing thing that happened to me was when I overtook Mr Lainson, who was returning home in his Rover. A few days previously he had been explaining to me that if every driver lifted their foot off the pedal the Company would save thousands of gallons of diesel a year. Being the gentleman that he is, he didn't say anything more to me about it.

In conclusion, I'd like to say that the thing that has given me the greatest pleasure is to have now completed twenty-five years driving with the Company.

WINTER 1963

Judging by the number of times it is mentioned in people's contributions, Premier has developed a sort of folk memory of the most awful weather that occurred nationwide in 1963. It was especially bad in the Haverhill Hills and the East Anglian Heights around Chrishall depot, and Premier vehicles ground to a halt. Sixteen buses were abandoned and sixteen crews walked home, some of them leading little groups of stranded passengers.

Even I was involved, for by a strange freak of nature the Fens were free of snow – more or less – and all the Pye buses arrived safely, so we were faced wtih plenty of vehicles, fairly free suburban roads round Cambridge and all the crews stranded up in the hills. Immediately a call went forth for volunteer conductors and for only the second time in my Premier life I went off to conduct Service 1, Fowlmere to Cambridge. I took 30s (£1.50) and checked a lot of seasons and weeklies. I was as scared and shy as in 1941 when M.J.G. took the tickets for me.

Joe Gogin remembers going prepared with extra shovels and a tow-rope on his early morning Pye contract and, sure enough, the coach got stuck and his passengers helped him dig it out and eventually they arrived at Pye's more or less on time.

Cyril Sadler couldn't get home from Haverhill to Bury as the road was blocked with snow and he slept

Winter 1963

in the bus. On another occasion he was stuck in a snow drift at Six Mile Bottom but he was dug out and arrived home 'tired, late and hungry'.

Harold Law's worst trip was going up from Clacton to Birmingham. He had just reached Northampton when the blizzard blew up, still with Market Harborough, Leicester and Coventry to go. He eventually reached Digbeth Coach Station at 4.30 a.m. instead of 8.30 p.m. 'I was most thankful', he commented, 'to think that we had moved from Barney Sharp's and were now staying at the Waverly Hotel, which had far more comfort. Mrs Pope, the manageress, opened the door after I had almost kicked it in to wake her. I'm pleased to say she made me a most welcome hot drink with a little "anti-freeze" dropped in.'

Harry Law had his worst journey from Cambridge to Edinburgh, through ghastly snow blizzards. He left at 6 a.m. and arrived at his destination at midnight. The coach, UVE 333, froze up several times on the bitter cold day, 'Was I pleased to arrive there safely.'

Harry Law's brother, Syd, had probably the hardest time of all. Here is his tape-recorded account of what happened:

Hallo. Here we are. [Dog barks. Silence] Hallo. Here we are again! The winter of 1963, as you know, was a very bad winter. And we had quite a lot of troubles through freezing up, but the worst was on a Wednesday morning. I got up at 5.30 a.m. because I knew there'd be a lot of trouble. Mr Grice rung up at 6 a.m. and told me to go straight out to March, as the March people couldn't start.

Anyway everything was so iced up I couldn't even get out of the yard. Mr Grice rang again at 6.30 a.m. and said, 'Why haven't you got yourself to March? You get to March straight away.' So with that I again attempted to go. Just before I got to Stretham I saw one of ours broken down. Fuel trouble again. Frozen. Well I got him going, filled his auto-vac, which took just about a gallon of diesel and said, 'I think you'll just about make it to Cambridge'. Then I carried on to March. I got that one going and by the time I got back to Stretham it was getting on for twelve o'clock. I rang Mr Gifford because I knew there were more down in the Fens who couldn't start, to see if anyone had gone out to them. He said they hadn't because there had been so much trouble locally. But he told me to come back to the garage and then he'd come out with me after dinner. Well, away we go into the fens and we got those three going after a bit. I think the last one just got to the Pye car-park as they were coming out to return home. Everything was running there but we pulled in to see they were alright and I reckon it was about a quarter to six when we got back to the garage.

Mr Frank Matthews was there and he said, 'I think you've had about enough of this today, my boy.'

'I have,' I said.

'Well, you get inside by that fire and don't come out again tonight.'

'I'm hoping that's just what I am going to do.' A very few minutes later the phone rang again. Poor old Herbie Cage. He'd just got through Ely and his fuel had frozen up. We had a job with that one that night. Anyway it was twenty past ten when we got back to Harston and I had had a rough day. I was only near a fire from one o'clock to two o'clock. The rest – I was frozen of cold nearly all day. Well, we thawed out that evening and went to bed.

As usual, I got up early the next morning and away we go again on different things. But it was the second morning after that that things went wrong again. The phone rang and it was Oscar Cornwell. He had a double-decker and he used to park at Hilgay Railway Station. Well poor old Fred Barker and I went out there. Of course we couldn't get any fuel through. The fuel line was frozen through and through so we had to crawl under the bus with a flare to thaw these fuel lines out. Well, we got the fuel circulating and were just about to start up when the fuel pump packed in and we hadn't got a spare fuel pump with us. We hadn't got much petrol in the truck to go about searching, so Oscar rang through to Chrishall and they sent one down by poor old Syd Pennell in his van – he was on freight at the time. He and Oscar met half-way and Oscar came back with the fuel pump. Of course the diesel was all frozen up again by that time, so we had to crawl underneath and thaw it out again and eventually we got going.

Oscar went to Pye's at Cambridge but I knew we'd got another at Sutton that wouldn't start. So I said to Barker, 'I reckon we'd better get to Sutton now.'

Of course, time was getting on, we were short on petrol for the truck and there weren't many petrol stations open. Anyway we managed to get to Sutton and pulled in there, onto the forecourt, and I said to the chap: 'Put us two gallons in, please, and give me a ticket for it.'

Well, he looked at me and he looked at the van and saw the name on the side; then he looked at poor old Fred Barker, who was black as the ace of spades through crawling underneath and he said: 'Well, don't tell me that you people need a ticket for petrol.' I told him that we certainly did.

When we got out on the road, I said to Barker, 'He's classed us as diddycoys, just because we're black as the ace of spades, especially with every kind of junk on the truck.' Anyways, I won't tell you what old Barker said.

We got the bus started but I don't think he went to Cambridge although he kept it running for several hours to charge the batteries up a bit. Then we came home and we'd had another full day out on the Fens, froze with cold, not a hot drink, not even at midday.

So that's some of the bad times with Premier Travel but there's a lot more I could tell you of bad times and good times but as you know I'd have to be here all day to tell you the full story. So all the very best for the book when you finish it and I hope I live long enough to get one to read.

Postscript. At a Board meeting on 7 February 1963, 'it was felt that the good work by the Staff in the severe weather during the past six weeks could best be recognised by a second Staff Dinner to be arranged on a Saturday evening in the near future'. Do the awful conditions of January and February 1985 warrant the same reward?

PREMIER EXPERIENCES 1955–75

J. Linsdell

I joined Premier on 1 October 1955. I was sixteen and it was my first job. I can remember being seated at a long table with a lino top and my first job was to analyse the excursion charts and tickets collected for the summer of 1955, which I seem to remember was a long hot summer – it must have been for the tickets were never ending. I was introduced to and fell in love with the Directors' typist, Pam Burgess, who worked behind me. Also in my part of the office was Mr Dodkin, who was my boss. Behind the partition in the old Phoenix office sat Mr Darby, who did the wages, and Eve Stanley who travelled in from Dunmow on Mondays, Wednesdays and Fridays.

On my first day I was called in to meet Mr F. N. Matthews, who spoke to me of his days at the County School where I had also been.

Shortly after I started, the Queen and the Duke of Edinburgh visited Cambridge and Mr Dodkin, Mr Darby and I almost ended up in prison. When the Royal car came down the main street it was followed closely by a large red 'object' with a flashing light. After the Queen had gone past, the 'object', a fire engine, stopped and firemen rushed into the Phoenix Assurance office on the ground floor. There was no fire: it was a false alarm. Mr Draper, the Manager, denied calling the brigade, so they proceeded upstairs to our floor. Mr Dodkin was

challenged and when asked if anyone had been on the premises just prior to the Queen's arrival at the railway station, he remembered that young Coleby – then an undergraduate – had been in. I understand that young Coleby was put through the mill by the police, who thought he had made the 'false alarm' call to disrupt the Queen's visit. He had not.

When I had completed the excursion analysis, I graduated to express analysis, which was much more exciting. Most of the operations at that time were on Service 5, with particularly heavy journeys from Leicester on peak summer Saturdays. Mr Dodkin had a chart on the wall which showed at a glance the 'ups' and 'downs' of revenue and PCM [pence per car mile] for each stage express service, together with the overall figures. Mr Lainson often used to explain these figures to me with such phrases as 'bottoms on seats', 'surgeon's knife' and 'fruit in the cake' – quite bewildering to me at the time. The 'surgeon's knife' was soon to come into operation when Nasser nationalised the Suez Canal in July 1956 and in December of that year petrol rationing came into force. Our services were slashed with only the main lines surviving in any volume and I can remember turning the handle of a black Roneo duplicating machine over and over again, printing leaflets to inform the public of the changes.

Among the other memories I have of the old Phoenix office were the walls of the corridor soaked with moisture during the winter, and the couple who lived upstairs above our office often talking about the problem. The man said to me one day, 'I have written to Jesus dozens of times but have never got any response.' A remark I found very puzzling until Mr Dodkin told me he meant Jesus College.

We used to be visited each Friday by a gentleman in a mac from Abbey Tyre, whom Mr Darby christened Uriah Heap because of his habit of rubbing his hands together. I caused great hilarity one day when, having answered the door bell, I announced that Mr Heap had come for his money.

One of my particular memories was of 'George', the poor tramp, and his visits to the office to collect his 'beer money'. Occasionally I interrupted meetings with other companies to collect 2s or 2s 6d [10p or 12½p] from Mr Lainson for George, who always wished me good luck and said 'Thankyou, my good man'. In January 1957 I moved on from the Phoenix office to Camps Road, Haverhill, where the natives taught me how to speak English proper.

In 1967 Sheila Hulyer and I undertook a complete ticket check, which included research into payments of a large proportion of tickets which were 'foreigners' – Eastern Counties, United Counties, Eastern National, Midland Red, etc. One such 'foreigner' was PSV. PSV tickets were of two types: one was the narrow print which were assembled in books of 100 and printed four to a page; the second were Lampson Paragon tickets produced for use in a booking office, where the volume of business meant a substantial turnover for a number of independent operators. Kings Cross Coach Station booking office was one such place and after checking the first type of tickets, which originated in general from agents in the London area and the Home Counties, we turned our attention to the Kings Cross Coach Station booking office sales.

It soon became clear that a large collection of tickets were being set aside because the total fare paid was less than the total shown on the passenger tickets collected by the Premier drivers on the London to Haverhill Service 38. The shortfall followed a pattern in that the total per ticket was often fifty per cent of the total paid by the passengers. Closer scrutiny of the tickets collected by the drivers, compared with the audit copy received by PSV accounts, showed that the tickets were identical in every detail except for the section showing total passengers and fare paid. In numerous cases the passenger tickets would read:

| 2 Adults. | Fare paid per person | £1 10s 0d |
| | Total Fare paid | £3 0s 0d |

but the audit copy read:

| 1 Adult. | Fare paid per person | £1 10s 0d |
| | Total Fare paid | £1 10s 0d |

It was clear that the numbers involved meant that someone was deliberately under-recording on ticket sales and it soon emerged that the passenger and fare section always produced a clearer carbon copy than any other part of the ticket.

When PSV were advised of our suspicions, they expressed considerable concern. Local operators, Whippet Coaches and Jennings Coaches of Ashen, were alerted to check their passenger tickets collected, and Yelloway of Rochdale were similarly advised. The clerk concerned was traced and it was found he had used a small piece of cardboard which he inserted under the passenger tickets and over the confirmation and audit copies. It was his intention, if a sharp-eyed superior had seen such an exercise, to pass the matter off as a method of ensuring that the most vital parts of the ticket, including the number of passengers (for charting), and the total fare paid (for audit and accountancy), were clearly readable on what were the third and fourth copies. By being aware of his own fiddle, he could quite easily chart the bookings, ensuring no overloading at the Kings Cross end, which would have caused an in-depth investigation. It so happened that the charts were completed, especially at weekends at Haverhill, by using the return times shown on the passenger tickets as a method of keeping the loadings under observation . These passenger tickets did, of course, bear the correct passenger total and fare paid and were the basis of the investigation which brought the fiddle to light. For the clerk concerned, prosecution and conviction followed.

Unfortunately, John Linsdell left us for ECOC and a larger field of enterprise in 1975. We miss his enthusiasm, sharp intelligence and eager sense of humour. It seemed very sad that he should go after twenty years.

THE MODERN COACHMAN ON A WEEKEND ABROAD, 1983

A.Nickson

My story starts at 8 p.m. on a Saturday evening in the South of France, in a village called Brignoles. As on previous Saturdays, Ray Beechill (another co-driver) and I were waiting for our coach, driven by Chris Woods, to arrive, so that we could return home after our weekend shuttle service from England to Monte Carlo.

At 11.30 p.m. our coach had still not arrived and a third driver had joined us, waiting for his connection. Just after midnight our coach arrived but Chris was not driving. The driver told us Chris's coach had broken down in Monte Carlo and asked if one of us could stay behind to co-drive when it was fixed. With Ray, Maurice Hall and Eamonn O'Leary all standing six foot or over and myself just over five foot, the argument was very short and decisive. I 'volunteered'. So started a weekend I shall never forget.

I wandered back to the village to find accommodation (very difficult if you don't speak French), but there was none available. My next thought was to go to the police station: the officer was not too pleased at being awoken at 2 a.m. and was unco-operative, so I spent the night in a toll-booth on the main autoroute. At 6 a.m. I rang the hotel in Monte Carlo to find out what was happening. I was told, 'Get to Monte, we are going to be here a couple of days'. So, up went the good old English thumb and down the autoroute I progressed for 150 miles.

The first lift I received was from a student; this was for a distance of about twenty miles. The second lift was far more interesting, the gentleman who stopped for me could speak very good English and it turned out that he was the Head of the Orthopaedic Department at the General Hospital in Cannes, and was on his way to work. At Cannes I was picked up by a young lady, who offered me a lift to Nice. We conversed with the aid of my English–French phrase book (she, I might add, had the French–English version), and when I asked at Nice how to get to Monte Carlo, she promptly took me to the railway station where she brought my ticket and showed me which platform to go to. I thanked her for her generosity and offered her a small token of thanks; she refused, saying that next year she would be coming to England for a holiday, and if she got into difficulty maybe there would be someone to help her. I thanked her again and boarded my train.

On arrival in Monte Carlo I was greeted by Chris Woods and Bill Lawrence with remarks such as, 'Had a nice day?', 'You look tired', 'How's the trip been?' It was then the bomb was dropped: 'Have an hour's sleep, because you are going home by train in two hours' time.'

The plan was to get a train to Nice, change to a sleeper, train to Calais, stopping at St Raphael to pick up thirty-one passengers who should have gone home on the coach the previous day; then over on the ferry and a coach would be at Dover with a driver to take the people home.

Easy? It was until we got to St Raphael: all the people climbed on board; Bill and I gave them their bunk numbers as the train pulled away. All of a sudden a passenger said with curiosity: 'Alan, they have left our luggage on the platform.' Thinking they were trying to wind me up, I replied, 'No need to worry, it will be on the train two minutes behind us.' Only then did Bill tell me it was true. So not only were the people two days late, they had no luggage either.

So off we went to find the guard, who informed us that at Marseille the train would stop for thirty minutes to take on extra coaches, and that it was possible that the following train could have the luggage on board. This train was due to arrive in Marseille as we were due to depart. We informed the passengers what was happening and then selected five men to run amok on the other train looking for the cases.

At Marseille we waited for the train hoping it would be early, so as to give us more vital seconds. Indeed, it did arrive two minutes early, so off we set, five English men in search of lost luggage, running in and out of the coaches, but to no avail. Our train started to pull away, and we five 'village idiots' just managed to clamber aboard. On arrival in Calais we were informed that the luggage was all intact at the station in St Raphael and would follow two days later.

People we greatly miss: (left to right) *H. Wynn, H. Impey, C. Jaggard*

We boarded the ferry for England. The crossing was rather boring and uneventful.

When we arrived we thought our troubles were over – some joke! The customs officer asked us where we had been and the following conversation ensued:

'To Monte Carlo.'

'How long for?'

'Ten days.'

'Where's your luggage?'

'On the platform at St Raphael station.'

'Oh, have you got your passports?'

'No.'

'Where are they?'

'In the cases on the platform at St Raphael station.'

'Oh!'

After that charade we found our coach but no driver, so Bill and I had to drive the people to London, Birmingham, Manchester, Leeds and York. We returned to Cambridge at 1.30 a.m. on Tuesday morning; I dropped Bill off, then went on to Haverhill, and the arms of my wife, who asked, 'Had a good trip, Love?'.

OBITUARIES

As can well be imagined, we have lost a great many good companions during our fifty years. Amongst them was *Horace Impey*, who died in 1981 and was one of the very few people who worked on both sides of the Company. He joined as a driver, took over the Huntingdon office from H. Wynn and later became a pukka travel agent, when we moved to attractive, if tiny, premises in the High Street. With the help of some good people he built up fantastic figures but the pressure was very great and after about ten years he opted for a quieter life in the parent Company. Very sadly indeed his health deteriorated and he died suddenly in his early fifties. The whole Company still misses the presence of a man of Horace's calibre who accepted challenge after challenge throughout his twenty-seven years with Premier. RIP

Leslie Clarke, cheerful, willing, able and extra-ordinarily popular with all his colleagues on the engineering side, died when hardly more than fifty. He was married to Sheila Matthews and together they bore the awful ordeal of losing their second son in a car accident almost outside their door. The shock penetrated both parents so deeply that ill-health took hold of them and Sheila underwent two vital operations. Her tragedy was compounded by Leslie's fatal illness. The power of grief is incalculable. RIP

Karl Wuebbelmann, ex U-boat prisoner of war, stayed on to work as one of our conductors on Service 44 for many years. His one fault, rigid punctuality, was also the source of his virtues – total reliability, strict honesty and a touching amazement that anything as unpredictable as life in Premier could succeed. We all miss him. RIP

A. Watson, Tiny to his friends, because he was tall and big, good-tempered and much respected by his passengers as well as ourselves, had a heart attack during a driving break and was found dead at the wheel. It was an extraordinary shock for all concerned, without warning or danger signals. All of us felt ashamed that we had had no opportunity to express our thanks to him for all his work for Premier. RIP

A. Rudderham has just succombed to a long, lingering, painful illness. He was a Fenman and was full of pride in his work and eager to add all sorts of additional services to his normal job as an express driver. He told us of the excitement he felt when he was asked to do a short Scottish Tour when laying-over in Glasgow from our service. He had never been over the area of the tour but he bought maps and guides and said he made quite a good driver–courier by anticipating what should have been round the next corner according to his very recently acquired information and nearly every commentary was accurate. His wife knitted beautiful dolls and he kept a row of them to welcome people aboard his coach. I have one dressed in the exact blue of our first Premier coaches. We remember him with great affection. RIP

13

The Birth and Early Growth of Premier Travel Agency

In the early months of 1956 one of our secretaries asked if we could arrange her Wallace Arnold Continental Holiday. Since both Wallace Arnold and Premier were members of PSV Operators it was fairly easy to contact the fast-growing Continental side of Wallace Arnold, and within about half an hour of Mrs B.'s first request, we had booked her tour to Spain. A fourteen-day holiday for two people cost at that time approximately £60, of which our share was ten per cent, or £6.

We were so intrigued by this instant income, earned in winter, when ordinary coach revenue was minimal, that we decided to follow seriously this promising extension to our business.

We looked first to our small booking office at Drummer Street Bus Station, which had been won after years of discussion by F.N.M. and E.A.L. with the local council. They had had to be convinced that Premier were handling a very fair, and increasing, proportion of the traffic in and out of the station and that it would be to the benefit of the travelling public if we had a permanent office there. The office had instantly become extremely busy in the summer months, with express services running on a daily basis and heavy excursion traffic building up annually. However, in the winter months, it merely ticked over as an enquiry office and a warm refuge for drivers waiting around for their next duties.

Luckily for our plans, it was too small to be used as a passenger waiting-room, a place which has so often become a dreary aspect of many coach and bus stations. We had a discussion with the clever Manager of our Drummer Street office, who had been one of our inspectors, and he was delighted to begin selling 'Dream Holidays for the Elderly', Wallace Arnold's excellent forerunner in the new market for the over sixties. He had instant success and very quickly built up a loyal clientele of first-time tourists. It is easier to follow the course of the ensuing travel pattern in Drummer Street than in the wider fields of agency that were spreading elsewhere in the Company. We found that after a season or two of British Coach Tours, the OAPs tended to become Continental Tourers (still mostly with Wallace Arnold from Cambridge), and, greatly daring and greatly to be admired, braved sea and air, foreign food and alien ways as pioneers of their generation. Nowadays, when a large number of British citizens depart annually for 'foreign parts', it is difficult to realise how insular, not to say parochial, the overwhelming majority of people were, only twenty-five years ago. It is true that a great number of men had travelled overseas in the services and a fair proportion of them had flown but the passengers I speak of were usually over sixty years old and accustomed to excursions to the seaside, plus an annual week at one of the more popular resorts. Now, thanks to the enterprise and salesmanship of both operators and travel agents, the English (and our East Anglians were amongst the first) were off to 'try anything once'. So we at Drummer Street inspired adventure, allayed anxieties and steered the elderly towards convivial overseas coach travel. The same pattern but on a smaller scale happened at our Haverhill and Saffron Walden bus offices.

At HQ it was less easy to begin. Our main office on the first floor of Market Hill was extremely busy and overcrowded. The whole building had been acquired by Watches of Switzerland in 1959, but after lengthy negotiations and thanks to F.N.M.'s persistence and bargaining skills, we had a long lease of the whole of the first floor and later the second, and, as a quid pro quo for certain structural adjustments, a small cubicle on the ground floor was allocated to us for a 'reception kiosk'. It was in this tiny space, 7ft by 5ft, that our very first Travel Agency, per se, was opened in Cambridge. There was no window, no hoarding, no exterior indication of its presence, but the *Cambridge Daily News* did its work for us and a judicious series of small ads were effective and people drifted in and booked with us. The extreme inaccessibility of this office, beautiful as it was inside, made it, in a sense, 'the buried acorn from which our great Agency

Oak has grown'. We took our subscriptions for the various travel manuals such as the *Air ABC Guide*, *Cook's International Railway Timetable*, the *Shipping Guide* and *Travel Trade Gazette*, all calculated to help us professionalise our new effort. We also contacted various non-IATA airlines and asked to be appointed agents.

We then followed the same procedure with a number of tour operators, and since the ABTA rules were not so all-encompassing in those days, people like Lyons Tours, Austria Travel, Yugotours and Paris Travel Services gave us their agencies. Wallace Arnold, by now impressed with our potential, Glenton Tours, Scottish Omnibus Tours (we were already coach agents for their Scottish services) and Scotia Tours added us to their list, so we were very shortly in business in the tiny office and felt moderately well-equipped, especially when Brinor, a London firm which acted as a rail and shipping ticketing agency, greatly enlarged our capability by giving us a twenty-four-hour guaranteed service. We still remember their contribution with gratitude.

On 12 December 1957, the Board discussed the future of developments in the travel agency side of the business: 'It was agreed that the first essential was to procure an expert with considerable experience in Agency work. From the balance sheet it was noted that the turnover last year was around £2,500 and that with expenses in the region of £1,250 per annum, the new business, to be any good, must increase its turnover to at least £15,000 per annum. It was resolved to develop the Travel Agency department to the full for a trial period of two years, and the Secretary was authorised to advertise in the trade journals with the object of obtaining an experienced Manager.'

Sixteen people replied, all with considerable experience and commanding salaries of between £700 and £1,000. After interviewing four applicants, a certain Mr D.W.R. of Leicester was chosen, at a salary of £750 per annum plus commission, ranging from 5 to 10 per cent on turnover. He joined us in March 1958 and a month later he

The Court House, Royston. PTA's most prestigious office

had secured direct agencies with Swans Tours, Sky Tours and many other operators. He reported bookings on 10 Continental, 19 British Tours and 22 miscellaneous holidays worth £770! He also suggested that we open a new office in Royston, an expanding town with no travel agency at all. This suggestion intrigued the Board since Premier had already had services in Royston for twenty years, so Mr R. and F.N.M. set about finding premises. In September, the very first custom-built office was opened at 21a High Street, with Mrs Cherry Orchard as Manager at a salary of £4 per week.

Gradually, like the rest of Premier, Cherry Orchard's approach grew more and more professional and successful (see her own account below). She became adept at picking out potential cruise or 'far away' passengers and sometimes it seemed that all Royston was holidaying at sea. The operating companies rewarded her with numerous complimentary cruises and flights all over the world and she travelled about to her heart's content. In 1971, a splendid new office was opened in the Old Court House in Royston and she took over its management with enormous confidence and zest. Unfortunately her health began to fail; retirement followed and sadly she died early in 1984.

Royston's first PTA office was soon followed by Saffron Walden, Huntingdon and Haverhill, and our purchase of Letchworth in 1965 completed the first chain of offices (see Appendix 4).

It was an extremely exciting period, since we were all bursting with enthusiasm and ideas, yet we were functioning in a totally new world. We experimented with administration, decor and shopfronts, publicity and folder design, brochure displays, travel wallets, passenger services, rewards and commissions, carpets, staff recruitment and strange 'traffic promotions'. At the same time we were also trying to professionalise ourselves, as we went along, in what must be the most complicated and sophisticated of all retail businesses. It was all very expensive and I was often blamed by those on the bus side of Premier for wasting their substance and pursuing a new fantasy world of foreign travel and sunshine holidays at the expense of new vehicles.

However, within a few years, Premier Travel Agency Limited, formally created as a wholly owned subsidiary of Premier in January 1964, had become the tail wagging the dog. As its total turnover leapt up year by year in a most spectacular way, we all understood that we had hit the boom in travel and we used it to take us on to the next phase of our journey.

RECOLLECTIONS OF A TRAVEL AGENT

Mrs H. Orchard

In July 1958 my personal life was in acute disarray and I needed a job to restore my confidence and provide the wherewithal for a new life. A friend brought to my attention the fact that Premier Travel, the bus company, was about to open a travel agency in Royston High Street, and it suddenly occurred to me that travel would be exactly right for me, so I wrote off to the Company Secretary who asked me to go and discuss the matter in Cambridge.

I was in high excitement at being granted an interview so quickly and went off by bus from Royston to Cambridge in good time to find the office in Rose Crescent by 3.30 p.m. The office entrance disappointed me: it was merely a passage with a tiny Travel Kiosk which doubled as a switchboard on the left-hand side as you approached the stairs. However, I thought, as I am here I'll go ahead; and so I asked the girl, 'Can you please tell me where the Premier Travel offices are?'

'Upstairs', she answered.

There I found someone else to direct me to Mr R.'s office and we settled down to the interview. He asked me several questions, as you might expect, then came the final one: 'Why do you want to become a travel agent, Mrs Orchard?'

I told him about my travels and about my general interest in running an office in Royston, where I was proposing to settle down. Presently, Mrs L. came in and told me about the new office which would soon be completed and about the challenge of the job. (I am convinced the desk at which I was interviewed was covered by a plush table-cloth but Mrs L. says 'Never'.) Anyway, they promised to let me know very soon. I thought I would never hear and that that was the end of that. And I went home.

The next day I got a letter offering me the post of Manageress at £4 per week, and on Monday 1 September 1958 I reported for duty.

When I arrived I was amazed to find Mrs L. and her young daughter, Vicky, busily painting the counter and generally helping to fix up 'my' office. It dawned on me that 'my' new company, in spite of its good notepaper, formal approach, and air of efficiency, was probably a fairly small concern. Later I was to find it was virtually a two-family company, the Matthews and the Lainsons, and that when you joined them, you immediately became part of their extended family.

I also found that my office was the very first travel agency opened by Premier – the other offices at Drummer Street and Saffron Walden were primarily bus offices. I have always been very proud of this special status.

The Royston office was an excellent home for a new venture. It occupied a central position very near the famous crossroads of the ancient town and from the window I could see the great Royston stone, sitting on its island of calm in the midst of the traffic. The premises were old, and low-ceilinged, but I had a very attractive bay window to show off my wares. Mr R. and Mrs L. had devised a long counter on one side, with reeded front; our brochures were displayed on a rotating circular stand; lovely National Tourist Bureaux posters adorned the walls and Mr R. had found numerous stands for various types of information. Underneath the counter were all the terrifying books of reference such as ABCs and time and fare tables.

Mr Bray often came to the office in the early days to explain the Premier services and time-tables, and Mr R. was constantly by my side in the first week or two. In fact, all the Directors made Royston a focus of attention in 1958–59. Later I was often alone for weeks!

At the back of the office was my 'bolt-hole', 'rabbit-hutch', 'storeroom' or 'the Manager's

PTA 'educational'. Cherry Orchard in India

office', according to the prevailing circumstances. Travel offices are extremely exposed to the public gaze and it is essential that this should be so because travel is a very personal concern, the one-to-one approach of agent and passenger is the prime source of good salesmanship. In recent years, counters with travel clerks sitting fairly close together have given way to individual desks, offering greater privacy. However, my counter, with its helpful tools carefully concealed below it, gave me confidence and a sense of space and security. The little partitioned office at the back gave me a breathing space to collect my thoughts, attempt my accounts, follow up my bookings and, best of all, escape the public eye.

I cannot stress enough the anxieties of those first few months. Every time the door opened my heart sank and I needed all my *savoir-faire* to find out what my potential traveller needed – especially if they wanted a coach ticket. Cruises, inclusive holidays, coach tours, theatre tickets, airline bookings (no IATA for me at that time) – I could cope with them all after a short experience, but British Rail, PSV coach tickets, even our own passenger enquiries sent me into a tizzy immediately! When I think now of the extensive training every newcomer to PTA receives, I know that my bewilderment and panic must be endemic to all budding travel agents.

To go back to the beginning, our opening day was celebrated by a party, attended not only by the Directors and supporting Premier people but also by generous local notabilities who offered their support. Reporters from the *Royston Crow* also came, and so started a very friendly relationship we have had with the paper ever since. They even helped me greatly in the early days with the format of advertisements.

Meanwhile 'my' office was duly launched and open for business. I suppose I can be grateful that in 1958 the great travel boom was only just beginning, so I was not inundated with potential holiday-makers; indeed, I sometimes felt very bored and alone.

One of my lighter moments in the early days was with a little old lady who asked me if I would do everything for her, so that she could have a cruise. So I helped her fill in her passport form and when I asked for her husband's nationality, she replied: 'Roman Catholic'.

I also liked the man who wanted a room with 'faculties' rather than facilities. I was quickly learning three things: first, that you have to be very interested in travel and people to do the job

Birthday Celebration Dinner

22nd December 1976
University Arms Hotel,
Cambridge

Edward Arthur Lainson Esq., MA, FCIT

'Bottoms on Seats', E.A.L., 1976

properly; secondly, the job satisfaction rating is extremely high; and thirdly, 'I had no time to stand and stare'.

PTA

A.W. Hill

My introduction to travel agency work was at our office in Royston High Street, as relief for Mrs Orchard when she was away or on her day off. As well as these periods, I used to take her in the old van, on Thursdays, to Wimpole Park, where the Americans were convalescing. How we managed to satisfy any of their travel requirements was a feat in itself, and required an awful lot of patience.

I also worked in the Saffron Walden office, at 14 Hill Street, in between duties as an inspector. This meant a lot of hard work, so when Mrs Kerr came it was a great relief. Then we moved to Emson Close, and the work became a challenge.

I remember opening the Letchworth office one Monday morning, and finding three gentlemen from India on the doorstep. I let them in and asked what I could do for them. They said they wanted to bring a member of their family to this country. I asked for his name and address. They gave me his name, but his address was impossible: 'He live in the forest in his village.' He had no passport, so I asked who was going to pay his fare. A large sum of money was immediately put on the counter. I hadn't got a clue what to do, so I phoned BOAC and outlined the situation to them. They told me

not to worry, so long as they paid the money. The man from BOAC explained: 'This is what we do. We send a runner into the forest with a camera. The Head Man of the village gives permission to photograph the man and he also gives the necessary details. A passport will then be applied for by BOAC and we will arrange everything. It is essential that you ask which sect he belongs to, so that we will know what food to give him.' While I was still working at Letchworth office, the same men walked in one day and introduced me to the fourth man, who thanked me for all the trouble I had taken to bring him to England. Then they produced a sum of money and said they wanted to bring over another member of their family. I knew what to do this time.

I enjoyed my work in the travel agencies because I had always had an ambition to be a great salesman. Although it was hard work, going as relief to a new office every day, it gave me great pleasure, when I first retired, to be able to hand over to Mrs Chapman a key to most Premier offices.

One of the greatest disappointments in my work with the Company was on the freight side. As I look over the papers of all I achieved, and how it was rejected by people who worked for Premier, I have proof of what was possible on that side of the Company. All that I have written can be proved, for I always kept records of all I did for the Company I was proud to work for.

The most treasured memory I have, was when the Directors asked me to act as Toast Master on 22 December 1976, at the birthday celebration dinner of Edward Arthur Lainson Esq., MA FCIT, one of our much loved Directors. It was a very great occasion.

14

Reports of Progress

POOLS AND LICENCES, 1961–67

G. Bray

In 1961 I was asked to undertake another new duty. The Company had recently decided to go into the travel agency business: the kiosk at Market Hill was turned into what was classed as a travel agency and Mr D.W.R. arrived to manage the new venture. Since the Company never nibbled at things but always jumped in at the deep end, within a few months Air Plan Holidays were developed. The idea was to charter planes to fly from Cambridge to anywhere you can think of and return the passengers a week later – the staff never had such a time:

'We've got three empty seats tomorrow. Do you want a trip there and back? Just the flight, you understand.' They went all over the place – for free.

The Air Transport Licensing Board (ATLB) had been set up to deal with licences and we had made an application to fly from Cambridge to Basle in Switzerland. We were opposed by BEA, and Premier was due to appear at the Aldersgate office of ATLB for the hearing. It so happened that there was no one available to attend since Mr L. was abroad and Mr F.N.M. had something else on, so he asked me to go. I told him I knew not the first thing about air travel but he just said, 'We've got some papers here, if you read them, you'll know as much as I do! Anyway you won't be on your own as Air Safari, our carriers, will also be represented.'

So I went along. Of course, there wasn't a soul about except the Clerk to the Court, so I asked him to point out the Air Safari representative when he arrived. But the gentleman didn't turn up and in due course the hearing began and I went into the box. There were eight or nine members on the panel, chaired by Professor Jack. I was well aware of Professor Jack's report on rural stage carriage services and, in fact, I was one of many who had been asked to submit my own views on the matter. I also knew that he had even ridden on some of the Premier services in the Huntingdon area whilst preparing the report.

On this occasion, however, he was in the Chair and I was in the witness box and all I could ask was, 'Will you please grant this application?' Full stop.

There was a silence, then the counsel for BEA got up and started to wipe the floor with me, asking me if I knew the length of the runway in Basle, and what planes were we going to fly, etc. I was getting fed up and cross and was suffering a mixture of emotions. Professor Jack, who could see what was happening, was very helpful to me and said: 'Mr Bray, you don't seem to know a great deal about this application.' I told him that was very true and I explained to him how I came to be there. He replied, 'Well, OK. That's one of the very few honest answers we've had in this court. I've heard of Premier Travel, of course, but I wasn't aware you were in this form of transportation. How long have you been?'

This was a question I could answer, 'About twelve months, maybe a little longer.'

'And how many passengers have you booked to Basle?'

Once again I hadn't a clue and that was that.

I reported to the Board that it had been a waste of time and that I was sure the application would be rejected. But we were successful, though the licence was never operated.

In the following years, the same pattern of publicity and licensing continued, with occasional applications to be made, such as for the Kidderminster to Clacton service. This again involved discovering the unsatisfied demand, although it was unopposed, so we obtained the grant and operated the service in the following year.

In 1964 there was an event of really great magnitude. My job had entailed visiting agents, witness-hunting, etc. and I had driven hundreds of miles either in an old pre-war car or in a second-hand Post Office van, which was a very reluctant starter. Then suddenly, there it was, a Brand New Car for me. It was a Hillman Imp and was my material token of success. I'm sure that at that period the Directors would not have bought a new car for themselves, yet I had been given one – it was really

The Eastlander en route at Cheltenham

something. And, of course, it made my job much easier. Previously I had had to make sure I kept the old car or van out of sight, parked well away from the call I was making, and now with this brand new car I could drive up to anywhere and invite my contacts to come for a drink: 'Right ho, I've got my car outside, hop in', and so showed it off and impressed them at the same time with the affluence of the Company.

The next big development got underway between 1965 and 1966 when we began pooled express services with other companies. Actually we had had a joint service with Percival Motors between Cambridge and Oxford for some years then but the start of real expansion was marked by our pool with Yelloway Motor Services of Rochdale. They operated from Lancashire to London, via Northampton and Leicester, and our service from Clacton to Birmingham tied in with their timetable at Leicester. At first there was an interchange of passengers, often involving longish waits

for connections, so the two independent companies decided to operate a direct pool service on Friday nights and Saturdays, in both directions between Clacton and Manchester, dividing at Manchester to form Service 74, across the Rossendale valley to Blackburn, and Service 75 to Blackpool via Preston.

This enterprise instigated a new type of record-keeping to ensure an accurate financial exchange between the companies at the end of each year. I remember that the bulk of the work was done initially by John Linsdell.

About the same time another major pool, the Eastlander, was formed. It came about in this way: in the five or six years that had elapsed since unsuccessful applications by Associated Motorways to operate a service from Cheltenham to Felixstowe and by Premier from Oxford to Clacton, to which I have already referred, there had been a change of General Secretary in Associated Motorways. Mr Geoffrey Webb had came on the scene with rather a different outlook and he proposed that the routes we had both applied for should be operated and developed jointly. We agreed, so a new application was submitted for two services, one from Clacton to Cheltenham via north Hertfordshire, Letchworth and Hitchin (which was basically an extension of the Premier route applied for from Oxford earlier); the other was the Associated Motorways route to Felixstowe, through Colchester, mid-Essex, Chelmsford and into Hertfordshire via Hatfield and St Albans, where the two routes arrived at the same time.

These applications attracted objections from Travel House (Luton) Ltd, who had been involved in the earlier proceedings and Grey-Green Coaches of Stamford Hill. In order to thwart the Premier/Associated Motorways application they put in a joint application themselves.

This was the start of a new approach, a new way of thinking by operators, whereby they decided that, since the Traffic Courts often made arbitrary decisions that pleased nobody, it might be better to sort things out among themselves, prior to going to court. There was then an almost one hundred per cent chance of agreed applications being granted as applied for.

Thus, in this case, for example, the four companies involved had a meeting prior to the sitting and agreed to form a pool service, with varying proportions of the revenue for each concern. The applications were amended accordingly and, except for the Metropolitan Area, were granted as applied for.

About that time the closure of the Bartlow–Saffron Walden–Audley End branch line took place and new road services were required, basically as rail replacements. Premier and Viceroy Coaches (F.C. Moore Ltd) of Saffron Walden applied to provide a rail replacement service via Castle Camps, Ashdon, Saffron Walden, Audley End, with the majority of the short journeys between Saffron Walden and Audley End being provided by Viceroy.

The timetable was considered by the Transport Users Consultative Committee (TUCC) for East Anglia. For geographical reasons, the substitute service operating through the centre of villages – notably Ashdon – was far more convenient for rail passengers than the former branch line. At the same time, a small number of journeys on the Linton–Saffron Walden service were diverted via Bartlow. The resulting timetable was not only devised to make almost immediate connections with the London rail service and, less conveniently, with Cambridge, but it was possibly the first in the

country to print these connections in a bus timetable. Incidentally, Service 59 is still operating on the same basis to this day.

The popularity of the service is illustrated by the unexpected but pleasing fact that the PTA office in Haverhill, some eleven miles from Audley End (the nearest railway station), received the Norwich Rail Division award for the best Rail Agent in the Eastern Area.

Another rail closure involved the Cambridge–Bedford–Bletchley–Oxford branch line. Numerous meetings took place with the railway authorities following their application for line closure and evidence was presented to the TUCCs for East Anglia and the East Midlands. Professor Pears, Chairman of the East Midland TUCC, commented at one sitting, 'Use it or lose it'. In the event permission was granted to close the Cambridge–Bedford (St John's) and the Bletchley–Oxford sections of the line.

Premier Travel had been operating the Inter-Varsity Express Service 39, between Cambridge and Oxford, since 1947. The service had been gradually increased, jointly with Percival Motors (Cambridge) Ltd, and ran via Royston, Hitchin, Luton and Dunstable. At the same time, Percival Motors (Oxford) Ltd operated an Oxford–Cambridge service via Buckingham and Bicester. As a result of the line closure all three parties met together and devised a pool service operating over the more populous route via Luton. They increased the departures to three times a day in each direction every Friday through to Monday, with diversions to Cambridge and Oxford railway stations, the latter pick-up being deleted after a few years.

The service took off very well but, considering that it began as a rail replacement service, it was odd that only the terminals could accurately be described as rail replacement points. This service really got underway by serving the points in the middle, Luton in particular. Nevertheless, these developments in pool operations meant that the old arguments in the Traffic Courts, though still occasionally necessary, were to a large extent eliminated.

However, the need to reach an agreement on the financial conditions between the various partners in the pool posed a new problem. There was a difference in the type of statistic for each service – no two were alike. It should and could have been possible to have some standard arrangement but each member had their own idea of what they

Inter-Varsity Express, Cambridge to Oxford, 1947

wanted. There was perhaps a bit of suspicion amongst certain operators: 'We've got to have this tied down . . . we've got to protect our part of the fare', etc. So it really started off quite a large volume of paperwork in offices.

There's no doubt in my mind that these pool services came in several years too late: in the past it had often been impossible to do anything about an unsatisfied need for services, simply because the onus to prove the demand had rested with the applicant. Services frequently failed to get off the ground for that very reason and when they subsequently did, they had to be developed for a much smaller market and at the same time attempt to wean some passengers back from cars. And that really is the conclusion I have reached about the years 1957–66.

Now we come to the years 1967–76, which, as far as Premier was concerned, and myself in particular, saw a further extension of the pooling services of the early sixties. There was the Morecombe–Southport pool that came in jointly with Midland Red, Ribble and Yelloway, and the Harwich–Bangor service jointly with Midland Red, both with new sets of statistics. Another that Premier introduced at the same time was Service 079, Cambridge to London Airport. This service was prompted by the idea that emerged from a meeting between BEA and Premier. BEA was interested mainly because of the expansion of PTA and a link from Cambridge to Heathrow was considered desirable. The application attracted objections from BR, ECOC and London Transport, all of whom pleaded abstraction of traffic. It resulted in a sitting where Lufthansa, BEA and one other airline and some passengers gave support. A licence was granted but it was restricted to passengers who were going to make a journey by air. Premier started this service with two journeys daily in each direction and it was very much a failure in its early years. It was decided that the service should reach Heathrow at 11 a.m., with a return time of 3 p.m. But it didn't do very well, in spite of intense publicity, especially in proportion to what had been expended on other sevices. On the publicity side, a coach was laid on one day and local politicians and representatives of all the travel agents were taken for a free trip to Heathrow and showed around the control tower, but none of this helped. It was operating at a loss and gradually went down to one journey until Premier decided that this wasn't doing us any good and it had to be done rather differently. So we decided to run it when we could afford to run and forget the planes it connected with; so we adopted a timetable that was operated

by a vehicle that had done a morning contract and would have had a lay-over until the afternoon and could go up to Heathrow and return. Surprisingly it began to carry more passengers and do reasonably well on this basis, quite well at weekends. On Saturdays and Sundays the costs were very much reduced and for the first time the service became profitable.

ECOC, who had objected originally, had had a change of Traffic Manager, and Mr Wade who was now TM suggested to us that they should come into a pool – their contribution would be an extension of the service from Cambridge to Peterborough and Huntingdon. I remember that it was agreed, because the route mileage from Peterborough to Cambridge was roughly half the mileage to Heathrow, that the division was one-third to ECOC, and two-thirds to Premier. The Peterborough/Huntingdon section subsequently proved disastrous, so sheer economics drove both of us to admit failure and the Peterborough section was withdrawn. However, the Cambridge–Heathrow service remained pooled. Thus Premier, who had developed the service, in spite of ECOC, found themselves a partner with ECOC, who still had one-third of it.

Here is another illustration, to my mind anyway, of what can be done outside the Traffic Commissioner's influence. Whereas Premier had initially operated under the condition that only air passengers could travel on Service 079, it had been subsequently amended to allow people who were going to wave them off to travel too. Now, because of the ECOC involvement and because of their Cambridge–London express service interest, it was possible to remove all restrictions and to pick up almost anywhere along the route, not only Cambridge, Baldock, Royston and Stevenage, but with pick-ups and setting down points at Mill Hill in London, through to Harrow, Hayes, and Heathrow, with day returns and singles for anybody and everybody. These changes were decided outside the Traffic Courts and simply submitted for approval; the whole structure of the service was changed – it became a first class operation.

All this happened in 1979 and I believe it is still operating along those lines, except that Premier has now acquired a 100 per cent interest in it.

In 1967 another interest was developed between companies in respect of representation. It had always been very difficult for independent operators to find booking agents and Premier was not alone in relying in many areas on what I call 'toffee shop' agencies – often newsagents, tobacconists, etc. They certainly helped greatly in building up

Service 5 at Bedford Coach Station, 1971

Premier's express services in the early days and the Company is always aware of its debt to them, yet they were an unprofessional outlet for the public.

As a result, however, of the new contacts, made through ECOC with the nationalised companies, the offices of the latter began to 'book Premier'. Midland Red had always done so but the slow and regular publicity drives and our personal contacts eventually permitted the removal of all restrictions and ECOC in Cambridge booked on all Premier departures. They had a larger booking office in Drummer Street bus station than Premier but we had, in my opinion, a much more efficient staff. Also both companies feared that information about the number of passengers carried could be used as evidence in the Traffic Courts.

Nevertheless, toes were dabbled gingerly in the water of co-operation. I remember that when Mr Boothby took over from Mr Fox as ECOC Area Superintendent, he and I arranged that we would book one another's excursions but not express services. The result was that passengers wanting to go to Yarmouth for a Saturday excursion, for example, would be told by ECOC: 'Sorry! we can't book you, as it's a Premier express service. If you go on Sunday, we can, because it's an excursion.' However, at least the thin edge of the wedge had gone in and within a year or two we agreed to act as full agents for one another.

This was a great step forward although at first only ECOC was involved. Then the new agency agreement also became the open sesame to ENOC and UCOC bookings. I was able to argue with them that, since they wouldn't and couldn't operate our services themselves, they might as well book on them and get ten per cent on all traffic booked in their offices. Both companies quickly agreed to this sensible and progressive relationship, beneficial to all concerned, and gave us full representation everywhere in their entire area.

So, from booking day excursions jointly with ECOC in Drummer Street, we had made a breakthrough of great significance, covering several counties on a professional basis, thus opening up much greater traffic potential.

The result was obvious. Our services began to develop more regular operations and the ease of booking was partly responsible for Service 5, Clacton to Birmingham, becoming daily throughout the year, because we were getting enough traffic to warrant it.

We in Premier, unlike most other independent companies, operated most of our express traffic away from our home base. Consequently we were more dependent on representation than many other companies, so it was a particularly important step forward for us. The fears expressed about too much knowledge of loadings failed to materialise

115

and, indeed, in one or two cases, the national companies didn't object to new Premier applications, being quite happy to enjoy ten per cent of any new service revenue.

ENGINEERING PROGRESS, 1966–85

M.J. Gifford

During the first half of these two decades we were ticking over reasonably well because, as well as the intake of new vehicles each year, we were able to purchase better class used vehicles, mainly from other operators, all with Harrington bodies. These were well built and in my opinion the most attractive coach design of the day.

Burlingham had ceased to manufacture coach bodies, so during the sixties we replaced the 24 Burlingham bodied vehicles in the fleet with 27 Harrington bodied coaches. This raised the Company fleet image considerably, but unfortunately Harrington ceased to build coach bodies about 1966. (Details of the fleet additions can be found in Appendix 8.)

Looking back, so much happened in this decade. We had built up a pretty good fleet of 51 vehicles, and it was gratifying to see the great improvement in our passenger carrying activities. Other branches of the Company had also been set up in Cambridge and were doing well. As mentioned in Chapter 5, we were always looking for a site in Cambridge, and in early 1973 F.N.M. acquired a piece of land in Kilmaine Close, Cambridge, big enough for a workshop and fuelling point to be erected. This was tremendous news and marked the start of two busy years of planning and development. As the plot of land was an unusual shape, a building 100 feet long and 50 feet wide was planned. It was positioned on the plot so that vehicles could get all the way round and would thus be able to enter the workshop at both front and rear. This building work was carried out by Kerridge of Cambridge. Inside the workshop we had a sunken floor work area linking four pits, and a ground level area to stand two vehicles for body repairs and painting; built onto the side of the workshop was the Spare Parts Stores Department, electrical repair shop, fuel injection repair shop and a rest room; outside we built the Tyre Repair Department, the engine-building workshop and we also had installed a twin post lift to enable us to steam clean chassis. In order to equip the workshop to the greatest advantage we contacted Messers Brown Bros, garage

equipment specialists, and they designed and produced the pit steel structure to fit in the sunken floor area. In May 1973, F.N.M and I went to Brown Bros' development planning offices in Swindon and discussed with their Mr Dorran the detailed layout of all the equipment that was to be installed in the works. It was difficult to realise that the wheels had been set in motion to have a new custom-built garage, fully equipped for the repair and maintenance of a fleet of vehicles. This was a very exciting period in our history. It had taken a long slow struggle of some thirty years to get this far, and when the development project was completed we moved from our Chrishall depot to the new Kilmaine Close works on 1 January 1975. In the same year the vehicle replacement programme was discussed and it was decided that, where possible, all replacements would be new vehicles. At the same time it was decided to standardise the fleet by having all Plaxton bodies fitted. This was a great step forward. As the fleet changes show (see Appendix 8), we purchased 4 new coaches in 1975 and 8 new coaches in 1976. On a personal note 1976 was a memorable year for me: it was the Company's fortieth anniversary and, included in the celebrations to mark this milestone, I was to receive a directorship of Premier Travel Services. It was a great honour indeed to receive this promotion.

In 1977 4 new vehicles were added to the fleet: PCE 601R, PCE 602R, RVE 650S and RVE 651S. An increase in traffic caused a vehicle shortage, so we also purchased 5 used vehicles to cover this situation: UTF 478M, UAR 925M, WUR 856J, URA 461K and YUS 244J. Another good move made in 1977, prompted by more frequent power cuts, was the installation of our own independent engine driven power generator. It is essential for us to have the air compressor working because much of the garage equipment is air operated and lights are needed to work in pits. There have been power cuts for various reasons during the seventies, and the generator has proved its worth in allowing garage working to continue and the computer to function.

In 1978 the Company purchased 6 new coaches: RVE 625S, RVE 653S, RVE 296S, RVE 297S, WEB 406T and WEB 407T. One thing we did this year, due to the continuous problems coach heating systems give, was to fit automatic radiator shutters on all the vehicles. These shutters work by having a thermostat in the engine coolant system, and the shutters will remain closed until a predetermined coolant temperature is reached. This allows the engine to warm up more quickly and, in turn, the heaters to distribute the warm air in the coach much sooner than with an open radiator. In cold conditions it is not unusual for a coach to travel from Cambridge to Birmingham and the radiator shutters to remain closed over the whole journey. This illustrates how a coach may travel quite a way and yet not raise the whole coolant system to the best operating temperature.

In 1979 we purchased 4 new coaches, WEB 408T, WEB 409T, WEB 410T and WEB 411T. In May Mr Roy Moore joined the Company to take over the running of the workshop, and it was a great relief for me to have someone who was willing to take over the responsibility of the maintenance and repair of the Company's fleet. But 1979 was also a sad year for me, in a way, because AEC vehicles of Southall had earlier been merged with British Leyland and we were subsequently informed that the manufacture of AEC vehicles would end, and the Southall works closed down. For twenty years we had been running an exclusively AEC fleet, and suddenly no more. This caused some concern because it takes a large capital outlay to build up a standardised fleet of 50 vehicles of another make, and other problems may

Eighty-four years with Premier. Jack and Maisie Gifford

emerge when changing from one make of vehicle to another. With this in mind I went to Sweden to the Volvo factory and to the DAF factory in Belgium to assess the merit of buying their chassis; both these chassis were very good. In the UK there was only one heavy chassis available and that was the Leyland Leopard, and this chassis was not comparable with the specification of our AEC vehicles. Roy Moore and I went to the Leyland works to discuss the position as to the future supply of AEC spare parts, and the possibility of modifying the Leyland chassis to a specification similar to our AEC vehicles. Agreement was reached in these discussions and modifications were carried out, and taking into account that we would be able to obtain spare parts for both AEC and Leyland from the same outlets that we had dealt with for many years it was decided that our vehicle replacement programme would be with Leyland Bus.

In 1980 we therefore purchased 10 Leyland Leopard coaches to our specification. These vehicles have proved successful since their purchase.

In 1981 no new vehicles were purchased. The changes made by the Department of Transport in their vehicle testing procedures meant that all PSVs would have to go to a Heavy Vehicle Test Station annually, unless the operator himself had approved testing facilities on his own premises. We therefore planned and had installed a rolling road brake testing machine. Following on from this, in consultation with Department of Transport officials, we set up an approved vehicle test lane, and when this was completed we were accepted as an official Department of Transport PSV Test Station.

In 1982 we took delivery of 5 new coaches: VAV 254X, VAV 255X, VAV 256X, VAV 257X and VAV 258X. These coaches were the first of the new Leyland Tiger 245 twelve-metre vehicles, and the first coaches to be painted in the Company's new livery of silver and blue. One of them was entered in the Brighton Coach Rally and won the trophy.

In 1983 we purchased 7 new coaches: FAV 254Y, FAV 255Y, FAV 256Y, FAV 257Y, GFL 527Y, GFL 528Y and GFL 529Y. These coaches were fitted with the new Plaxton Paramount bodies. The first 4 were fitted with normal height coach bodies, and the last 3 were fitted with high floor bodies. These 3 Highline coaches were up-market vehicles, and were fitted out with a toilet, coffee machine, fridge, video equipment and drivers bunk. They work on a shuttle contract to the South of France. One of these coaches was entered in the Brighton Coach Rally and we again won a trophy.

Partnership: Leyland and Premier celebrate '1000', 1983

Also in this year we expanded further by acquiring the business of Percivals Anglia Coaches, complete with the property, and this is currently being developed to become the Company's central workshop and Administration Department.

In 1984 two new coaches were added to the fleet: A638 OEB and A695 JER. The former was rather special. It was the 1000th Leyland Tiger chassis produced by Leyland Bus. It was fitted with a Plaxton Highline body, it incorporated many modifications and was launched at Kilmaine Close with considerable publicity. This vehicle was also entered in the Nice Coach Rally, and put up a good performance. A695 JER is working on an American contract running from Wentwaters to London Airport.

During 1984, after attending a preview of the new Metropolitan Cammel Weymann (MCW) Metroliner coach, it was decided that we would purchase the first Metroliner to be built, and as the Motor Show at the National Exhibition Centre was towards the end of the year, we thought it would be nice to enter it in the exhibition on the MCW stand. An extraordinarily high specification was drawn up and the coach entered the Show. It was a great success and when all trials and tests had been carried out we took delivery in January 1985. Three more MCW Metroliners have been ordered and are in production. These are of slightly lower specification than the Show coach and delivery is expected in April or May 1985.

This outline of my memories of Premier makes it

quite apparent that the garage staff were never looking for work. To such stalwarts as Sid Law, Fitter; Alf Wisbey, Stores Department; Roy Scarr, Fitter (still on active service); and those who are not now with us, much credit must go. Fitters and all other maintenance staff rarely get in the limelight, but they have been vital to the success of the Company. It has given me tremendous satisfaction to have witnessed the Company's growth over the past four decades, and I am happy to have played a small part in it.

EDUCATION

S.E. Pennell

Another thing the Company did to me was to send me on a driving instructor's course to High Ercol, near Shrewsbury. At that time it was the heavy goods and passenger transport vehicle training centre. I liked the idea but I'm not much of a scholar and I reckoned it would be beyond me. Still I went and in the first week I nearly did my nut. The lecturer asked for questions and I said, 'You've been waffling on for a week and I can't make head or tail of you or what you've been talking about.'

At the end of the second week we had to take tests. I finished up fairly well. Of course my driving was OK but the paperwork – 87 per cent! When I got my results the Chief Instructor said, 'Well, what do you think now?'

When I got back, I went to see the guvnors.

'What happens now?'

'Back to driving.'

'What about the money? Now I've got a certificate am I on the same or am I going to get more?'

The terms were very favourable and we had a good meeting.

I carried on as instructor for many years until my arm went and I had to come off driving and that was the end of that chapter.

Driving Instruction No. 1

Frank Grice said to me one day, 'I've got a bloke coming through for his test – will you take him?'

'What's his name?'

'Cage.'

'Not Herbert Cage? He's a bloke I knew in the war. We used to call him Scatty. He'd had a lot of Indian sun on him.'

Well, dear oh dear! I took him round Peas Hill. There was a man on a ladder against the Guildhall; his mate was at the bottom. Cagey never stopped; never slowed down. Just went through like the

Roy Scarr, surgeon-engineer (top), *and his mate, T. Sabnani*

Devil. The bloke at the bottom ran for his life; the man on the ladder yelled; old Scatty laughed – doubled up over the wheel. Remember it was his first lesson.

Driving Instruction No. 2

F.N.M: I want a PSV Licence.
S.P.: What the hell do you want that for?
F.N.M: I want a PSV.

So I took him out and gave him a few lessons and he decided to have a go.

S.P.: How did it go?
F.N.M: B..... well failed.
S.P.: Well I'll be b..... You'll have to go again.

A little more tuition and he went up and passed. It pleased him no end and it meant a fiver for me.

Perhaps because I did so well academically at High Ercol, perhaps because I began to develop arthritis in the arm in 1969 and couldn't drive anymore, I was sent up to Head Office, 15 Market Hill, and there I started on office work – journey cards, waybills, ticket checks. I learnt them all. So they gave me Drummer Street office to manage. That was hard because sitting in those cramped conditions gave my legs beans and I don't reckon I was out of pain for about five years. I liked the work, saw a lot of my old mates and was busy as hell. Frank Grice used to pick me up each day. All the time he was Traffic Manager he had a way of getting people to do things for him. He was having a bad time in the seventies himself but he still looked after me. Then my days with Premier ended when I had two hip operations – one very good, the other a total failure. I send best wishes to you all.

SUCCESS

G. Bray

It also happened in the late sixties and early seventies that PTA was expanding and I was introduced to a new form of representation. I joined, on behalf of Premier, the SKAL Club, which I had never heard of before and thought it must be something to do with drinking lager. A Cambridge and East Anglian Branch had been founded, which included Luton and adjoining towns, and although my motives for joining may have been the wrong ones, the SKAL meetings provided another point of contact with agents and thus improved my reception and the image of the Company as I toured around with our publicity.

I also became a member of the local Travel Trade Club (TTC), which was the social club for members of the counter staffs. They used to have sponsored evenings and by becoming a member of the Luton TTC I met up with the local agency staff, who were normally the only direct contact with our passengers, apart from the coach drivers. So I was able to assess the popularity, or otherwise, of Premier in yet another area. All in all the sixties and early seventies saw our whole representation and publicity put on a fully professional basis.

Another improvement came about in 1969 with the introduction of driver training. As a result of a serious programme of 'classroom' training, I was able to demonstrate the vital part a driver's paperwork played in producing accurate and up-to-date statistics, required both for the financial exchanges of pool services and to fulfil legal duties. The staff responded well to these training sessions, we had very good results and improved things no end.

Around the same period, management meetings were started. Certain members of Premier's staff who were in management in the various operational departments depended on each other in day-to-day matters to a very great extent but hardly ever had any formal contacts. Engineering, Traffic, Statistics, Training, Personnel, Finance were all interrelated and so it was agreed that we should hold management meetings twice yearly, and report our conclusions to the Board. We met in Owen Webb House in Cambridge and discussed anything and everything that was going on and so built up a picture of what was happening in every department. The results of our discussions were a valuable aid in future planning: it was no longer a matter of 'so and so thinks we should do this' or 'we've always run it this way'; we had something solid on which to forecast. In my opinion, a new era in policy-making had begun and it has proved very useful. This was altogether a time of many, many meetings.

As a result of new legislation, local authorities were coming into the picture to a much larger extent in respect of stage carriage services, which, since the days of the Windmill timetable, had withered away or been reduced. By this time, the preponderant mileage of the Company was on express services. A regular series of meetings was set up with local authorities to discuss rural bus services. There had already existed, prior to this, two platforms for discussion with LAs. One was the North Herts' Joint Transport Conference, which met twice-yearly at Letchworth, and the Huntingdonshire Passenger Liaison Committee,

Captain at the wheel. F.N.M., 1973

which met twice-yearly in Huntingdon. But these organisations were very much an annual reiteration of problems. Local authorities were not then empowered to assist financially any schemes that were put forward, but by the early seventies that had changed. Financial assistance was made available to any operator of stage carriage services in rural areas and, as he that pays the piper always calls the tune, operations were revised after these discussions. Initially they were with non-professional people, without any knowledge of transport, someone from the Supply Department, for example, so it was often very difficult to convey more technical aspects of bus operation to well-meaning laymen.

Also in those days, we had the start of concessionary fares on local services, whereby LAs used to make payments for senior citizens, handicapped people and so on. This, too, called for discussion and certainly there were many more hours spent on discussion about the operation of a bus fleet than ever before. An additional problem arose because the LAs were used to working on a district basis but it became clear that it had got to be done on a county basis, so most of the counties appointed a professional bod to the post of Transport Liaison Officer. I personally welcomed this very much because it then became possible to say to the professional man, who had had operational experience, 'this is the situation . . . it's your job to put it into the politician's mind'. It made things much easier and much more rational.

Premier had particular difficulties as the Saffron Walden–Haverhill–Chrishall triangle was not a big area but did involve four counties. It had problems which were always overcome, but one county's attitude to a proposal was sometimes different from that of the neighbouring county and many compromises had to be reached. One thing that caused a lot of problems was the different counties' attitude towards concessionary fares: Suffolk, for instance, had one system and one set of conditions; Essex used to work on a district basis, as did Hertfordshire; but Cambridge had a county basis. There was therefore no standardisation and I still think it was marvellous that the conductors agreed to have anything to do with concessionary tickets. For example, a route like Chrishall to Royston, Service 43, even via Barkway, Barley and Reed, is only twelve miles long, yet you have three different counties and three different systems. It was a wonder to me that the schemes ever got off the ground. I remember that there were efforts by the then Government to standardise concessions on a national basis and I personally deputised for Mr Lainson at two or three meetings on the matter at Sardinia House. Then there was another change of government in 1974 and the whole thing got ditched and has never been reintroduced. Subsequently both Suffolk and Cambridgeshire agreed a swings and roundabouts method of simplifying the matter, but not so the other two counties. Of course, another set of statistics had to be prepared for concessionary fares. And yet other sets were needed to deal with new legislation that had been passed in the sixties and seventies. Fuel-tax remission enabled operators to be reimbursed for stage carriage mileage. Of course, Premier operations required vehicles to run on stage, express, excursion and contract mileage – occasionally all in one day – and it was a major operation to sort out the stage mileage from the vehicles' daily records. But a considerable amount of money was involved and this remission of tax assisted enormously in the maintenance of our rural services.

The legislation that was introduced to assist operators by the New Vehicle Grants also helped in this area of operations. To begin with, when Mrs Castle was Minister of Transport, these were set at 25 per cent of the cost of the vehicle, provided that at least 50 per cent of a vehicle's total mileage was on stage-carriage operation during the first five years of its life. This was subsequently amended to 50 per cent of the first two years plus two distinct periods on stage carriage in the subsequent three years. Eventually it was further amended to 50 per cent of each individual year.

This last revision tightened up the system considerably and meant that the Traffic Department had to know where it stood at any particular time. The paperwork had to be kept up to date and the total mileage had to be broken down and recorded against each vehicle daily, then weekly. This was then divided into stage and non-stage, keeping a running total, so that I could say to 'Traffic', 'such and such a vehicle has done more express than stage, so it must come off express altogether, otherwise the 50 per cent figures will not balance when the period is up in so many days'. These figures were audited very thoroughly every year and the department was determined nothing would go wrong.

Two further pools came into being in the mid-seventies. One was Dunstable–Glasgow with Western SMT. The other was Liverpool–Clacton joint with Crosville and Yelloway. Again more pool statistics were kept and another illustration of how the paperwork, which had started off on such a small scale, continued to grow. Indeed, by this time it had become quite voluminous under so many different headings but in my opinion the causes of that increased paperwork were very beneficial to the industry, the public and everyone else who participated in it.

My work was really assisted by our move to Kilmaine Close in May 1974. For the very first time there was enough room to spread all this paper around and to organise it so that we knew where everything was – with room to move. What a delight that was.

Now we come to the last period as far as my contribution to the Company is concerned and it takes us up to my retirement in March 1982. By then life really had become a continual battle to keep on top of statistics. Fuel tax, bus grants, pool settlements and concessionary fares made the paperwork a never ending job with volumes of paper arriving every day.

When I had originally come off the road twenty years earlier, I was hardly ever in the office but was going round the field to try and sell things and improve our representation. By this time, however, I had become absolutely desk-bound. Perhaps we were lucky but we certainly had no problems on government audit, or nothing that wasn't easily put right. The people who came to audit were quite friendly and I was rather pleased to be told on one occasion how they wished that every firm could present their statistics in our fashion.

But statistics continued to grow and there were further poolings in the late seventies. We developed a pool with York Bros: the old Bedford–Cromer service had not been all that buoyant and Messrs York Bros of Northampton also had a service from that part of the East Midlands to Cromer, so we were able, after discussion, to arrive at a mutually beneficial basis on which to pool our efforts. The load factor and the receipts per mile increased for both companies and only one vehicle went through, other than on peak Saturdays, and carried all the passengers. It meant discontinuing certain intermediate points which were used very little but that was the only cost in terms of traffic. It provides a further example of what can be easily achieved by co-operation.

The last pooling arrangement I was involved in was the pooling of effort to provide excursions and tours with two other companies, as J.A.M. explains in Chapter 18. But again here were two further pools necessitating further statistics, and I would like to say here and now that it would not have been possible, given the labour force and the facilities available at either Market Hill or Kilmaine Close, without the expertise of Mrs Bernardini, alias Miss Flack, alias Heather, as I call her who never ceased to amaze me. The volume of work which she would get through, which was hardly ever queried when submitted to other companies for scrutiny, speaks for itself.

Also around this time, or just prior to this time, there was a change in Road Licensing laws, resulting in considerably less paperwork, on the one hand, and a redefinition of stage carriage services, on the other. The latter had always been defined by a minimum fare of 11p. This was changed, so that the new yardstick became a passenger making a journey of thirty miles or fifty kilometres, as the official wording put it. This meant that overnight many more services which had been classed as express became legally and technically stage carriage services; and then of course they qualified for bus grant and fuel-tax remission. Thus the initial saving on paperwork which had resulted from the licensing changes produced an even greater volume of paperwork when the stage carriage service was redefined – because of the fuel records and so forth.

Although paperwork is possibly the least important part of the joint operating effort it is essential that it is done efficiently to substantiate claims and refunds. It would be unthinkable not to do it because we would deny ourselves the benefits of the new legislation.

I don't think I've left much out of this account, which ends with my retirement in 1982, except perhaps to say that all the foregoing represents a very interesting and enjoyable thirty years, made possible by the friendship and understanding of the then Managing Director, Mr E.A. Lainson, who gave me every encouragement and to whom I will always be indebted.

Postscript by E.A.L.

Geoffrey Bray is a remarkable man, whose career with Premier spanned more than thirty years. His analytical faculties, combined with a very engaging personality, earned him friends throughout the passenger transport industry, who greatly respected his integrity and grasp of detail. It is to his efforts that much of the progress and success of Premier is due.

15
Infusion of Youth

Early in 1966 an influx of young executives started to change the face of Premier. Not, of course, that any of those in charge were growing old – they were all in their prime and have remained so until this day. It was just that in the harsh fifties, Premier had had to discard the junior administrators and for about ten years took on no other middle management. So with the diversification programme between 1958 and 1965, it became apparent that the Company needed some vigorous new blood and new techniques.

This was brought to the Board's notice, in the first place, by R.C.H.D., who urged the employment of a resident accountant, since the enormous growth in turnover, added to increased responsibilities as Company Secretary, was too much for any one man. This was reinforced by the young, newly qualified accountant who audited the annual accounts for 1966, and who was horrified at the inadequacy of our bookkeeping, especially that of PTA. He strongly recommended that we employ a full-time accountant; we advertised, he applied and was unanimously voted into the job.

And so it was that P.S. Andrews, chartered

Youth at the helm. R. L. Sargent with some Managers: (left to right, standing) *John Cain, Letchworth; Ian Slater, Huntingdon; G. Mould, St Ives;* (seated) *Jennifer Howlett, Saffron Walden; Carole Goodenough, Thetford; R. L. S.; Gill Scott, Cambridge*

The Finance Director, P.S. Andrews, FCA

accountant, joined Premier on 1 August 1967, at the age of twenty-four. Since that moment he has had a whale of a time guarding, protecting, increasing and managing the finances of the whole group. Professionalism is a marvellous weapon and a trained mind is a joy to behold. He has computerised almost every department and now, surrounded by twenty-first-century technology, he still remains sane and has also had time to learn one or two Premier lessons about the imponderables of the human side of finance. The Company to which he has dedicated the last eighteen years and of which he has been Financial Director since 1972 thrives on his knowledge, skill and relentless appetite for work.

Two years before Peter Andrews, Renford Sargent came as a boy of twenty in answer to an advertisement for a trainee travel clerk. He took to travel like a duck to water, was Manager of Rose Crescent's new office within a couple of years, became General Manager before Jack Robinson got out of bed, was made a Director of PTA in 1976 and became a Group Director in December 1982. There is no doubt at all that this vigorous, go-getting young tycoon, not yet forty years old, has been almost totally responsible for the very substantial and influential position now enjoyed by

PTA. He himself tells most of the story in Chapter 16 but someone else has to put into words the value of his contribution to the Group; his ideas flash out like short sharp shocks to the senior members of the Company but even he sometimes bows to their judgement.

He and Peter Andrews became close friends as well as colleagues and seemed to spend twenty hours a day discussing the future and present potential of Premier, to the great benefit of the Company. Renford married Christine Rule, possibly the most beautiful girl ever employed by the Company, and they have two children.

At the same time, another young and valuable addition to the staff arrived at PAL, which had been going through very difficult times. B.V. Burnett came from the RAF and so fitted easily into the slot of Assistant Air Traffic Controller, and later Airport Superintendent. The whole plan that had been behind the enterprise then gradually came to fruition: efficiency and honesty marked its progress; passenger carryings increased and that happy word, profit, suddenly became a reality.

Farewell! M.M.E.L., 1971

The next step forward was the return of John A. Matthews to the Premier fold in 1969. He had joined the Company at the age of seventeen in 1947 but left, to relieve financial pressures, in 1953. The Board had often spoken of the need to have another Matthews in the Company and when the post of Road Transport Training Officer came up, John agreed to join in that capacity. He quickly organised 'schools' for every member of the firm and it became quite normal to open a door and find a blackboard in position and an assortment of office and road staff sitting grimly on plastic chairs, whilst the more intricate problems of their jobs were formalised before their eyes.

This training was extremely useful to the professional transport world but, of course, once done, left no more to do, so the Training Officer turned to the many opportunities of traffic development. In 1972 J.A.M. was appointed a Group Director and when Premier Travel Services was set up to look after the transport operations of the Company, he became its first General Manager and Director.

His father would have been delighted to see his original plan to have both Frank and John in Premier now realised, and very often it seems that the same warmth and sincerity that W.F.M. brought to the Company is back with us again, in double measure.

Thus in five years, four new people, capable and eager, had come into the Company and the way was open for change. The Woman on the Board read the signs, sighed half-pleasurably, half-regretfully, gave in her resignation on 19 June 1971 and retired.

Whether leaving work voluntarily or compulsorily, the sudden collapse of a world of friendship, talk, planning, thinking, scheming and working in partnership is nearly as traumatic as divorce. Avoid it.

16

The Continued Growth of Premier Travel Agency

PREMIER TRAVEL AGENCY, 1965–85

R.L. Sargent

I commenced work in 1965 with the beautiful Eliane Kestleloot – no small incentive for working with a struggling company. At that time it was well-endowed with eccentrics, including Thomas, the black Labrador of the Chairman, who was responsible for surprising many ladies with his wet nose at our travel agency counter (the dog, not the Chairman). Eliane, a trained travel agent, was running the Market Hill kiosk and was the only person who really knew what she was doing in PTA [not true] and, with hindsight, it is not difficult to see why we were not taken seriously by the travel trade. Those other, longer established, more professional companies, particularly in Cambridge, would, in later years, come to rue the manner in which they disregarded the Premier potential.

However, Premier was a 'beautiful' place to work, mainly because of the Chairman, Arthur Lainson, who made just about everybody feel important all the time, and Frank Matthews, who was generally reckoned to possess the business acumen that kept Premier going. He was held in great esteem by everyone and feared by most. These two totally different characters made a great impact on all who came into contact with them. Others that come to mind from that era are Harry Wynn, the 'gravel voiced' payer of wages, whose London cabbie's humour was appreciated by all; Linton Linsdell, football referee, raconteur and pursuer of young ladies; Narajen Singh, the singing Sikh, who enthralled Premier children one Christmas with his version of 'Babyface', accompanied by Ann Bailey on piano; Uncle Bert Hill, whose stories were not always completely accurate, but who was a great Premier ambassador and friend. There were also many Company marriages, the most important to me being my own to Christine. Her most poignant early memory of Premier is that on completion of her three-month trial period she was rewarded by being given the other half of her free bus pass, in place of a salary review. This frugal approach is still apparent today and has no doubt contributed to our success. My principal memory of those early days was the extraordinary loyalty of the staff, and the uncomprehending looks on the faces of the Board when someone announced they were leaving (even for three times the salary they were earning with Premier). In fact, certain Board members were quite bitter about losing their protégés.

PTA has come a long way since those early days, thanks to many dedicated people including J.H. Northmore and the PTA executive (P.S.A., Vicky Lainson and myself). January 1974 saw my appointment to the position of General Manager, a mere boy of twenty-nine. The turnover of PTA for 1973 was £1.2 million; For 1984 it was £10.8 million, plus Premier Holidays Ltd, now turning over £5.5 million. The Board decided to support me, young as I was, and began by gradually closing the unprofitable offices at Bedford, Ware, Peterborough and Ramsey. They were replaced by even more unprofitable offices at Mildenhall and Swaffham [see Appendix 4]. Later we were to acquire Thetford Travel in 1978 and Clayden's of Bishop's Stortford in 1980. With Thetford Travel came Margaret Beatty, a Director of that company, who became my Personal Assistant and greatly contributed to the development of PTA.

The Board were persuaded that 'good housekeeping' alone was not sufficient to ensure the future nucleus of PTA. The process of improving our existing locations began in some cases by renovating offices and in others by moving to better positions in their respective towns. A new corporate logo was designed for our travel agencies, later updated and used throughout the group. Our improved image attracted more experienced staff; and training schemes, career structures, staff pensions all helped to sell Premier to new staff and clients alike. We were thinking bigger and more long term and this approach was also beginning to influence the attitudes of the much longer established PTS.

Dennis Rule became very important to us in his new role as Group painter, decorator, plumber, carpenter, brochure distributor and morale booster for overworked travel staff.

We were able to establish our own long-service lunch as more and more staff decided that PTA was to be their future. The first phase of the new PTA was accomplished. We had achieved credibility with our staff.

Business improved spectacularly in the late 1970s and in 1979 it was apparent that we should either expand our number of travel agencies to keep pace with the emerging large multiples, or diversify further into our own four operations. We opted for the latter and I think this decision will eventually prove to be one of the most significant in Premier's history. We began in 1980 with our first Channel Islands brochure, a natural extension of our activities at Cambridge Airport, and carried 786 passengers, booked only through our own travel offices. In 1985, under the management of Susan Papworth and her young team, we anticipate carrying around 14,000 passengers, booked by travel agents from all over the UK.

In 1981 Premier Holidays America came into being in the cellar of our Rose Crescent travel agency, initially offering advice and bookings for Cambridge people travelling to the USA. The popularity of this department, under the direction of Chris Bailey, became evident immediately and the following year we had sufficient confidence to produce the first Premier Holidays brochure. Since then its progress has been astounding. In 1985 we anticipate carrying 12,000 passengers, again booked by the major travel agents of the UK.

In 1982, upon the appointment of Roger Balsom, from Thomas Cook, came our first China and Faraway brochures. Study China Travel was acquired from Mr and Mrs Cecil Kline to help establish us in this exciting new market. Mr Balsom's meticulous planning ensures a steady flow of complimentary letters concerning these products.

In 1984 Premier's Conference and Incentive Department arrived under the experienced management of Christine Poynter. This department will not only handle company conferences abroad but will also deal with the important incoming market of the UK.

The newly incorporated Premier Holidays commences trading in 1985, equipped to handle in excess of 30,000 holidays worldwide. It is quite extraordinary that a Group that has been in business for fifty years has received genuine national and international recognition for the first time, as a result of developing these successful tour programmes. This recognition has obviously benefited all parts of the Group and it is very gratifying to see Premier entering its second fifty years with such a splendid balance of old and new.

It has been said before that 'It's all about people' and this does sum up Premier's attitude towards life and business. E.A.L. and F.N.M. in particular have done a marvellous job in holding together all parts of Premier. The stability which they provide is just as important as the exciting new developments.

I have known many contributors to Premier's success during my twenty years with the Group, and those I particularly remember are regrettably no longer with us. They were Ann Bailey, John Northmore, Bert Hill, Horace Impey and Cherry Orchard. Those who are still with us include Audrey Kerr, Sheila Brennan, Roger Barker, Ian Slater, John Morgan, John Cain, and Bob Pool, plus all members of the ten-year Luncheon Club [see Appendix 4]. Finally special mention must be made of Granny Chapman, my secretary for eighteen years, and comforter-in-chief when times get tough.

SAFFRON WALDEN OFFICE

A. Kerr

Early in December 1963 the Minutes record that Mrs Audrey Kerr had been engaged to cover the Saffron Walden office at a salary of £5 per week. Twenty-one years later, here is her story of the growth and development of one of the most attractive and successful offices in the Company.

I joined Premier Travel Agency after an interview with Mrs Lainson and Mr F.N. Matthews at 14 Hill Street on 16 December 1963. Hill Street office was situated in premises owned by Messrs Rookes and the office-cum-shop was squeezed between Rookes' Wallpapers and Paints on one side and the lavatory pans and sinks on the other. The office had apparently been used by Premier Travel for years as a chart room for the buses. It was a very small office and for the first few weeks all I sold was bus tickets on a very old-fashioned machine, which, to my horror, ran out one day and try as I might I could not refill it. Fortunately the

PTA's leading ladies: (left to right) *Audrey Kerr, Cherry Orchard, Elizabeth Chapman*

passenger was not travelling for a few days so I tactfully asked her to come back the next day – and I spent the rest of the afternoon trying to make the copies (of which I think there were four) come out in the correct way; instead they would keep shooting out of the top. However, I eventually mastered it and was greatly pleased with myself.

Business gradually picked up after a great amount of advertising – having talked the paper boys into delivering a form of leaflet and given talks to WIs in surrounding villages, amongst other things. Fridays were the highlight: it was pay day and, as happened in our Royston office in those days, I had to run out at 16.05 to catch my pay packet, which the driver of the bus threw to me as he went by on his way to Radwinter. If by any chance I was on the telephone or had a client and missed the bus, the following Friday I had to be very dexterous and catch two pay packets.

One morning I undid the door and the telephone was ringing. The following conversation took place:

'Premier Travel Agency, good morning.'
'What time does the bus leave?'
'Where to, Madam?'
'Walden of course!'
'Where from, Madam?'
'Here of course!'
'Where is here, Madam?'
'At my home of course!'

After about five minutes of this I eventually found out that the lady lived at Chesterford and it was the Eastern Counties bus she wanted, not even ours.

Obviously I had some funny requests from, as I thought, potential clients. They came in the wrong door and asked for paint or a loo seat, in spite of the numerous travel posters around the walls.

However, there was great news in store. A new row of shops was being built in Emson Close and in June 1964 Premier moved to what was then a dream of an office, with super pigeon-holes for the manuals. I felt that I was in the lap of luxury. The move itself was an absolute scream: Mrs Lainson and the late Mrs Hill plus a few others helped, but we found that half the things we needed were in the old office and there seemed to be a continuous stream of coming and going up and down the Common Hill. After this move we took on two juniors.

The next excitement was the closing of the Saffron Walden railway line when we got the British Rail licence. After spending my lunchtime in the booking office with the BR clerk I really felt quite knowledgeable about rail tickets and I scrounged their ticket rack and old fashioned date stamper (now in a museum I think).

But to more serious things about Saffron Walden. The most significant moment came when we put in for IATA. I had a couple of days training with BEA, who at that time were at Kett House, Cambridge. Colin Robson was a great help as was 'Charlie' Chaplin and his crew at Kett House. After that followed a day's ticketing course at Pan Am, where I met Don Lane. In those days several snoopers were around before the proper inspection, so all had to be on their toes with the right answers. Nevertheless, you could somehow 'smell them out', and after one such gentleman had cross-questioned me for ages and said he would go away and consider where and when to go, he then asked where he could get the bus to Audley End Station – that was the give away. My husband was working part-time and was going to the bank, so offered to escort him to the High Street to show him the stop (of course he knew why he had come). Anyhow, he (my late husband) was quite nervous about the answers I had given and having left the said gentleman at the bus stop, called at the local hostelry to calm his nerves. Before he could swallow his drink, the aforementioned gentleman was at his elbow; he treated my husband and told him to tell his wife all was well. She was OK.

The actual inspection was done by Don Lane of Pan Am and to my and Mrs Lainson's utter joy, Saffron Walden obtained the first IATA licence in the Group. We had a wonderful party to celebrate and all the Air Reps came. Unfortunately a successor of mine destroyed my scrap books and photographs of this great occasion, so I am unable to produce the 'evidence'.

I left my dear Saffron Walden for about five years, doing training and relief work, but I was delighted to return in a lower capacity to a very different, but still delightful office and was made to feel so welcome, not only by the staff but also by a number of 'old' clients. How gratifying it is to be remembered. Saffron Walden has really gone from strength to strength in spite of losing a couple of big business houses, who went to the wall.

I have certainly enjoyed my twenty-one years with Premier and only wish I had started in travel years before I did.

PREMIER TRAVEL AGENCY

E. Chapman

October 1966 saw my arrival at Premier Travel Agency, Rose Crescent (the premises now occupied by John Peters, opticians), as a 'temp'. I have now been there eighteen years.

I joined as secretary to John Henry Northmore, the first General Manager, and Renford Sargent,

who is now a Director of the Group, but at that time was Manager of the Cambridge Branch. John Northmore had only preceded me by about a month and came to Premier from Frames Tours, bringing with him a wealth of experience. It must have taken great courage for John Northmore, who was in his mid-fifties, to uproot himself from a company in which he had worked for many years, and join a company where much was expected of him, and indeed obtained from him. There is no doubt he played an important part in laying the foundation of the growth of PTA to its present size. He was a well-known figure in the travel industry and was respected by all who had contact with him. Sadly, John Northmore died in 1971, whilst still with the Premier Group; it was a great pleasure to have known and worked with him.

Mrs Lainson then took the PTA reins again for a spell, subsequently handing over to John Tyler, who was with the Company for only a short time. A trio of Peter Andrews, Renford Sargent and Vicky Lainson then took over. How the little rooms at 15 Market Hill resounded with the fiery, though constructive meetings held there. Time progressed and eventually Vicky flew off to Australia to marriage and a son, Renford Sargent was promoted to General Manager and together with Peter Andrews set about expanding PTA to the prestigious Company it has now become.

During my eighteen years with the Premier 'family' (what a true ring there is to Mr Lainson's pet word), I have seen the number of travel agency branches grow from 7 to 14 and witnessed the birth of our tour operating sections, offering holidays to America, the Channel Islands, China, India and 'Faraway' to all points East. This explosion has instigated the setting up of yet another Company within the Premier Group, Premier Holidays; the up-dating of the Premier fleet of coaches to incorporate the high-specification vehicles demanded these days by the travelling public; the arrival of those gurgling, squeaking computers (I will honestly admit I quickly sidle past them with eyes averted as this age of computer technology leaves me cold); and the building of our new coach depot at Kilmaine Close.

On a note of celebration, the Company was delighted to share with Mr E.A. Lainson the honour bestowed on him when he was awarded the OBE in 1976, and the splendid 65th birthday dinner held for him in the same year in Cambridge. People in the transport world from all over the UK came to join the festivities. How magnificent was the birthday cake in the shape of a Premier bus, down to the smallest detail, created by the chef.

[Incidentally, Mrs Cherry Orchard enjoyed enormously the honour of speaking on behalf of PTA at the dinner.] Another happy occasion was the 50th birthday party of Mr Frank Matthews held in Harston Village Hall. Both of these functions were arranged by a committee of representatives from all sections of the Premier group.

There have, of course, been some sadder moments during this time – the death of many of my colleagues in the Company, particularly 'Uncle Bert' Hill, Cherry Orchard, Horace Impey, Anne Bailey, with whom I was particularly associated; many happy times were shared wtih them. I remember the departure of the Group's Head Office from 15 Market Hill, where Premier started in 1936. A little of Premier's heart will always remain within those walls.

As I write this, in December 1984, Renford Sargent and Peter Andrews are now Directors of the Premier Travel Group, positions attained with a great deal of hard work, headaches and humour (I secretly like to feel I have played a small part in their success). I am still secretary to Renford, and also to Margaret Camp, his Personal Assistant, and I feel proud to have entered the Company at just about its real expansion stage and seen it grow to attain its present size and reputation.

A VIEW OF PTA

J.J. Morgan

I remember my first days with Premier Travel, just over ten years ago, as Manager of our Bedford office.

Times were very different then. The Bedford office was small and people often used to pass by without noticing it. Customers were few and far between and most bookings came from wardens from the prison opposite. It came as no real surprise that this office was subsequently closed to concentrate on other larger and busier Premier offices.

I can recall, when working in Halstead, ordering a taxi for passengers because our coach had failed to stop and so left them stranded. They were going on a day's outing to Clacton. We therefore rang Colchester to hold the coach until the taxi caught up. However, the taxi driver dashed in to state he could not carry all five passengers, as they were rather elderly, carried walking sticks, and had to travel with their legs outstretched. I therefore got my car and carried the remaining passengers, following the taxi at high speed to Colchester. The

passengers arrived in a rather nervous condition, this being their annual pilgrimage to the seaside. It took almost five minutes to get the old lady in the back seat out of my two-door car; she managed to get her head stuck against the roof and it was not until we had removed her heavy overcoat that we were successful.

On one occasion a lady came into our office to buy a ticket to Christchurch. I said this would be rather expensive and looked up the return air-fare – approximately £800. She then said she had gone last month for approximately £10 return. I then realised she meant Christchurch, Dorset and not New Zealand.

ROSE CRESCENT

N. Morgan

I joined the Company in November 1970, when Anne Bailey was Manageress and Renford Sargent had just set up the Business House Department. These were the days when Mrs Lean wandered between Rose Crescent and Market Hill, wanting to know who had taken her bins. Tom the Labrador would sit on the doorstep gnawing a bone, but a phone call from Panton Street, pressed to his ear, would send him home. Only Cambridge and Saffron Walden had IATA then and the office with its own loo was the exception rather than the rule.

During my first days at PTA, Mary Eyres booked a flight to Germany and took a cheque which 'bounced' and turned out to be stolen. The CID were amused by the thief's sense of humour, as he had given his fictitious address as the Department of Criminology!

John Matthews was at this time teaching decimalisation to us all at Market Hill in small groups. Our slogan was 'Get away with PTA'. At one time I understand an advertising company was commissioned to think up new slogans. The first showed some suitcases with the words 'These old bags have got a new look' and was rejected in case it offended older passengers. The second, 'We'll go as far as you want', also got rejected on the grounds of bad taste.

Anne Bailey's favourite story was of a client who wanted to go to Africa. When she enquired which part of Africa, he replied 'The jungle bit'. Enough to tax the best travel agent! Mr Lainson used to come and help us behind the counter and talk enthusiastically to clients about the Azores and Russian ships.

We also served clients by candlelight in the course of 1974, brought about by Ted Heath's 'three-day week', which resulted in power cuts and coffee brewed over paraffin heaters. The summer that year brought further problems. Court Line collapsed and many Clarkson holiday-makers lost their holidays. There was no 'bond' in those days, although clients eventually got their money back. There was also trouble in Greece that year and the pound was floated for the first time. Mr Lainson would tell me off for saying 'clients' or 'customers', he always insisted (quite rightly) on calling them 'passengers'. I was also given a magazine article to read about Mr Lainson. He had said, 'We can do anything from a fourpenny bus ride to a trip around the world.' It stayed with me.

I encouraged my brother and husband to join the Company. Paul came whilst still at school as a brochure stamper and worked his way through Drummer Street, Rose Crescent, Ely, Ticket Office and Business House. I married John as the opposition in 1973 and converted him the following year. I finally left in January 1976 when expecting Duncan and missed it all very much.

I'm sure I've left a lot out as memories fade, but I've enjoyed reliving it all and writing about it.

17
Forty Years On and a New Board

On 16 January 1976 a special meeting was convened to celebrate the fortieth anniversary of the first Board meeting of Premier Travel Ltd. The Minutes of that first meeting were read by Mr E. A. Lainson, Chairman and co-founder of the Company; the 1936 Minutes had been written by him in his capacity as Company Secretary.

From small beginnings Premier Travel has grown into a substantial Group and it is in recognition of this, and of the merits of the senior management, who have made it so, that the Directors are pleased to announce the following appointments:

Mr R.C.H. Dodkin, Group Secretary, to be a Director of Premier Travel Services Ltd.

Mr M.J. Gifford, T. Eng AMIRTE. Chief Engineer, Premier Travel Services Ltd, to be a Director of that Company.

Mr R.L. Sargent, General Manager, Premier Travel Agency Ltd, to be a Director of that Company.

Mr B.V. Burnett, General Manager, Premier Airlines Ltd, to be a Director of that Company.

Mr G. Bray, to be Traffic Manager (Commercial) of Premier Travel Services Ltd.

In a way, Premier's future began with these fortieth anniversary appointments. They caused an

The new Board, 1976: (left to right, standing) *R.L.S., P.S.A., R.C.H.D., F.N.M., B.V.B.;* (seated) *J.A.M., E.A.L., M.J.G.*

explosion of effort, enthusiasm and adventurous planning and, ten years later, at the end of Premier's fifth decade, they have already brought a rich harvest to the Company and all its members.

It all began with my retirement in 1971, followed by the appointment of J.A.M. and P.S.A. to join E.A.L. and F.N.M. on the Board in 1972. There the four thought about the future, while they watched over the progress of the other young managers. They also pondered over the best way to acknowledge the irredeemable debt owed by Premier to its senior management throughout the history of the Company. They achieved this double on that auspicious day in 1976.

Yet another change took place at the end of that year when, on his 65th birthday, E.A.L. relinquished his Managing Directorship to F.N.M., keeping his role as Chairman of the Company. It was a marvellous birthday because F.N.M. and many others organised a splendid celebration party, even by Premier's high standards, and he was overcome with pride and humility and gratitude. Shortly afterwards he and all his family grew ten feet tall when he was awarded the OBE. ''e be OBE 'e be' became our slogan.

F.N.M., who had for so many years played the part of junior Director quietly and generously, was now head of a lively young team, strengthened by the backing of the senior members. The combination worked wonders. R.L.S.'s PTA world leapt ahead, as his account in Chapter 16 shows. M.J.G. groomed Roy Moore in Premier ways until he was ready to become Chief Engineer in 1983. John Matthews bought the best coaches to be had – not one by one but by the dozen, and so transformed the PTS fleet into one of the most modern and attractive in the country. R.C.H.D. took all the challenges in his stride, only insisting that the new Company Secretary should be ready to take over when he was sixty-five, in May 1981. B.V.B. was ready and is now comfortable in the hot seat. G.B. also felt the need to have a 'clean break' retirement and since his work-load had grown and grown and grown it was an understandable, if much regretted decision. David Hurry has taken part of his place and should have a fine life ahead.

Throughout this fifth decade F.N.M. and P.S.A. have managed together to make money and property work for the Company in a constructive way. Painlessly and practically, the infusion of youth has proved a great stimulus to endeavour; to those of us who were in at the beginning, it seems like a replay of the days when E.A.L., aged twenty-four, began it all and when F.N.M., aged twenty-two, joined him in building our 'beautiful' Company.

King's and Premier, 1983

18
Let the Board Speak

THE FIFTH DECADE

J.A. Matthews

I rejoined the Company in 1969 as Training Officer. Under the rules of the Road Transport Training Board, the levy paid by the Company could be recovered, if proof could be given that members of the staff had received adequate and formal preliminary and updated training for their work. Accordingly I set up classes, organised people to attend courses at High Ercol and increased the overall efficiency of the staff, as well as obtaining substantial repayments of our forced investment in the Training Board. This work enabled me to look into the bus and coach side of Premier Travel and find its strengths and weaknesses, together with the problems of traffic and engineering and the general economics of passenger transport.

I was particularly pleased to be able to work again with Mr Grice and Mr Gifford after so many years and to assist them in finding solutions to the many problems that were around at the time. In the first few years, we were able to persuade the Board to invest in additional vehicles to alleviate some of the inter-hiring, then a major feature of our operations. We were soon able to operate our services mainly with our own updated fleet. This was particularly beneficial since grant-aided vehicles had become available.

During this period Geoff Bray and I spent about three months hard labour looking at the stage carriage services, with a view to preparing packages for the County Councils, who were now in a position to support financially unremunerative rural services. This was done in an unique way, because we became the only company in the country to 'hire' vehicles to the Councils on a 'day-basis', which enabled them to incorporate unremunerative services, extend market-day services and run in-filling journeys as they wished.

I was also able to join the many managerial meetings that G.B. has already mentioned and quickly assimilated an overall picture of the operations of the Company. The private hire department was only ticking over at this period but I could see the potential that was available between contract hours. The emphasis in the early seventies was on the latter work and contracts covered about 30 per cent of our total operations. The proportion occupied by express services was about 37 per cent with stage carriage approximately 26 per cent. Private hire held an insignificant proportion at 7 per cent.

In 1972, after becoming a Director, I was able to participate in the Board's deliberations about future planning and when it was decided a year later to form a subsidiary company, Premier Travel Services, I took responsibility for the operations and economic efficiency of the new company.

We had bought our first grant-aided vehicle in 1971/72, followed by two more in 1972/73 and another two in 1973/74, then we acquired eight new type vehicles in 1975/76 with long-distance passenger appeal. Perhaps the most significant changes we made in our replacement programme were the new type of coach and the colour scheme. The colour changed from our distinctive, rather dull blue to a two-tone blue. The staff balloted for this change and its introduction was a great stimulus to morale. All this prepared us for our future expansion of express services. It also had very satisfactory financial results. Profits in 1976 were ten times those of 1974.

In January 1975, the Company stabilised its administration and engineering at Kilmaine Close, which gave us the opportunity to streamline our services and also a platform from which to expand. It was a great disappontment to us all when we learnt of Frank Grice's decision to leave the Company. It immediately left a very great void in the Traffic Department, which I tried to fill, together with K. Worland, who proved himself to be a great asset.

But the summer of 1975 was extremely difficult for both of us, and through being forced into the hot-seat, I was able to take a more serious view of vehicle productivity. So together, G.B. and I started another exercise, with the help of his excellent records, to reschedule existing services and

The Board and its Directors or why it works so well: (left to right, above) *Mr and Mrs Frank Matthews, Mr and Mrs Bill Burnett;* (below) *Mr and Mrs Renford Sargent, Mr and Mrs John Matthews*

introduce new ones, always, of course, within the restrictions of the stage-carriage grant vehicles.

Between 1976 and 1980 there was continual battle to update the fleet and we recorded in October 1979 that all C registrations had been replaced. It is significant to note that in the first few months of the eighties, ten new Leyland Leopards were introduced, which rejuvenated the fleet in one fell swoop and counteracted the cessation of the AEC. Another result was that during 1980, in spite of losing some passengers, our pvm had increased by 25 per cent.

In 1980, when the new Road Transport Act, with its de-licensing provisions, came into force, we sat on the fence and watched developments in other parts of the industry. However, in order to combat any inroads into our excursion traffic, ECOC, Messrs Youngs of Rampton and PT joined forces under the umbrella of Companion Tours, named by G.B., which operated successfully until disbanded in 1984, when NBC decided not to participate any further. Excursion traffic went up by 60 per cent during the period of Companion Tours' operations.

Another landmark was achieved in 1980 when our turnover exceeded one million pounds, and in 1981 the revenue of private hire escalated by 100 per cent. Of course, much of this success is due to the unique harmony between traffic and engineering in Premier, to an extent that is not always enjoyed by other companies. (Personal friendships do help in our case!) Other aspects of our success were the rail strikes of 1981, which greatly enhanced our opportunity to develop the potential of coaching. The 'Age of the Coach', as we know it today, began at this point. The following year saw Premier's small toe dipped into the deep waters of continental travel, when we sent three coaches to

Spain for a three-week tour, for the World Cup. It also marked the introduction of the new silver and blue livery, suggested by R.L.S., now adopted throughout the Group.

The tour to Spain certainly whetted our appetites for overseas operations and the Board reacted by ordering our first High-line vehicles for the 1983 season and as a result we became heavily involved that year in coach-touring and shuttle services to the South of France and Austria. We celebrated the launching of the 1000th Leyland Tiger on 11 October 1983, at Kilmaine Close – this was our fourth High-liner.

In 1983 we acquired, in addition, four Leyland Tiger express coaches to cope with our involvement in limited stop service with ECOC and the heavy involvement with National Express on Service 5, now identified as Service 905, in which Premier enjoys a substantial majority holding.

Our express service operations were further developed in 1984 with the introduction of the Premier/Yelloway 879 Service, twice daily, between Cambridge, Manchester and Rochdale, in both directions. In the latter part of 1984 we concluded negotiations on pooling the Premier/Percivals Cambridge–Oxford Service 39 into the new and extensive National Express Yarmouth–Bristol Service 747, in which Premier and Percivals enjoy a substantial holding. The year closed with a tremendous upsurge in express mileage, and the introduciton of our first MCW Metroliner.

With an increase of some 42 per cent in our operational mileage in two years, and the prospect of further development, we had to look for assistance. In March 1985 Barry Parsison joined us as Manager of our new Coach Tours Division, with a brief to break into the coach holiday market. Who better than Barry, coming from National Holidays, to set up our Coaching Holiday Programme for Autumn 1985/Spring 1986 and Summer 1986? Ian Roberts, who left United Northern Coaching Division in April 1985 to join us as Assistant General Manager, has brought assistance in the increased volume of administration, in the enhancement of our image and in the installation of new systems. Both Barry and Ian have a strong, secure platform on which to continue building.

In May 1985 we introduced second-hand double-deckers to cope with the increased number of passengers on certain stage routes, thus making operational economies. These vehicles are also used to advertise to the general public the many travel opportunities offered by the Premier Travel Group. Three more MCW Metroliners joined the fleet in May and June and a Royal Tiger in July, bringing the total fleet to 64.

Building on the foundations cemented during the 40s, 50s and 60s has been easy, because the direction was always sure and steadfast. Without the stalwarts of the older driving, engineering and administrative staff, coupled with excellent younger serving staff members, Premier could not have

Three good men and true: (left to right) *D. Hurry, Bob Read, D. Rule*

Hope for the future, 1984 teenagers: (left to right, back) *Mark West, Richard Gower;* (centre) *Kevin Jay, Louise Silk;* (front) *Richard Rutherford, Darren Lebbon*

won and retained the respect of the industry during the last fifty years. We look forward to 1986, our Golden Jubilee, and wonder what might be in store for the next decade.

CELEBRATIONS

E.A. Lainson

The first christening of a Premier vehicle took place in April 1950. It was our first 53-seater, Daimler double-decker luxury coach and was named 'County of Cambridgeshire' by Alderman E.G. Gordon-Frost, Chairman of Cambridgeshire County Council, in the presence of the Eastern Area Traffic Commissioner, Sir Alfred Faulkner, and members of his staff. A luncheon at the University Arms Hotel was attended by Mr R.S. Crouch of Transport Vehicles (Daimler) Ltd, Mr G. Nowell and Mr Haggerty of Wilks and Meade, together with a large company of staff, shareholders and others. We all thoroughly enjoyed the occasion and were very grateful to the County for giving us their support. The registration number of this vehicle was HVE 401 and its sister vehicles, HVE 402 and 403, were later named 'County of Essex' and 'County of West Suffolk', with the consent of the authorities concerned.

After an interval of more than thirty years, the Directors placed an order with MCW Ltd for four Metroliner coaches with Cummins engines. These vehicles are of integral construction, which gives greater stability, weight reduction and consequently more comfort for passengers. We wrote to Cambridge City Council asking whether the Mayor of Cambridge would consent to christen the first vehicle 'City of Cambridge'. Councillor E. Cowell, the Mayor, most kindly agreed to do this for us and we had a short ceremony outside the Guildhall on 1 February 1985. This was followed by a buffet lunch in the coach on the Gog-Magog Hills, from which the Mayor, his wife and some of his staff were able to obtain a bird's eye view of their city. We greatly appreciated their co-operation on this day.

Our third christening was performed by the Lord Mayor of Birmingham, Councillor Reginald Hales, outside the Council House on Friday 10 May 1985, in the presence of representatives of Premier Travel, MCW Ltd, Stuart Johnson Ltd and the press. It is noteworthy that John Parke, representing the technical press, had been present at our first naming ceremony thirty years before. Following the ceremony, we were entertained by the Birmingham City Council to a buffet lunch at which the Lord Mayor was present. We were then taken on a tour of the City Hall, through all the principal rooms, redolent with history, including the Birmingham City Museum.

Apart from this being the first Civic Lunch to which Premier representatives had been invited, the whole occasion was both memorable and full of interest. We felt very privileged to be welcomed in such a signal fashion. Reference was made to the fact that MCW, as manufacturers, and Premier, as operators, had very long associations with Birmingham and the West Midlands.

This occasion formed a fitting climax to nearly fifty years of effort.

Christening of the 'County of Cambridgeshire' by the Chairman of Cambridgeshire County Council, 1950

THE SUMMING UP

F.N. Matthews

Some may hold the view that to devote the whole of one's working life to one company must produce a narrow, limited field of vision. This cannot be further from the facts if the organisation that one has been exclusively involved with is similar to the Premier Travel Group.

I was reminded only last year, in a strangely roundabout way, of my first tangible link with Premier when I received a letter from a Mr D.J. Bright of Faversham, Kent. He told me that he had recently read Noel Millier's article in the *Commercial Motor*, 'Premier believes British is premier', and recalled that in August 1946, as an orderly corporal attached to the BAOR at Bad Oeynhausen, he had typed my first letters to Arthur Lainson. It was certainly dereliction of Army duty on both our parts, although we may be

excused, perhaps, as our task there was almost at an end and young minds tended to look eagerly to a new and somewhat unknown future.

The saga of Premier's progress has been splendidly presented in the preceding pages by many of those who have also spent most of their working lives with Premier. I will not attempt to add to their story in general. Instead, I offer my version of some of the turning points and salient milestones that have marked the long, often turbulent, almost always uphill route that has led successfully to Premier's Golden Jubilee.

Arthur Lainson regularly reminds us that 'It's all about people', and there is no doubt that the many people connected with the Company in various capacities over the years have made it what it is today. At a very early stage in the life of Premier it was decided to ask the staff to elect their own representatives to act on their behalf in negotiations with the Board on wages and conditions. This practice, with one or two minor diversions, has been maintained to this day, and has been accompanied by a long history of loyalty, dedication and resolution. This was aptly illustrated as recently as April 1985 when, in an effort to assist the Company to retain long-established contract bus services in the face of cut-price competition, the staff voluntarily offered to defer their annual wage award for one year.

On the theme of loyalty, it is worth mentioning that since its formation, emergencies excepted, Premier has been served by only one major supplier of fuel (Shell), one banker (Lloyds), one firm of accountants since the Companies Act 1948 (Slater, Dominy and Swann/Spicer and Pegler), one estate agent (Douglas L. January and Partners) and basically by only two insurance companies (Phoenix and Cornhill). Long established connections with other professional bodies and with suppliers have cemented a firm foundation of mutual understanding and trust.

Much has been written of the growth and expansion of Premier Travel Agency; but the quite unforeseen spin-off to the Group as a whole must be recorded. Gradually, then in an increasing flood, came the splendid surge of a cash flow that dispelled all liquidity problems. Coaches and buses, properties and plant we purchased without incurring the often penal interest charges that borrowed money attracts. Moreover, we were, for the first time, in a position to pay promptly and regularly, thereby demonstrating both confidence and stability to our bankers, creditors, competitors and the business world in general. Not least important was the visible enhancement of the Group image, which attracted tangible advantages from many quarters.

It has been said that success is never won without the risk of failure and that the greatest achievements have been won by taking the greatest risks. Certainly Premier has never been afraid of failure, as may be illustrated by one or two examples.

In 1965, in order to secure the ground floor shop of No. 7 Rose Crescent with a frontage of just ten feet, we had to commit ourselves to a lease of the whole ground and first floor unit at a substantial rent. This financial burden had to be borne for two years before we were able to sub-let the whole of the first floor on a nourishing profit basis. Similarly, the decision to purchase the freehold land and to build the comprehensive Kilmaine Close engineering complex in 1974/6 required great resolution and no small measure of bravery at a time when our resources were more than stretched. It is ironic to reflect that far less courage was required in 1984 to embark upon the substantial property developments now in progress.

One of the principal tenets of Premier's progress has been the exemplary strength and unity of leadership displayed by those in command at all levels. The old sergeant major's saying, 'Don't do what I do – do what I tell you to do', has never been acceptable within Premier. Having the courage to change the tactical emphasis without losing strategic direction has been one of the mainstays of our flexible but firm leadership. This has been proved again and again over the years and recent events provide a shining example of this policy in practice. Deregulation in 1980 led to major shifts of power within the public and private sectors of the bus and coach industry, including the formation of British Coachways. To a traditionally independent company such as Premier, the challenges of this new era were both appealing and exciting, although the uncertainties were well signposted. Having borne the heat and burden of cross-subsidisation and the slow but steady build-up of our express services network, with and without joint operators, it was decided that the opportunities for expansion presented by delicensing should be pursued within the existing long established and well tried framework.

Further, although the strength of the Group has led to the temptation to diversify beyond the sphere of travel and transport, we have consistently maintained a firm resolve to stay with what we know and do best. In any event, what broader, more consuming and fulfilling function can there be than the movement of people by all forms of transport, for business or pleasure?

Reaching the pinnacle of our Golden Jubilee not only enables us to look back and reflect upon the steep path we have climbed and to savour the view with the contentment of a job well done; it also provides a vantage point from which to view the route ahead. The next peak along our journey can clearly be seen across the intervening plateau, and plans for achieving our objectives for the next decade are already well-laid. May we be privileged to record a similar success story when marking the Diamond Jubilee of Premier's progress in 1996.

PROSPECT

E.A. Lainson

After half a century in passenger movement one's early impressions may be expected to have changed materially.

Meeting the staff of Harston and District Motor Services in 1936 made me realise, not for the first time, that the one cardinal essential for success and happiness is the team spirit – people count.

Nothing that has happened over the years has changed this view.

We at Premier have been extremely fortunate in having been able to gather together, in increasing numbers, a team of men and women who have given loyalty and good will to our passengers and to the Company.

There are good reasons for their spirit – interest in their often very demanding job and lack of carping criticism on the lines of 'them and us'. It should always be 'we' and almost always has been thus.

A glance at the Honours Board of long service members (see p. 79) is the surest testimonmial to the family spirit. The biggest challenge to management and staff in the years ahead is the preservation of this spirit.

Another factor is looking on the bright side, which is sometimes difficult. Our attitude, even in dark days, has always been that the glass is half full, not half empty.

141

Appendixes

1
Summary of the Premier Travel Group, 1936–86

1936	Premier Travel Limited	Founded
	Undergraduate Roadways	Incorporated
	Harston and District Motor Services	Incorporated
	Royal Blue Coaches, Cambridge	Incorporated
1945	Weeden's Motor Services	Acquired
1946	Gill's Motor Services	Acquired
1947	Drayton's Motor Services	Acquired
	W.H. Thorne, Clacton (Service 35)	Acquired
1949	Long's Coaches, West Wratting	Acquired
	G.F. Burgoin (Haverhill) Limited (trading as Grey Pullman Coaches)	Acquired
1952	Allenways Limited (Service 67)	Acquired
1960	Premier Airlines Limited	Incorporated
1964	Premier Travel Agency Limited	Incorporated
1973	Premier Travel Group	Incorporated
	Premier Travel Services Limited	Incorporated
1978	Premier Transport Limited (dormant co.)	Incorporated
	Thetford Travel Limited (dormant co.)	Acquired
1982	Study China Travel Limited	Acquired
1983	Percivals Anglia Limited (dormant co.)	Acquired
1984	Premier Holidays Limited	Incorporated

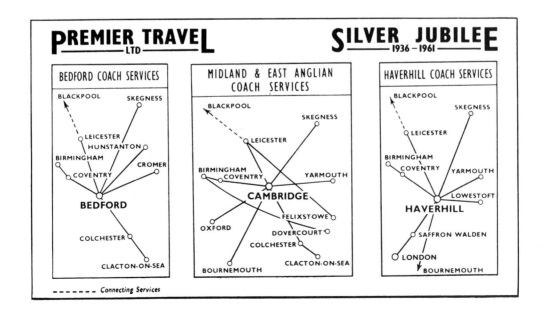

2
Directors and Company Secretaries

Sir Christopher Magnay	Chairman	1936–38
Capt. C.J.P. Kirk	Director	1936–38
E.A. Lainson	Director	1936–
	Company Secretary	1936–39
	Chairman	1938–86
	Group Chairman	1973–76
	Managing Director	1943–76
	Group Managing Director	1973–76
N.C.P. Thompson	Director	1936–44
	Managing Director	1936–43
	Company Secretary	1939–43
R.A. Howard	Company Secretary	1943–48
	Director	1943–48
M.M.E. Lainson	Director	1943–71
	Managing Director (PTA)	1964–71
W.F. Matthews	Director	1944–59
F.N. Matthews	Director	1948–
	Company Secretary	1948–60
	Managing Director (PAL)	1960–
	Group Managing Director	1976–
J.A. Matthews	Director	1972–
	Group Director	1973–
	Director (PTS)	1973–
P.S. Andrews	Director	1972–
	Group Finance Director	1973–
R.C.H. Dodkin	Company Secretary	1960–81
	Director (PTS)	1976–81
	Group Company Secretary	1973–81
M.J. Gifford	Director (PTS)	1976–
B.V. Burnett	Director (PAL)	1976–
	Group Company Secretary	1981–
R.L. Sargent	Director (PTA)	1976–
	Group Director	1982–

3
Club 25 Members

Name	Dates	Years Service
E.A. Lainson	1936–86	50
S.E. Pennell	1936–80	44
H. Bird	1937–70	33
F.R. Barker	1937–82	45
M.M.E. Lainson	1939–71	32
M.J. Gifford	1941–86	45
F.A. Grice	1942–75	33
E.W. Day	1945–80	35
H. Law	1945–76	32
A. Wisbey	1945–86	41
H.F.W. Wynn	1946–72	26
R.C.H. Dodkin	1946–81	35
M. Francis (Mrs)	1947–83	36
H.W. Lee	1947–86	39
E.P. Law	1947–73	26
S.J. Law	1947–86	39
F.N. Matthews	1947–86	39
A.W. Reeves	1947–75	28
W.J. Aldous	1948–86	38
G. Bray	1949–82	33
R. Scarr	1949–86	37
R. Scrivener	1949–86	37
W. Ruffle	1949–80	31
R. Roope	1949–86	37
C. Jaggard	1949–78	29
J.B. Gower	1949–86	37
R. Mumby	1951–86	35
A.W. Hill	1951–81	30
N. Bell	1953–86	33
R. Baker	1953–86	33
H.J. Impey	1954–81	27
L. South	1956–86	30
H. Bernardini (Mrs)	1957–86	29
C. A. Sadler	1960–86	26
F. J. Gogin	1960–86	26

Total number of years served 1206

4
Premier Travel Agency

Premier Travel Agency and Premier Airlines 10-Year Service Members

Mrs H. Orchard	1958–84	Mr R. Barker	1972
Mrs A. Kerr	1964	Mr R. Pool	1973
Mr R.L. Sargent	1965	Miss L. Dowling	1973
Mrs S. Brennan	1966	Mrs A. Parker	1973
Mrs E. Chapman	1966	Mr I. Slater	1973
Mr B. Burnett	1967	Mrs V. Titmarsh	1973
Mrs C. Toyer	1967–82	Mrs P. Constable	1973
Mr S. Dartford	1971	Mrs J. Cripps	1974
Mrs P. Claridge	1971–83	Mr J. Morgan	1974
Mr C. Parish	1971	Mrs A. Smith	1974
Mr C. Camp	1971	Mr R. Cane	1975
Mrs M. Fereday	1972	Mrs J. Curtis	1975

Opening Dates of PTA Offices

	1st Office	2nd Office	3rd Office
Saffron Walden	March 1947	1966	
Huntingdon	May 1947	1968	1976
Haverhill	July 1949	1970	1978
Drummer Street, Cambridge	September 1952		
Rose Crescent, Cambridge	September 1956	1966	1976
Royston	September 1958	1971	
Letchworth	March 1965		
Peterborough	March 1969 (Discontinued)		
Ely	January 1970		
Bedford	December 1970 (Discontinued)		
St Ives	April 1971	1974	
Ware	June 1971 (Discontinued)		
Halstead	November 1972	1983	
Ramsey	October 1972 (Discontinued)		
Mildenhall	December 1973	1984	
Swaffham	October 1974	1983	
Thetford	January 1978		
Bishop's Stortford	May 1980		

5
Stage Carriage Services, January 1985

Service No.	Route	Acquired From	Date
1	Cambridge–Harston–Fowlmere–Royston	Harston Motor Services	1936
2[1]	Cambridge–Harston–Barrington–Royston	Harston Motor Services	1936
9	Cambridge–Sawston–Ickleton–Chishill	Weeden's Motor Services	1945
10	Arkesden–Clavering–Bishop's Stortford	Weeden's Motor Services	1945
11	Saffron Walden–Clavering–Wendon Lofts	Weeden's Motor Services	1945
*12	Duxford–Fowlmere–Melbourn–Royston	Premier Travel	–
*14	Saffron Walden First Town Service	Premier Travel	1959
*16[2]	Royston Town Service	Premier Travel	–
26	Royston–Barley–Pelhams–Bishop's Stortford	Drayton's Motor Services	1947
*27	Royston–Barkway–Brent Pelham–Royston	Premier Travel	–
*28	Barley–Buntingford	Premier Travel	–
*29[3]	Linton–Hadstock–Saffron Walden	Premier Travel/Viceroy	–
38	Haverhill–Radwinter–Saffron Walden	Grey Pullman	1949
43	Royston–Elmdon–Saffron Walden	Drayton's Motor Services	1947
44/45	Haverhill–Kedington–Balsham–Cambridge	Long's Coaches	1949
46	Linton–West Wratting–Newmarket	Long's Coaches	1949
49	Weston Colville–Haverhill	Long's Coaches	1949
52	Haverhill Town Service (2)	Premier Travel	1969
54	Haverhill Town Service (1)	Premier Travel	1960
55	Haverhill–The Thurlows–Bury St Edmunds	Grey Pullman	1949
56	Haverhill–Great Bradley–Newmarket	Grey Pullman	1949
*57	Haverhill Town Service (3)	Premier Travel	–
59	Haverhill–Saffron Walden–Audley End (rail replacement)	Premier Travel	1964
60–9	School contracts, also available to the public	Premier Travel	–

Notes: * New services using former service numbers
[1] Joint service with ECOC
[2] Joint service with H.V. Richmond
[3] Joint service with Viceroy Coaches

Discontinued services. Since our main expansion in 1947 and 1949 a great many changes in stage carriage operation have taken place, notably the withdrawal of all the Huntingdon services (17–22, 24–5) in 1975. Amalgamations of a number of rural routes have rationalised the services required in the eighties and the streamlined network detailed above should be able to withstand all political changes

148

6
Long-Distance and Express Services, January 1985

Service No.	Route	Acquired From	Date
3	Haverhill–Cambridge–Boston–Skegness	Undergraduate Roadways	1933
4	Huntingdon–Cambridge–Norwich–Yarmouth–Hemsby	Royal Blue	1936
5[1]	Birmingham–Leicester–Cambridge–Clacton	Empire's Best	1937
34	Luton–Bedford–Boston–Skegness	Premier Travel	1949
*37	Cambridge–Saffron Walden–Bishop's Stortford–Gatwick–Brighton	Premier Travel	New
38	Haverhill–Bishop's Stortford–London–Heathrow	Grey Pullman	1949
39[2]	Cambridge–Hitchin–Luton–Oxford	Premier Travel/Percivals	1948
40[3]	Northampton–Bedford–Hunstanton–Cromer	Premier Travel/Yorks Travel	1959
72	Haverhill–Cambridge–Southampton–Bournemouth	Premier Travel	1957
74[4]	Clacton–Cambridge–Leicester–Blackpool (1)	Premier Travel/Yelloway	
79	Cambridge–Stevenage–West London–Heathrow	Premier Travel	1964
83[5]	Ipswich–Cardiff, Eastlander joint service	Premier Travel/Others	1964
88[6]	Hemel Hempstead–Luton–Carlisle–Glasgow	Premier Travel/WSMT	
89[6]	Cambridge–Bedford–Northampton–Glasgow	Premier Travel/WSMT	

New numberings introduced in the seventies for pool services

355[7]	Colchester–Cambridge–Nottingham–Sheffield–Leeds		
747[2]	Lowestoft–Yarmouth–Norwich–Cambridge–Bedford–Oxford–Swindon–Bristol		
747[2]	Lowestoft–Cambridge–Hitchin–Luton–Aylesbury–Oxford–Swindon–Bristol		
747[2]	Cambridge–Bedford–Milton Keynes–Oxford–Cheltenham–Gloucester		
783[5]	Ipswich–Chelmsford–Harlow–Stevenage–Aylesbury–Oxford–Newport–Cardiff		
876[4]	Cambridge–Bedford–Northampton–Leicester–Preston–Blackpool		
877[4]	Clacton–Cambridge–Leicester–Derby–Manchester–Oldham–Rochdale–Blackburn		
878[4]	Clacton–Cambridge–Northampton–Derby–Manchester–Bolton–Preston–Blackpool		
879[4]	Cambridge–Bedford–Leicester–Derby–Bolton–Rochdale		
905[1]	Birmingham–Coventry–Northampton–Bedford–Cambridge–Clacton/Norwich–Yarmouth		
792[8]	Felixstowe–Ipswich–Bury St Edmunds–Cambridge–Peterborough		

Notes:
* New service using former service number
Key to joint operators:
[1] National Express
[2] Percival Motors (Oxford) Ltd and National Express
[3] Yorks Travel Ltd, Northampton
[4] Yelloway Motor Services Ltd
[5] Tourmaster Coaches, Grey–Green Coaches and National Express
[6] Western SMT Co. Ltd
[7] Yelloway Motor Services Ltd and National Express
[8] Ambassador Travel Ltd, formerly ECOC

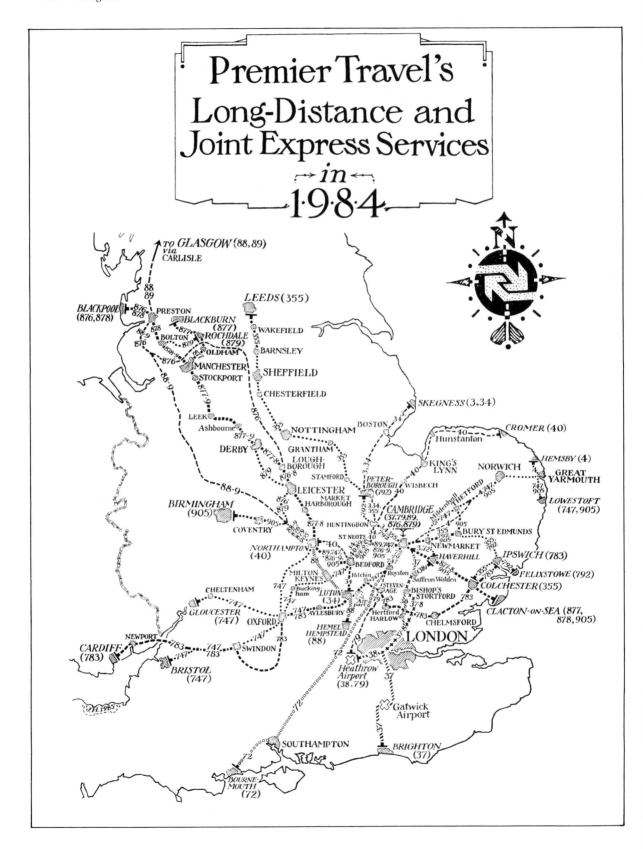

Service No.	Route	Acquired From	Date

Discontinued services (1985)

Service No.	Route	Acquired From	Date
6	Great Chishill–Saffron Walden–Clacton	Weeden's Motor Services	1945
7	Heydon–Chrishall–Clavering–London	Weeden's Motor Services	
28	Chrishall–Heydon–Barley–London	Drayton's Motor Services	1947
35	Clacton–London	W.H. Thorne	1949
37	Berden–Saffron Walden–Lowestoft–Yarmouth	Premier Travel	1950
65	Ramsey–Huntingdon–Cambridge–Southend	Premier Travel	1952
66	Newton–Saffron Walden–Haverhill–Ipswich–Felixstowe	Premier Travel	1952
67	Birmingham–Coventry–Harwich–Dovercourt	Allenways Coaches	1952
70	Leicester–Felixstowe	Premier Travel	1953
71	Worcester–Cambridge–Clacton	Premier Travel	1956
76	Kidderminster–Clacton	Premier Travel	1962
80	Cambridge–Luton Airport	Premier Travel	1964
82	Harwich–Bangor via Stonebridge	Premier Travel/Midland Red	1965
81	Cambridge–Ilfracombe	Premier Travel	1964

7
Operational Fleet, January 1936– December 1955

(With grateful thanks to PSV Circle Publication No. R.F. 2 for valuable corroboration)

Date Acquired	Reg. No.	No. of Seats	Make	Body	Original Operator
Jan. 1936	VE 3002	14	Reo	–	Harston Motor Services
Jan. 1936	VE 4993	30	Gilford 1680T	–	Harston Motor Services
Jan. 1936	VE 8761	20	Gilford AF6	–	Harston Motor Services
Jan. 1936	VE 855	26	Reo 26	–	Harston Motor Services
Jan. 1936	WG 334	32	Gilford 1680T	Wycombe	Harston Motor Services
Jan. 1936	YE 439D	28	ADC	–	Royal Blue Coaches
Jan. 1936	VE 919	29	Maudsley	–	Royal Blue Coaches
Dec. 1936	BVE 668	25	Bedford WTB	Duple	New to Premier Travel
Mar. 1937	WG 1284[1]	32	Gilford 1680T	Wycombe	W. Alexander
May 1937	CCE 568	35	Dennis Lancet	Duple	New to Premier Travel
June 1938	HX 4364	20	Gilford AS6	Duple	Crouch End Luxury Coaches
Feb. 1941	TF 1555[2]	32	Leyland TS1	Alexander	Rowe of Cudworth
Feb. 1941	TM 8465[3]	30	Gilford 1680T	–	Strawhatters of Luton
Sept. 1943	ECE 879	28	Bedford OWB	Duple	New to Premier Travel
Jan. 1944	ECE 948	28[4]	Bedford OWB	Duple	New to Premier Travel
Sept. 1944	EER 242	28[4]	Bedford OWB	Duple	New to Premier Travel
Sept. 1944	MO 8513[5]	30	Dennis	Duple	Windsorian Coaches
Aug. 1945	EER 570[6]	32	Bedford OWB	Duple	New to Premier Travel
Sept. 1945	BCE 372[7]	20	Albion Victor	Duple	Weeden's Motor Services
Sept. 1945	CUR 921[8]	26	Albion PK114	–	Weeden's Motor Services
Sept. 1945	EER 99	28[4]	Bedford OWB	Duple	Weeden's Motor Services
Sept. 1945	ECE 794	28[4]	Bedford OWB	Mulliner	Weeden's Motor Services
Sept. 1945	CVE 12	32	Dennis Lancet	Duple	Weeden's Motor Services
Sept. 1945	CVE 424	20	Bedford WTB	Duple	Weeden's Motor Services
Sept. 1945	WG 1273	32	Gilford 1680T	Wycombe	Weeden's Motor Services
May 1946	MJ 2154	32	Gilford Hera	–	Gill's Motor Services
May 1946	WG 329	32	Gilford 1680T	–	Gill's Motor Services
May 1946	EW 7332	20	Bedford WLB	–	Gill's Motor Services
May 1946	JF 2725	20	Bedford WLB	–	Gill's Motor Services
July 1946	AG 6221	33	Leyland TS1	Alexander	Western SMT
July 1946	GJ 5124	28	Leyland TS3	United	Mascot of Norwich
Feb. 1947	FER 241	32	Bedford OB	Duple	New to Premier Travel
May 1947	ENK 387[9]	32	Dennis Lancet	Duple	Drayton's Motor Services
May 1947	DRO 972	20	Dennis Pike	Duple	Drayton's Motor Services
May 1947	JH 4429	20	Gilford AS 6	Duple	Drayton's Motor Services
May 1947	CWD 840	26	Bedford WTB	Duple	Drayton's Motor Services
May 1947	WG 1286	31	Gilford 1680T	Wycombe	Drayton's Motor Services
May 1947	FD 9601[10]	26	Leyland SKP 3	–	Drayton's Motor Services
May 1947	BFD 955[11]	32	Bedford WTB	–	Drayton's Motor Services

Date Acquired	Reg. No.	No. of Seats	Make	Body	Original Operator
May 1947	BAJ 161	26	Bedford WTB	Plaxton	Drayton's Motor Services
Jan. 1948	GCE 442	31	Bedford OB	Mulliner	New to Premier Travel
Jan. 1948	GCE 654[12]	33	Daimler CVD6	Wilks & Meade	New to Premier Travel
Jan. 1948	GCE 655	33	Daimler CVD6	Wilks & Meade	New to Premier Travel
Apr. 1948	BU 7601[13]	54	Leyland TD 2	Eng. Elec.	Oldham Corporation
June 1948	GER 422	29	Bedford OB	Duple	New to Premier Travel
Aug. 1948	DW 6924	48	Leyland TD 2	–	Red & White Motor Services
Aug. 1948	DW 6944	48	Leyland TD 2	–	Red & White Motor Services
Oct. 1948	GER 217	35	Dennis Lancet	Duple	New to Premier Travel
Oct. 1948	GER 140	33	Leyland PS1/1	Wilks & Meade	New to Premier Travel
Jan. 1949	GER 141	33	Leyland PS1/1	Wilks & Meade	New to Premier Travel
Jan. 1949	GER 834	33	Leyland PS1/1	Wilks & Meade	New to Premier Travel
Apr. 1949	GER 835	33	Leyland PS1/1	Wilks & Meade	New to Premier Travel
Apr. 1948	JY 6739	48	Leyland TD 4	Weymann	Plymouth Corporation
Apr. 1949	JO 8456	48	AEC Regent	Weymann	Long's Coaches
Apr. 1949	JO 8663	52	AEC Regent	Weymann	Long's Coaches
Apr. 1949	AOP 777	54	Daimler COG	Birmingham RCW	Long's Coaches
Dec. 1949	GV 2405	32	Gilford Hera	Duple	Grey Pullman
Dec. 1949	ACF 272	29	Bedford DB	Duple	Grey Pullman
Dec. 1949	ACF 672	29	Bedford DB	Thurgood	Grey Pullman
Dec. 1949	AGF 194	29	Bedford DB	Duple	Grey Pullman
Dec. 1949	BGV 261	29	Bedford DB	Duple	Grey Pullman
Dec. 1949	BGV 401	35	AEC Regal	Willowbrook	Grey Pullman
Dec. 1949	BGV 719	29	Bedford OB	Duple	Grey Pullman
Dec. 1949	CS 4326	27	Leyland SKB 2	Burlingham	Grey Pullman
Dec. 1949	HA 9797	20	Bush & Twiddy	–	Grey Pullman
Dec. 1949	GV 5160	26	Bedford WTB	Duple	Grey Pullman
Dec. 1949	GV 9861	32	Bedford OB	Duple	Grey Pullman
Dec. 1949	GV 5552	26	Bedford WTB	Duple	Grey Pullman
Dec. 1949	GV 8751	32	Bedford OB	Mulliner	Grey Pullman
Apr. 1950	HVE 36[14]	35	Dennis Lancet	Mulliner	New to Premier Travel
Apr. 1950	HVE 242	29	Bedford OB	Mulliner	New to Premier Travel
Apr. 1950	HVE 401[15]	53	Daimler CVD 6	Wilks & Meade	New to Premier Travel
May 1950	HVE 707	35	Dennis Lancet	Duple	New to Premier Travel
June 1950	HVE 402[16]	53	Daimler CVD 6	Wilks & Meade	New to Premier Travel
July 1950	HVE 403[17]	53	Daimler CVD 6	Wilks & Meade	New to Premier Travel
Nov. 1951	JY 3642	48	Leyland TD 3	Weymann	Plymouth Corporation
Jan. 1952	ANT 471	35	Dennis Lancet	Yeates	Salopia Coaches
May 1952	FTD 195	55	Daimler CWG	Brush	Haslingden Corporation
Oct. 1952	CVP 438	54	AEC Regent	Metro-Cammell	Birmingham Corporation
Jan. 1953	BGA 60	56	Leyland TD 5	Metro-Cammell	Glasgow Corporation
July 1953	HWA 277	56	Leyland TD 7	NCB	Sheffield Corporation
Nov. 1953	BLH 887	52	AEC Regent	LPTB	London Transport Executive
Nov. 1953	CXX 380	56	AEC Regent	LPTB	London Transport Executive
Jan. 1954	DLU 225[18]	55	AEC Regent	LPTB	London Transport Executive
Mar. 1954	DGX 285	56	AEC Regent	LPTB	London Transport Executive
June 1954	DLU 227[18,19]	55	AEC Regent	LPTB	London Transport Executive
June 1954	DLU 242	55	AEC Regent	LPTB	London Transport Executive
Nov. 1954	ECP 138	56	AEC Regent	LPTB	London Transport Executive
Dec. 1954	DYL 827	56	AEC Regent	LPTB	London Transport Executive
July 1955	DGX 195	56	AEC Regent	LPTB	London Transport Executive

Date Acquired	Reg. No.	No. of Seats	Make	Body	Original Operator
Oct. 1955	DGG 916	56	Daimler CWA6	NCME	Glasgow Corporation
Nov. 1955	GNN 664	56	Daimler CWA6	Duple	Mansfield DT
Nov. 1955	GNN 665	56	Daimler CWA6	Duple	Mansfield DT
Nov. 1955	CCX 651	55	Daimler CWA6	Duple	Huddersfield Corporation
Dec. 1955	CCX 652	55	Daimler CWA6	Brush	Huddersfield Corporation

Notes

[1] Burnt out near Foxton Station in July 1944

[2] The first Leyland owned

[3] Bought for £50 from a travelling salesman and was called Tom Mix because it leapt forward when starting

[4] Utility Bedford with wooden seats

[5] Used Normal Control, i.e. driver not in cab

[6] First non-utility Bedford in Britain

[7] Stripped of seats and engine and used as an office at Godmanchester until May 1956

[8] Presented to Cambridge County Council Road Safety Committee in January 1952 for use as a demonstration bus

[9] Sold to Messrs Flatt of Long Sutton

[10] First rear entrance type owned

[11] Sold to A. Keyner of Aylsham

[12] First Daimler owned

[13] First double-decker owned

[14] Originally ordered by A. Drayton of Barley in 1947

[15] A luxury double-decker christened 'County of Cambridgeshire' at a ceremony at the University Arms Hotel

[16] A luxury double-decker christened 'County of West Suffolk', without ceremony

[17] A luxury double-decker christened 'County of Essex', without ceremony

[18] Built with special bodies for the Blackwall Tunnel

[19] Withdrawn from public service and converted to a 'tree-lopper'

8
Fleet Additions, January 1956–January 1985

Date	Registration Numbers	Remarks
1956	No purchases made	
1957	GUF 130, 131, 136, 157, 190, 394	Six second-hand double-deckers
1958	GUF 173; CDR 748, 750, 756	Four second-hand double-deckers
	HOM 677; KGY 940	Two second-hand AEC coaches
1959	GKP 262, 266, 656; BWY 979, 986, 993	Six second-hand double-deckers
	UVE 333	New AEC Reliance coach
1960	BWY 985, 988; BTR 312; CWX 667; FWX 821	Five second-hand double-deckers
	XMT 54, 55, 56	Three second-hand AEC coaches
1961	LKK 863, 859	Two second-hand double-deckers
	TMM 829; GFU 700; MKL 511; 138 EMF; LKT 993, 998, 999	Eight second-hand AEC coaches
1962	DCK 204, 205, 206, 208, 211, 212, 214, 215, 217, 218	Ten second-hand Leyland double-deckers with enclosed platforms
	LKT 984; XHN 573; 201 EMP	Three second-hand AEC coaches
1963	UDK 313, 314; UAF 281; 772 EMU; 199 EMP; 86 UME; 75, 76 TML	Eight second-hand AEC coaches
1964	AVE 444B, 555B	Two new AEC Reliance Coaches, 11 metres
	LUC 202, 203, 204, 206, 207, 208, 209, 211, 225; MLL 519, 795, 819; 83, 85 UME; ROC 161	Fifteen second-hand AEC coaches
1965	DCE 800C, 801C	Two new AEC Reliance coaches
	UDK 311, 312; MDK 916, 917, 918	Five second-hand AEC coaches
1966	FCE 132D, 133D	Two new AEC Reliance coaches
	DCK 219	One second-hand double-decker
1967	GER 501E, 502E	Two new AEC Reliance coaches
1968	KCN 913, 916, 917, 919, 920	Five second-hand AEC coaches
1969	LJE 991G, 992G	Two new AEC coaches, 12 metres
	VDV 794, 795, 796, 797, 800, 803, 805, 806	Eight second-hand London Transport Buses
	631, 632, 633 WKL	Three second-hand AEC coaches
1970	OVE 232J, 233J	Two new AEC coaches, 12 metres
	YBD 79, 80, 81, 82; 83 BNV	Five second-hand AEC coaches
1971	NMU 6, 7; AMX 8A, 9A; BOF 854C, 855C	Six second-hand AEC coaches
1972	VER 261L, 262L	Two new AEC coaches, 12 metres
	FMK 129B; DWD 104C	Two second-hand AEC coaches
	316, 317, 318, 319, 322, 323, 326, 328 NJO	Eight second-hand double-deckers
1973	XVE 814L, 815L	Two new AEC coaches, 11 metres
	MMX 103C, 104C, 105C; BVO 1C, 3C, 6C, 7C, 9C, 10C	Nine second-hand AEC coaches
1974	OVE 550M, 551M; GER 913N, 914N	Four new AEC coaches
	HLP 10C, 11C	Two second-hand AEC coaches
1975	JVE 370P, 371P, 372P, 373P	Four new AEC coaches
1976	KVE 906P, 908P, 909P, 907P; NEB 346R, 347R, 348R, 349R	Eight new AEC coaches
1977	PCE 601R, 602R; RVE 650S, 651S	Four new AEC coaches
	UTF 478M; UAR 925M; WUR 856J; URA 461K, YUS 244J	Five second-hand AEC coaches

Date	Registration Numbers	Remarks
1978	RVE 652S, 653S, 296S, 297S; WEB 406T, 407T	Six new AEC coaches
1979	WEB 408T, 409T, 410T, 411T	Four new AEC coaches
1980	BVA 784V, 785V, 786V, 787V, 788V, 789V;	
	CJE 425V, 453V, 454V, 455V	Ten new Leyland Leopard coaches
1981	No purchases made	
1982	VAV 254X, 255X, 256X, 257X, 258X	Five new Leyland Tiger, 12 metres
1983	FAV 254Y, 255Y, 256Y, 257Y	Four Leyland/Plaxton Paramount
	GFL 527Y, 528Y, 529Y	Three High-line Leyland/Plaxton
1984	A638 OEB	1000th Leyland Tiger coach
	A695 JER	Leyland/Plaxton High-line
1985	B192 JVA	First MCW Metroliner coach, 'City of Cambridge'
	B244 JVA	Second MCW Metroliner coach, 'City of Birmingham'

TIME SHEET.

Trade _ConductRess_   Name _M WatKins_   Week ending } _August 6th 19 4 8._

	WHERE WORKING AND WHAT DOING	Hours	MATERIALS	TOTAL HOURS
Saturday	9 30 AM (B STORTFORD Ser 3) (S WALDEN 13 13) 11 30 PM	14		13
Monday	9 30 AM (B STORTFORD Ser 3) (S WALDEN 13 13) 11 30 PM	14	DOUBLE TIME	26
Tuesday	9 0 AM (S WALDEN Ser 11 14) 5 - 30 PM	8½		8½
Wednesday	2 15 (B STORTFORD Ser 26) 12 0	10		9
Thursday	12 30 (S WALDEN Ser 11 13) 11 0 PM	10½	Time ½ Hrs	12½
Friday	9 15 (Service 28) 9 0	12		12

Amount due £ _7 : 6 : 8_   TOTAL HOURS _80½_

"GUILDHALL" Form No. **130.**   T&H-852

10

The Rise and Fall of the First Premier Inclusive Holidays

or

How it Really Worked in the Jolly Boardroom

5 January 1950

'Why don't we start a sort of combined holiday, using Service 5 and one of those hotels in Clacton or Walton or whatever?'

'Good idea – why don't you get going and find out if it has any chance.'

12 January 1950

'We've contacted a number of hotels – the Apsley House seems quite interested. We couldn't cope with more than one 29-seater – I'm sure of that. I reckon we could charge about £14 10s [£14.50] from Sunday to Sunday – better keep the Tourists separate from that Saturday traffic.'

'Be sure you draft out good agreements between the hotels and the Company and keep a decent profit margin in your costings.'

16 February 1950

'The Royal Hotel's agreement will be ready for you three to sign and seal within the next few days.'

'Good. What about the brochure? We need a really first class job – must be ready for bookings to open in March.'

23 February 1950

'The Royal has bought up the Westcliffe and our passengers will go there. They say it is much more luxurious.'

'That's really good. What about the brochure?

'It's at the printers except for the photographs. You should have the proofs by next Thursday.'

'Well done – jolly good – let's have a drink.'

30 March 1950

'Here's the final copy of the brochure. What do you think?'

'Not bad at all – nice wording – like the layout – what happens next?'

'Off to the Midland Agents tomorrow to distribute it.'

11 May 1950

'How are the bookings going?'

'Horribly slowly. Agents say they are interested but nothing happens.'

'Perhaps E.A.L. should make a second tour?'

'Good idea – soon as possible.'

25 May 1950

'Bookings are awful – we're bound to make a hefty loss in June. We'll have to sell the hotel accommodation separately – it's totally disappointing.'

'Never mind, it's a new venture – needs building up. Public must believe they are good value holidays.'

22 June 1950

'Still only dribs and drabs. Shall we surrender the rest of our hotel bookings?'

'No – don't do that because it'll ruin our chances in 1951 – we'll just soldier on this year and see what happens.'

9 November 1950

'Here are the dismal accounts for the season. We've spent about £1,000 and taken £600. What about next year?'

'Well, we'd better get on with it as soon as possible. Contact the Westcliffe and we'll go and see them.'

23 November 1950

'How did you get on with Mr Harnett?'

'Very well – we've booked accommodation for a minimum of 15 people outside the peak season and 28 in July and August.'

'Lovely! How much for?'

'£6 15s [£6.75] per person and if we charge 13 guineas out of season and 15 guineas in, we should be alright.'

9 August 1951

'Bad news – the Westcliffe have sold our remaining accommodation and we can't fit in our late bookings.'

'Have a look at the agreement.'

'Will do but there's not much hope.'

No news remains for the 1952 season but in June 1953 we were assured of a full quota of passengers for the first big week. On 27 August 1953 we carried 51 passengers and by now we were back at the Royal Hotel. In September 1953 it was agreed to have a go in 1954. Then in December the Royal opted out and word went forth: 'Cut out all references to Inclusive Holidays in 1954 publicity.'

'Oh, Blaast.'

Notes